Law Express

Q&A

Question&Answer

EQUITY
AND TRUSTS

3rd edition

John Duddington
Former Head of the Law School
Worcester College of Technology

D0293373

PEARSON

Harlow, England • London • New York • Boston • San Francisco • Toronto • Sydney • Auckland • Singapore • Hong Kong
Tokyo • Seoul • Taipei • New Delhi • Cape Town • São Paulo • Mexico City • Madrid • Amsterdam • Munich • Paris • Milan

Pearson Education Limited
Edinburgh Gate
Harlow CM20 2JE
United Kingdom
Tel: +44 (0)1279 623623
Web: www.pearson.com/uk

First published 2012 (print)
Second edition published 2014 (print and electronic)
Third edition published 2016 (print and electronic)

ISBN: 978-1-292-06661-5 (print)
978-1-292-06663-9 (PDF)
978-1-292-06664-6 (ePub)
978-1-292-06665-3 (eText)

British Library Cataloguing-in-Publication Data
A catalogue record for the print edition is available from the British Library

10 9 8 7 6 5 4 3 2 1
19 18 17 16 15

Front cover bestseller data from Nielsen BookScan (2009–2013, Law Revision Series)

Print edition typeset in 10/13pt Helvetica Neue LT Pro by 71
Printed in Malaysia (CTP-PJB)

NOTE THAT ANY PAGE CROSS REFERENCES REFER TO THE PRINT EDITION

Contents

Supporting resources

Visit the **Law Express Question&Answer** series companion website at
www.pearsoned.co.uk/lawexpressqa to find valuable learning material
including:

- **Additional essay and problem questions** arranged by topic for each chapter
  give you more opportunity to practise and hone your exam skills.
- **Diagram plans** for all additional questions assist you in structuring and writing
  your answers.
- **You be the marker** questions allow you to see through the eyes of the examiner
  by marking essay and problem questions on every topic covered in the book.
- Download and print all **Before you begin** diagrams and **Diagram plans** from
  the book.

Also: The companion website provides the following features:

- Search tool to help locate specific items of content.
- Online help and support to assist with website usage and troubleshooting.

For more information please contact your local Pearson sales representative or
visit **www.pearsoned.co.uk/lawexpressqa**

Acknowledgements

To my father, Walter Duddington, who first encouraged me to become a lawyer, and who would, I think, have been an equity enthusiast; to my wife Anne, for her constant support, loyalty and technical expertise over many years and without which my books would never begin to be written; to my daughter Mary, for her seemingly faultless proofreading and sense of fun which keeps me going; and to my son Christopher for just being himself.

I would also like to thank the staff of Pearson, especially Hannah Marston for her endless encouragement, cheerfulness and practical guidance, and all the reviewers who sent in such helpful comments on preliminary drafts of this book. I have considered them all and adopted most of them. I would indeed have adopted more had space permitted.

In preparing this new edition I have made changes to all the chapters to reflect alterations in both the law and in the importance accorded to certain areas at the expense of others. The chapter on charities has been extensively revised to take into account developments in the law on public benefit and Chapter 11 now includes the Inheritance and Trustees' Powers Act 2014 and the Supreme Court decision in *Pitt* v *Holt*. Other particular changes have been to Chapters 8 and 13 to incorporate the seeming inability of the courts to decide if a bribe received by a fiduciary from a third party is held on trust for the principal and to Chapter 5 to note the helpful decision on *donationes mortis causa* in *Vallee* v *Birchwood*. Meanwhile Chapter 12 on breach of trust has been revisited in yet another attempt to make what is a complex area slightly more comprehensible.

Finally I still continue to visit the ground of Worcestershire County Cricket Club where, during quiet passages of play, many of the ideas for the questions in this book first come to my mind!

Readers should know that this book is based on sources available to me on All Saints' Day, 1 November 2014.

John Duddington

Publisher's acknowledgements

Our thanks go to all reviewers who contributed to the development of this text, including students who participated in research and focus groups which helped to shape the series format.

What you need to do for every question in Equity and Trusts

Equity and trusts exams have a mixture of questions ranging from very technical questions on areas such as constitution of trusts to questions dealing with theoretical areas such as the nature of a resulting trust.

First, you need to have an appreciation of exactly what equity is about. If you have not, this will be obvious throughout your answer. Equity is not easy to pin down and it certainly cannot be defined with absolute precision. However, it is possible to acquire a feeling for a flavour of equity such as the broad outlines of its history and the existence of the equitable maxims.

You will not go far, however, before you discover that many areas are controversial. One example is the extent to which equitable remedies are discretionary. A poor answer will simply say: 'Equitable remedies are discretionary.' A good answer will first ask: 'What is meant by discretion?' So the message is to avoid bland over-definite statements and instead ask questions as you go along.

You must also remember that equity needs to be seen in contrast to the common law and so just because you are studying equity does not mean that you should leave behind your knowledge of, for example, contract and tort. Questions in an equity exam may ask about the relationship between equity and the common law, one instance being the extent to which flexibility in the application of the law is unique to equity. If you can illustrate your answer by reference, for example, to the common law of negligence then this will immediately improve your marks.

You must also make sure that you are absolutely clear on the fundamental principles and concepts of equity. Make sure, for example, that you understand the nature of a resulting trust as compared to a constructive trust, and a charitable trust as compared to a non-charitable purpose trust. However, when you delve deeper you will find that there may be dispute about the exact nature of, for example, a resulting trust and it is here that you start to score marks. Remember that in the end you may have to say that a particular point remains uncertain. A good example of this is exactly who a fiduciary is and what are the duties which a fiduciary owes. Do not feel that you should come to a black and white conclusion.

Above all ask questions, put your book down and *think* about the subject, and be adventurous in your reasoning!

Guided tour

What you need to do for every question in Equity and Trusts

What to do for every question – Identify the key things you should look for and do in any question and answer on the subject, ensuring you give every one of your answers a great chance from the start.

Equitable remedies and doctrines

How this topic may come up in exams

This area is a familiar one in equity exams and a very common question is an essay on equitable remedies. This gives you the opportunity to gain extra marks by looking across the whole subject and looking at remedies in the context of trusts, as well as equitable remedies in general. You can also expect problem questions on areas such as specific performance and injunctions as well as on equitable doctrines. In this chapter you will find a problem on undue influence.

How this topic may come up in exams – Understand how to tackle any question on this topic by using the handy tips and advice relevant to both essay and problem questions. In-text symbols clearly identify each question type as they occur.

 Essay question   **Problem question**

Before you begin – Use these diagrams as a step-by-step guide to help you confidently identify the main points covered in any question asked. Download these from the companion website to add to your revision notes.

Answer plans and Diagram plans – A clear and concise plan is the key to a good answer and these answer and diagram plans support the structuring of your answers, whatever your preferred learning style.

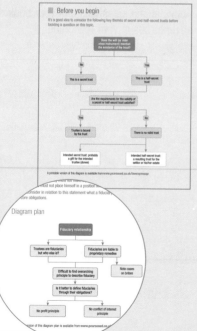

■ Before you begin

It's a good idea to consider the following key themes of secret and half-secret trusts before tackling a question on this topic.

A printable version of this diagram is available from www.pearsoned.co.uk/lawexpressqa

Answer plan

→ Explain and evaluate the core meaning of the term 'fiduciary'.

→ Outline the well-recognised categories of fiduciary relationships and then give instances of where the courts have held relationships to be fiduciary in more controversial cases.

→ Identify and analyse the core fiduciary obligations: the 'no profit rule' and 'no conflict of interest rule'.

→ Are they two rules or one? Does this matter?

→ Conclusion – link the idea of a concept of a fiduciary to the principles on which fiduciary obligations rest.

Diagram plan

Answer with accompanying guidance – Make the most out of every question by using the guidance to recognise what makes a good answer and why. Answers are the length you could realistically hope to produce in an exam to show you how to gain marks quickly when under pressure.

Answer

(a) The first question is whether there is certainty of intention to create a trust or just a request which Tom can comply with or ignore as he wishes. In **Re Hamilton** [1895] 2 Ch 370 CA Lindley LJ said that the courts must look at all the words used by the testator or settlor to see if, on their true construction in the context of the particular gift, a trust was intended.[1] The test asks what the actual intentions of the person were, looking at the words as a whole, rather than concentrating only on particular words. Here the gift is 'to Tom, and it is my wish that he will hold this sum to provide Eileen'.[2] It is suggested that the words 'it is my wish' do not imply any intention by Paul to place Tom under an obligation to hold the £10,000 on trust for Eileen. However, it is important to look at the gift as a whole[3] (**Comiskey v Bowring-Hanbury** [1905] AC 84) and here the will goes on to say that Tom is to 'hold this sum' which looks like the language of trusts. This can be contrasted with **Suggitt v Suggitt** [2011] EWHC 903 (Ch) where the words used were: 'And I express the wish (without

[1] A mention of this general principle is an excellent way to begin an answer in certainties.

resolve disputes over beneficial entitlement to the family home (see e.g. **Baumgartner v Baumgartner** (1988) 62 ALJR 29).

In England the courts have been less adventurous. In a series of cases in the 1970s, Denning MR sought to develop what he called 'a constructive trust of a new model' (**Eves v Eves** [1975] 3 All ER 768 CA). The existence of a fiduciary relationship was not required to found such a trust: instead, one would be imposed 'whenever justice and good conscience require it . . . it is an equitable remedy by which the court can enable an aggrieved party to obtain restitution' (Denning MR in **Hussey v Palmer** [1972] 3 All ER 744 CA). However, this idea was not approved by Bagnall J, who, in **Cowcher v Cowcher** [1972] 1 All ER 943 HC insisted that: 'In any individual case the application of [established rules of law]

Case names clearly highlighted – Easy-to-spot bold text makes those all important case names stand out from the rest of the answer, ensuring they are much easier to remember in revision and an exam.

Make your answer stand out – Really impress your examiners by going the extra mile and including these additional points and further reading to illustrate your deeper knowledge of the subject, fully maximising your marks.

✓ Make your answer stand out

■ Read Dunn (2008). This article looks at the role of charities in promoting social reform and the increasing role of the state in promoting social welfare. It then looks at the rules which restrict the political activities of charities.

■ Mention the different approach taken in the United States. There is a very useful summary of the US cases in the judgment of Carnwath J in *Southwood v A-G.*

■ Look at investigations undertaken by the Charity Commission into particular charities, e.g. the investigation into OXFAM (in 1991).

■ Look at the activities and objects of any charity and see if, in your opinion, the boundary between charitable and political activity is crossed.

■ Could the restriction on the 'political activities' of charities be an infringement of their rights under Article 10 of the European Convention on Human Rights, which provides for freedom of expression?

■ In *Aid/Watch Incorporated v Commissioner of Taxation* (2010) 241 CLR 539 the High Court of Australia held that there is no longer any prohibition in Australia on charities having political purposes. The court specifically recognised the public benefit in charities campaigning for both changes in the law and in government policy.

Don't be tempted to – Points out common mistakes ensuring you avoid losing easy marks by understanding where students most often trip up in exams.

! Don't be tempted to . . .

■ Concentrate too much on the public benefit issue to the exclusion of the others.

■ Go through all of the heads of charity set out in section 3 of the Charities Act 2011 and in each case decide if the law has changed. This will take you too long and you will not have time to discuss the issues.

■ Discuss whether the Charities Act 2006 (now Charities Act 2011) has changed the law without explaining exactly what its provisions are.

Bibliography

Bibliography – Use this list of further reading to really delve into the subject and explore areas in more depth, enabling you to excel in exams.

Andrews, G. (2002) Undue influence – where's the disadvantage? *Conveyancer and Property Lawyer*, 66: 456.

Baker, J.H. (2002) *Introduction to English Legal History* (4th edn). Oxford: Oxford University Press.

Baker, P. (1993) Land as a *donatio mortis causa. Law Quarterly Review*, 109: 19.

Guided tour of the companion website

 Book resources are available to download. Print your own **Before you begin** and **Diagram plans** to pin to your wall or add to your own revision notes.

 Additional Essay and Problem questions with **Diagram plans** arranged by topic for each chapter give you more opportunity to practise and hone your exam skills. Print and email your answers.

 You be the marker gives you a chance to evaluate sample exam answers for different question types for each topic and understand how and why an examiner awards marks. Use the accompanying guidance to get the most out of every question and recognise what makes a good answer.

All of this and more can be found when you visit
www.pearsoned.co.uk/lawexpressqa

Table of cases and statutes

■ Cases

▮ Statutes

■ International Conventions

Nature of equity and trusts

1

How this topic may come up in exams

This area will almost certainly contain essay questions in your exam rather than problems but of course you must check in your case. The nature of equity is a fertile area for general topics but in some cases answers on these areas have been left to later (see Chapter 13), as they require you to use material from particular topics to illustrate your answer and it is more appropriate to look at these questions when these topics have been covered.

◼ Before you begin

It's a good idea to consider the following key themes of the nature of equity and trusts before tackling a question on this topic.

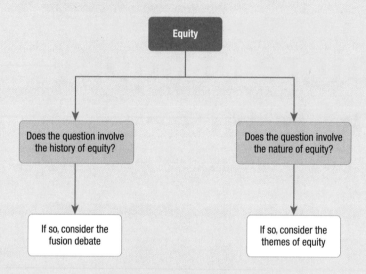

A printable version of this diagram is available from **www.pearsoned.co.uk/lawexpressqa**

🖎 Question 1

'There is no single concept of equity.' Critically consider this view of equitable jurisdiction.

Answer plan

→ Explain that there is no single concept of 'equity' as compared to, for example, the law of contract.

→ Consider attempts to encapsulate the term 'equity'.

→ Shift the argument to an attempt to identify certain distinguishing characteristics of equity and see if we can draw these together to arrive at a single concept of equity.

→ Can we conclude by saying that the concept of equity is a discretionary system based on the twin ideas of providing a remedy for unconscionable behaviour and that of intervening where the application of strict rules would cause injustice?

Diagram plan

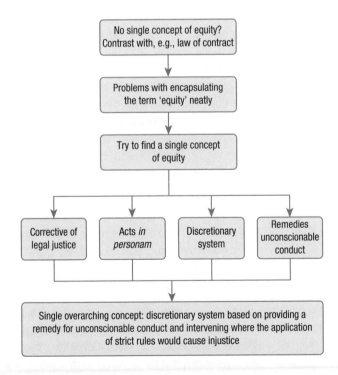

No single concept of equity?
Contrast with, e.g., law of contract

↓

Problems with encapsulating the term 'equity' neatly

↓

Try to find a single concept of equity

Corrective of legal justice | Acts *in personam* | Discretionary system | Remedies unconscionable conduct

Single overarching concept: discretionary system based on providing a remedy for unconscionable conduct and intervening where the application of strict rules would cause injustice

A printable version of this diagram plan is available from **www.pearsoned.co.uk/lawexpressqa**

Answer

As applied to equity, this statement means that there is no single concept that can, by itself, encompass all the areas where equity operates.[1] By contrast, for instance, one could say that the fundamental concept of the law of contract is concerned with legally enforceable agreements and how breaches of them are remedied. This does not tell us everything but it does give us an overriding view of the law of contracts. Is this statement about equity true?

This is an important question as equity is often contrasted with the common law. However, if we are not sure what equity is then how can it be contrasted with something else?

There is no doubt that it has always been difficult to encapsulate the term 'equity' neatly. For example, Hanbury's *Modern Equity* (2012, p. 3) simply states that 'Equity is the branch of the law which, before the Judicature Act of 1873 came into force, was applied and administered by the Court of Chancery'. This sounds more like a description than a definition as it does not tell us precisely *what* law was administered by the Court of Chancery.[2] Another simple definition might be that equity consists of the body of rules which was developed to mitigate the harshness of the common law and originally applied by the Court of Chancery, but this, although true, is also more of a description than a definition. Instead textbooks usually concentrate on describing the features and characteristics of equity. For instance, Graham Virgo in *The Principles of Equity and Trusts*, spends one page on 'What is Equity?' and 24 pages on its features and characteristics.

[2] Throughout the answer, as here, keep coming back to the contrast between a definition and a description.

One argument is that to fit equity into some neat formula would work against the very notion of equity[3] as equity works through more generalised concepts than the common law. However, we do need to be able to give some idea of what equity covers and the challenge is to arrive at a concept of equity which will be workable without placing equity in too much of a straightjacket.

[3] This point is important in any discussion of the nature of equity so do stress it.

Equity is an area where there is a layperson's idea of what it is and a lawyer's idea. Here we are concerned with the legal idea of equity. However, it is worth starting with the layperson's view: such a person might well answer that the concept of equity is that of 'fairness' but not only is this not sufficiently precise but it overlaps with administrative law where the notion of fairness in decision making is well known.[4]

[4] This link to another area of law will gain you marks. Remember that law is a unity and so knowledge of intersections between different areas is always going to boost your exam performance.

[5] Here you are starting to earn those extra marks: rather than just confining yourself to a discussion of whether we can identify a concept of equity you are branching out and asking if we can identify certain characteristics of equity.

[6] This is a familiar point to make in the discussion but you need to develop it to show that although equity does operate as a kind of corrective to the common law this is not the only way in which equity works.

[7] Notice how, in this example, we have *first* shown how equity usually does follow the law as this is of universal application, but then, as Aristotle suggested, show how equity acts as a corrector of strict legal justice in particular cases. There is, incidentally, no need to set out the details of the formalities in the Wills Act.

[8] This is an essential issue for this question: do emphasise it.

Similarly, words such as justice, mercy, and conscience are often used as synonyms for equity but lack sufficient precise meanings. Is it possible to broaden out our search[5] and start from how equity operates and see if this leads us to a meaningful concept.

A starting point is found in the *Nicomachean Ethics of Aristotle* (Book 5) where the distinction between justice and equity is found by regarding justice as dealing with what is lawful but there is a need to have a kind of corrective to legal justice.[6] This is because a law is obviously universal in that it applies to all in particular situations without being able to take account of individual circumstances. Worthington (2006) refers to this principle of Aristotle's as distinguishing between bright line rules and fact sensitive rules in that the latter lend themselves to discretionary justice. Thus whereas equity will normally follow the rule that any gift to take effect on death must comply with the formalities in the Wills Act 1837 (as amended) it will be prepared to enforce exceptional cases where the formalities have not been complied with as in the cases of secret trusts and *donationes mortis causa*.[7] Similarly in **Inwards v Baker** [1965] 2 QB 29 a father suggested to his son that he should build a bungalow on land owned by the father. The son did so, although there was no formal conveyance to him, and on the father's death it was held that the son could remain in the bungalow for as long as he wished. Had there been no equity[8] the lack of a formal conveyance would have prevented the son's claim, and indeed equity itself would normally hold that this was so, but here the equitable doctrine of proprietary estoppel was applied to allow the son's claim.

However, there are other cases where equity intervenes that are concerned with quite different matters. One example is the maxim that 'equity acts *in personam*'. This means that equity has jurisdiction over the defendant personally whereas the common law would grant an order against his property. This is the idea behind the equitable remedies of specific performance and injunction which are directed at the defendant personally to do or not to do a thing. If they are disobeyed the defendant may be committed to prison for contempt. Once again we have identified a characteristic of equity but have not captured its actual concept.

Another characteristic of equity, but one which does not lead us to an overall concept, is that it is a discretionary system as the common law will grant a remedy if the claim is made out, but equity has discretion to refuse a remedy if, for example, the claimant has not come with clean hands. Thus in **Coatsworth v Johnson** (1886) 55 LJQB 220 a

[9] There is a good deal of background detail which could be given about this case, for example we could refer to *Walsh* v *Lonsdale* (1882) 21 Ch D 9. However, this would distract from our point: there was a claim to an equitable remedy which the court, in its discretion, denied.

[10] This is an excellent example as we have two reasonably similar situations where the result was different. It also has the merit that it does not take long to explain!

[11] This conclusion neatly rounds off your answer as it shows a real attempt to grapple with the question and attempt to develop a concept of equity.

[12] Clearly, if you had time, you could look at particular cases and see if they all rest on preventing unconscionability.

tenant who claimed equitable relief as he only had an agreement for a lease of land and not a deed had himself not looked after the land and so was in breach of the covenants.[9] Equity refused relief. However, in areas such as remedies for breach of trust, often involving tracing of assets on an insolvency, the system is anything but discretionary.

Another idea that may lead us to a concept of equity is that of unconscionability, which has gained increasing ground in the resolution of disputes involving equity. In ***Bank of Credit and Commerce International (Overseas) Ltd* v *Akindele*** [2000] 4 All ER 221 unconscionability was accepted by Nourse LJ as the appropriate test in cases where it is alleged that trust property has been knowingly received in breach of trust. However, Lord Nicholls in ***Royal Brunei Airlines Sdn Bhd* v *Tan Kok Ming*** [1995] 2 AC 378 at 392 rejected it as the test in cases of knowing assistance in a breach of trust.[10] He felt that it was unacceptably vague and preferred the term 'dishonesty'. Although it is clear that unconscionability does not run right through equity as a principle there is no doubt that it is gaining ground, especially in Australia in decisions on the family home (see e.g. ***Baumgartner* v *Baumgartner*** (1988) 62 ALJR 29).

Can we draw all of this together? One could say that the concept of equity is that it is a discretionary system based on the twin ideas of providing a remedy for unconscionable behaviour and that of intervening where the application of strict rules, as in ***Inwards* v *Baker*** [1965] 2 QB 29, would cause injustice.[11] If we substituted 'unconscionability' for injustice we would come too close to resting a large part of equitable jurisdiction on the one word 'unconscionability' but the cases do not justify this.[12]

 Make your answer stand out

- Keep the idea of a concept of equity in mind throughout your essay: this is what you are asked to do.

- Spend some time on the word 'concept' and note that it is deliberately broad: the issue is not whether we can find some form of words which have the precision of a statute.

- Do not be dogmatic – this answer requires a thoughtful approach.

- Read Watt (2009), especially pp. 26–45 on the character of equity and pp.108–113 on unconscionability. It has some really excellent and illuminating ideas.

- Read Worthington (2006) in more detail, especially her ideas on whether equity really does have distinctive features.

Don't be tempted to . . .

■ Just go with the familiar definition of equity as correcting the harshness of the common law. The examiner will have read this countless times but will reward you if you think in a more adventurous way!

■ Go off the point by going into too much detail on points of law. For example, there is no need to explain the essential requirements of a secret trust or, still worse, how it differs from a half-secret trust. By now you will have lost the plot completely. Instead just mention secret trusts as in the answer.

■ Think of just one possible area and leave it at that. Instead, as in the question, consider various possibilities.

Question 2

Critically evaluate the statement 'a study of the history of equity can teach us valuable lessons for equity today'.

Diagram plan

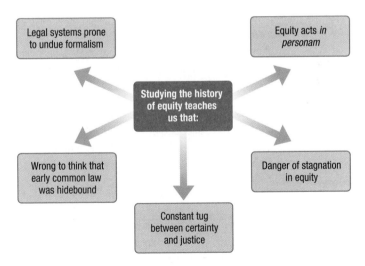

A printable version of this diagram plan is available from **www.pearsoned.co.uk/lawexpressqa**

Answer plan

➡ Explain how equity originally developed and consider the lessons for today from this.

➡ Now look at the later history of equity and show how to some degree there was a period of stagnation.

➡ Explain that this is not entirely true and give examples.

➡ Consider whether there is any evidence of stagnation in equity today.

Answer

[1] As ever, you could take the opposite view and argue that the history of equity is indeed just history but you would really be saying that the question is pointless! However, the argument would be interesting.

[2] This is vital, as the answer could go hopelessly wrong at this point. You could easily find yourself enmeshed in a lengthy account of how equity developed and leave yourself no time at all to actually answer the question. This is a good example of where, in an exam, you may have far more information than you can usefully use and you need to stop yourself and continually refer back to the question.

[3] This is all you need say on this point, as what is important for us today is what equity did rather than the actual way in which it developed.

A study of the history of equity is not an end in itself but can teach us valuable lessons for today.[1]

The first lesson comes from the way in which equity originally developed. One could summarise[2] this by saying that, although the early history of equity is in parts obscure, it is true to say that there were increasing complaints about the ability of the common law courts to deal with a variety of matters and there is evidence of increasing rigidity by the mid-fourteenth century. Some examples were that juries were bribed or intimidated so that a litigant could not obtain justice; the writ system had become an obstacle to the proper development of the law; and the procedures of the common law courts were often unsatisfactory, ill-suited to deal with cases which required the personal attendance of the parties and witnesses and where it was necessary to command a party to actually do, or not do, something. The common law courts were far better suited to disputes concerning land where, rather than deal with an individual direct, his land could be taken from him.

For these, and other reasons, litigants took to petitioning the King's Council to do justice and by the mid-fourteenth century this practice was becoming increasingly common. It was by this means that what we now know as equity eventually developed.[3]

There are three lessons to be drawn from this. The first is the obvious one that legal systems are always prone to undue formalism and they need to stop and remind themselves that they are there to serve the interests of justice. The second point is that, as we have seen, the common law courts acted against the litigant's land but equity acted against the person and this is still an indispensable feature of equity's jurisdiction today as it is the origin of the maxim that equity acts *in personam*. Thus this reminds us of the continuing importance of the equitable remedies of specific performance and injunction by which equity can command an act or restrain an individual. Recent examples of the importance of these are what were known as Mareva orders (now known as freezing orders) and Anton Piller orders (now known as search orders), both of which can be granted even before the issue of proceedings. Had equity not developed in response to the need for court orders to act against the person, these remedies might not have existed today. Finally, it is wrong to say that in this early period the common law was entirely hidebound, as there is evidence, for example, from the early cases of the remedies of specific performance and injunction being granted by the common law courts. The contemporary moral here is that perhaps there is not as much difference today between equity and the common law as we think and that fusion might be possible.[4]

[4] This is a really good point which the examiner may not expect and for which you can expect due credit. It leads directly to the very topical question of whether there is really all that much that is distinctive about equity and, if you have time, you would do well to say more on this.

Another way in which the study of the history of equity teaches us lessons for today is by looking at the history of equity in the period of the late seventeenth to the mid-nineteenth centuries when equity began to turn in on itself.[5] This development was probably inevitable as far as trusts were concerned, as the actual administration of a trust needs to be governed by clear rules. But in addition there was a reluctance to extend equity into new fields as when, in *Gale v Bennett* (1772) Amb 681, the Court of Chancery declined to give relief against unfair terms in contracts. Much later, in 1818, Lord Eldon said, in *Gee v Pritchard* 2 Swan 402 HC, that nothing would give him greater pain 'quitting this place' than recollecting that he had done anything 'to justify the reproach that the equity of this court varies like the Chancellor's foot'.

[5] The logic here is that we have moved on from early history and here again there are lessons to be drawn.

[6] This is the kind of approach which sets a good answer out from a poor one. It is essential, in questions such as these, to stress that there is no simplistic answer.

Even so, equity at this date was by no means stagnant.[6] When the Statute of Frauds was passed in 1677, it quickly developed the doctrine of secret trusts and redeveloped the rules of *donatio mortis causa* to deal with cases where property had been left outside a will. Also this was the era when the maxims were developed as a guide to equitable jurisdiction. Nevertheless, it is difficult to avoid the impression that equity had lost its early vigour. It could be said that this phase lasted until fairly recent times with, for example, the restrictive decisions of Lord Simonds as Lord Chancellor in cases involving public benefit in charitable trusts such as *Gilmour v Coats* [1949] AC 426 HL and *Oppenheim v Tobacco Securities Trust Co Ltd* [1951] AC 297 HL.[7] What is clear is that, at present, there is renewed vigour in equity. In Australia, for example, there has been a revitalised interest in, and utilisation of, equitable doctrines, remedies and institutions. One example is the development of a jurisprudence based on unconscionability to

[7] There is no time to go into this area in detail: all you need is to give enough information to show that you understand the issue.

resolve disputes over beneficial entitlement to the family home (see e.g. **Baumgartner v Baumgartner** (1988) 62 ALJR 29).

In England the courts have been less adventurous. In a series of cases in the 1970s, Denning MR sought to develop what he called 'a constructive trust of a new model' (**Eves v Eves** [1975] 3 All ER 768 CA). The existence of a fiduciary relationship was not required to found such a trust: instead, one would be imposed 'whenever justice and good conscience require it . . . it is an equitable remedy by which the court can enable an aggrieved party to obtain restitution' (Denning MR in **Hussey v Palmer** [1972] 3 All ER 744 CA). However, this idea was not approved by Bagnall J, who, in **Cowcher v Cowcher** [1972] 1 All ER 943 HC insisted that: 'In any individual case the application of [established rules of law] may produce a result which appears unfair. So be it: in my view that is not an injustice . . . in determining rights, particularly property rights, the only justice that can be attained by mortals . . . is justice that flows from the application of sure and settled principles . . .' Since then, however, the idea of a remedial constructive trust, which is what Denning MR was referring to, has been taken up by Lord Scott in **Thorner v Major** [2009] UKHL 18 and in **Stack v Dowden** [2007] UKHL 17 the House of Lords[8] seems to have departed from the rule that, in determining the beneficial interests in the family home the courts need to find the intentions of the parties. This had threatened to place the law on this area in a straightjacket, as seen in such cases as **Burns v Burns** [1984] Ch 317 CA.

What this really illustrates is the constant tug in equity between those who desire certainty and those who wish equity to strike out in pursuit of justice. This is true of all legal systems and not just of equity but it is still a lesson worth learning from history.

[8] This part of the answer began by saying that there was some stagnation in equity and then it described attempts by Denning MR, among others, to develop the law and how this did not meet with success in England. Now, finally, and to gain your extra marks, you must show how more recently the picture has changed. In this way you have covered the whole topic.

✓ **Make your answer stand out**

■ Read more on the early history of equity – any standard textbook on equity will start you off but for more detail go to Baker (2002).

■ To give a contemporary flavour to your answer, look in more detail at the debate on the remedial constructive trust and other areas. Begin with Etherton (2008).

■ Look at the debate on whether equity and the common law should indeed in time converge. See, for example, Honoré (2003). He argues that one major creation of equity, the trust, could be introduced into other legal systems. One could then go on to argue that, if so, what is distinctively equitable about it?

Don't be tempted to . . .

- Give an account of the history of equity. This is not what is asked for and will earn you a very poor mark. The question is concerned with the *lessons* of history.

- Equally do not give too much detail on present-day developments. It would be easy to go right off the point by, for example, giving lengthy accounts of cases involving disputes over beneficial entitlements to the family home. Instead, keep the idea of lessons from history in mind.

Question 3

'The so-called "fusion debate" is simply "old hat" and is only of historical interest.' Critically consider this statement.

Diagram plan

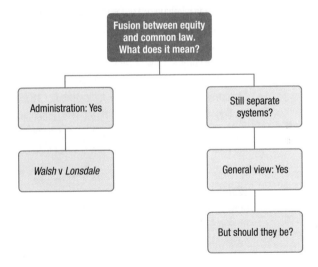

A printable version of this diagram plan is available from **www.pearsoned.co.uk/lawexpressqa**

Answer plan

→ Explain that the administration of common law and equity is fused as a result of the Judicature Acts.

→ Provide an example of this: *Walsh* v *Lonsdale*.

➔ Set out the view that equity and the common law are fused as systems of law and then subject this to critical analysis.

➔ Critically consider the view that integration between the common law and equity is possible in future.

➔ Show briefly in conclusion how this last point shows that the fusion debate is not dead.

Answer

[1] This is an absolutely fundamental point, which you should make at the start and gain credit for a clear answer.

[2] This is the second point and this requires much more thought. In this first paragraph you have set out the main lines of this essay and so it is an ideal start.

[3] In this essay you need to mention just enough history to make your answer understandable but you must resist the temptation to mention too much, as the question is clearly about equity today.

[4] The facts of this case have been set out in detail as they are of such importance. Students often oversimplify this case and here we have gained extra marks by showing the interaction of common law and equity.

There is no doubt that the actual administration of equity and the common law are fused by the Judicature Acts[1] but are equity and the common law themselves fused[2] so that it is no longer correct to speak of equity and the common law as distinct systems? It is suggested that they are still separate systems and so the debate is not just of historical interest.

Prior to the Judicature Acts 1873–1875, equity and the common law were separate systems so that if one wanted an equitable remedy or if the case concerned a trust then it was necessary to bring the action in the Court of Chancery, which administered equity.[3] Since the Judicature Acts that has changed and equitable remedies are available in all courts alongside common law remedies and, for example, a court may award common law damages and/or an injunction for breach of contract. Moreover, section 25(11) of the Judicature Act 1873 (the rule is now in section 49 of the Supreme Court Act 1981) recognised that equitable and common law rules are applied side by side by providing that where the rules of equity and common law conflict then equity shall prevail.

An example of administration of both systems in the same courts is **Walsh v Lonsdale** (1882) 21 Ch D 9 CA,[4] where the parties had agreed on a lease of a mill for seven years. Rent was payable quarterly in arrears but the landlord was entitled to demand a year's rent in advance. However, the agreement was not contained in a deed as required to make it binding in law (this requirement is now in section 52(1) of the Law of Property Act 1925). The tenant entered into possession and paid rent quarterly in accordance with the lease. The landlord then demanded a year's rent in arrears and when the tenant refused to pay he brought a common law claim for distress. The issue was whether the terms of the agreement for a lease could be relied on. The court held that equity could be applied and here the maxim 'equity looks on that as done which ought to be done' meant that, as the parties had agreed on a lease, equity would consider this as good as a lease. Thus as the agreement allowed the landlord to claim payment of rent in advance, the landlord's claim succeeded.

[5] This is the essential point that the examiner will be looking for, so do make sure that you emphasise it and, above all, show that you understand it.

The vital point is that this result would have been the same before the passage of the Judicature Acts but the claim would have had to have been heard in two different courts:[5] the common law courts would have heard the distress claim and the courts of equity would have dealt with the equitable principles. Now the same court can deal with both. However, the actual principles were different and we must now examine whether this is still so.

The general view is that equity and common law have not fused. This was expressed in a well-known metaphor by Ashburner (Browne, 1933): 'the two streams of jurisdiction, though they run in the same channel, run side by side and do not mix their waters'. This view has been contradicted, most notably by Lord Diplock in **United Scientific Holdings v Burnley Borough Council** [1978] AC 904 HL, who said that this 'fluvial metaphor' is 'mischievous and deceptive' and that the two systems of law, common law and equity, were indeed fused by the Judicature Acts.

[6] This approach will gain you marks. A poor answer would just say that Lord Diplock was wrong as, of course, equity and the common law are different systems and otherwise, for example, this book would not have been written!

It is not entirely clear what Lord Diplock meant.[6] He may have been referring to the fact that we should now consider common law and equity as different streams of law which operate together rather in the way that, for example, one might use both contract and tort in one action. This is, of course, true. On the other hand, he may have meant that they are in fact one system so that the distinctive features of both can no longer be seen and they are merged into one. The truth is, however, that this is not so, as a moment's thought will make anyone realise. Equitable and common law remedies operate together but are not governed by the same principles, as shown by **Patel v Ali** [1984] Ch 283.[7] Here the court used its equitable discretion[8] to decline to order the equitable remedy of specific performance for the sale of a house as this, due to the personal circumstances of one of the sellers, would have amounted to 'hardship amounting to injustice'. The court did, however, award the buyers their remedy at common law – in this case, damages – on being satisfied that they would be paid.

[7] *Patel* v *Ali* is a really excellent and easily remembered case to illustrate this point. It is easy with a case with memorable facts like this one to let the facts crowd out your explanation of the legal principle. Do not let this happen!

[8] It is important that you mention this as discretion in the grant of remedies is one of the characteristics of equity which distinguishes it from the common law.

Examples of the difference between legal and equitable rules are found throughout the law. For example, the rules on the running of the burden in freehold covenants differ in common law (see ***Austerberry*** v ***Oldham Corporation*** (1885) 29 Ch D 750 HL) from those in equity (see ***Tulk*** v ***Moxhay*** (1848) 1 H & Tw 105 HC) as at common law the burden does not run at all but in equity it does run where the covenant is negative.[9] On a broader level, Millett J (as he then was) wrote (1998) that: 'The common law insists on honesty, diligence and the due performance of contractual obligations. But equity insists on nobler and subtler qualities: loyalty, fidelity, integrity, respect for confidentiality, and the disinterested discharge of obligations of trust and confidence.' He was speaking in the context of equity and commerce but his words can, it is submitted, be applied to all areas in which equity engages, and are particularly relevant to the equitable concept of the fiduciary.

[9] This is all the detail you need to give here, as you have shown that you are aware of the fundamental difference between the approaches of common law and equity.

The fusion debate has been revived from another angle by Worthington (2006) who suggests that it is time that equity and the common law were fully integrated.[10] She points out that it is untrue to say that it is only equity which permits the exercise of discretion; so does the common law. She instances, for example, the discretionary element in deciding whether a duty of care exists in tort or if a consumer contract contains unfair terms. At times, on the other hand, equity has no discretion at all: for example, in deciding if equitable proprietary remedies should be awarded or not. She makes the telling point that, if there were discretion here, the law of insolvency would turn into a farce. Moreover, she rightly draws attention to the increased willingness of the common law to adjudicate according to the standard of reasonableness following on from ***Donoghue*** v ***Stevenson*** [1932] AC 562 HL.[11]

[10] We have outlined the obvious point that equity and common law do in fact have different characteristics but now we are taking the answer further by asking if this should always be so in the future. If you are aiming for high marks then this is exactly what the examiner is looking for.

[11] Mention of a case from a completely different area, even one as celebrated as this, will gain you credit.

This in itself shows[12] that the fusion debate is not merely of historical interest but that, instead, the extent to which equity and the common law are fused is part of the ongoing debate on the relationship between these two complementary systems of law.

[12] Here you are linking the views quoted in the previous paragraph to the quotation in the question.

 Make your answer stand out

- Look at the article by Duggan (1996). He looks at whether both equity and the common law aim at 'efficient outcomes' and argues that they do. Nor does he consider that equity is 'motivated by altruistic concerns'. Look at some of the cases which he quotes and compare his view with that of Millett J mentioned in the article.
- Read Worthington (2006). It is not very long and is extremely useful on this area and on others.

■ Look in detail at other cases and areas to evaluate the extent to which equity and the common law are fused – one possibility is the law on trusts of the home.

■ Read also the answer (in Chapter 13) to the question: 'Does equity have a future?' This develops some of the ideas found here.

! Don't be tempted to . . .

■ Give a detailed historical account of how equity and the common law developed as separate systems of law.

■ Fail to distinguish between fusion of the administration of equity and the common law and fusion of them as actual systems of law.

■ Set out facts of cases and not link them to the fusion debate.

■ Fail to give examples of how equity and the common law are still separate systems.

■ Fail to mention the views of Worthington.

www.pearsoned.co.uk/lawexpressqa

 Go online to access more revision support including additional essay and problem questions with diagram plans, You be the marker questions, and download all diagrams from the book.

Equitable remedies and doctrines

How this topic may come up in exams

This area is a familiar one in equity exams and a very common question is an essay on equitable remedies. This gives you the opportunity to gain extra marks by looking across the whole subject and looking at remedies in the context of trusts, as well as equitable remedies in general. You can also expect problem questions on areas such as specific performance and injunctions as well as on equitable doctrines. In this chapter you will find a problem on undue influence.

▉ Before you begin

It's a good idea to consider the following key themes of equitable remedies and doctrines before tackling a question on this topic.

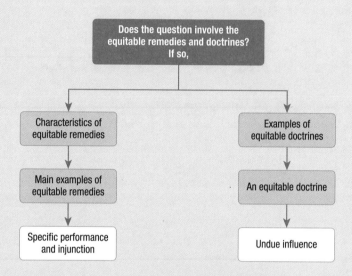

A printable version of this diagram is available from **www.pearsoned.co.uk/lawexpressqa**

 Question 1

'Although the jurisdiction to grant equitable remedies is discretionary, the exercise of the jurisdiction is dependent on recognised principles.' (Virgo, 2012, p. 715)

Critically consider this statement in the light of case law on the application of discretion in equity.

Answer plan

→ Start by explaining what discretion in equity actually means.

→ Look at cases, showing how equitable discretion has actually been applied by the courts.

→ Look further than the obvious areas and consider the remedial constructive trust.

→ Conclude by pointing to the fundamental point that there are no rigid rules governing the grant of equitable remedies.

Diagram plan

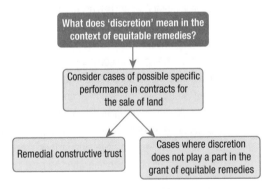

A printable version of this diagram plan is available from **www.pearsoned.co.uk/lawexpressqa**

Answer

[1] It is impossible to actually *define* what is meant by discretion but you do need to spend some time 'considering' what it can mean. You should not aim at very precise points in an answer in this area though as equity does not operate in this way.

[2] A mediocre answer would simply give a list of cases illustrating the exercise of discretion in the grant of equitable remedies. The cases are important but first you need some principle.

[3] This is one of those cases where a detailed account of the facts really does help to add value to your answer as in the next paragraph we show how exceptional hardship would result from the grant of this order.

[4] You need to pin down exactly what discretion means in this context. Thus in this case we have pinpointed the exact area where the court exercised its discretion.

[5] The advantage of using this case is that you are looking at equitable remedies and discretion in more depth in one particular area and contrasting two cases.

We first need to be clear exactly what is meant by discretion in this context.[1] Discretion means in ordinary language that there is an element of choice whether to do something or not and so, applied to equity, this would mean that the courts when considering if to grant an equitable remedy have a choice whether or not to do so. However, if we stopped here that would give a misleading impression because although a court, when awarding equitable remedies has some discretion, it is not a complete discretion. The court cannot simply do what it feels to be just in the circumstances and it must be emphasised that the fact that equity is a discretionary system should not lead to the idea that equity is all about vagueness.[2] It has been said that 'there is a real danger in simply assuming that equity stands for flexibility and vagueness. Equity needs to be principled and equity needs to be clear' (Virgo (2003)).

Patel v Ali [1984] Ch 283 HC illustrates the discretionary character of equitable remedies. A contract had been made for the sale of a house but a year later the sellers had not moved out. There is a well-established principle that equity will normally grant specific performance of a contract for the sale of land. The usual explanation for this is that each piece of land is unique and so an equitable remedy can be granted as common law damages would not be an adequate remedy. However, in this case the reason for the delay was that one of the sellers,[3] Mrs Ali, became seriously ill with bone cancer. She later became pregnant and had a leg amputated. As a result she needed help with household duties and shopping. A month later she gave birth to their second child. Her husband was subsequently in prison and later she gave birth to their third child.

In these circumstances the court held that if specific performance was granted and Mrs Ali had to move out, there would be 'hardship amounting to injustice', in the words of Goulding J. The fact that a person would suffer hardship in having to complete a sale was not in itself enough to justify the court in refusing an order for specific performance. Hardship would, said the court, only justify the refusal of an order in an exceptional case.[4] This was one.

Another case involving the grant of specific performance (SP) in a sale of land involving equitable discretion but with a different result[5] is *Matila Ltd v Lisheen Properties Ltd* [2010] EWHC 1832 (Ch) where the purchaser of two apartments had lost its bank funding partly through the downturn in the property market and used this as the reason for being unable to complete the sale. However, the court granted SP and held that it was only in extraordinary cases that hardship can be a reason not to grant SP. Although inability to perform a contract for financial reasons could raise the defence of impossibility (see **North East Lincolnshire BC v Millennium Park (Grimsby) Ltd** [2002] EWCA Civ 1719) there was no evidence here that it was impossible to obtain the necessary finance to complete the purchase.

Here we see equitable remedies in action. There is no absolute discretion in the grant of them but instead equity applies certain broad principles to guide it in deciding whether to grant a remedy. This case also illustrates another principle which guides the court in the exercise of its discretion in the grant of equitable remedies:[6] if specific performance had been granted the court would have acted *in personam*. This means that failure to comply with an order such as specific performance or injunction is contempt of court punishable with imprisonment. Thus had specific performance been awarded in **Patel v Ali**[7] and Mrs Ali had not complied with it then she could have been committed to prison. A glance at her circumstances will show how wrong that would have been.

The case of **Co-operative Insurance Society Ltd v Argyll Stores (Holdings) Ltd** [1998] AC 1 HL shows how the exercise of equitable discretion is often based on general equitable principles and, because these are general, different courts may apply different principles leading to different results. Specific performance was asked for by the claimant landlords of a covenant by the tenants of a lease of a supermarket to keep it open during the usual hours of business. The lease had still 19 years to run. The supermarket was an 'anchor store' in a shopping centre and its closure would badly affect the viability of the rest of the centre. The Court of Appeal[8] granted the order on the principle that an equitable remedy can be granted where damages would not be an adequate remedy. Roch LJ held that damages would not compensate the claimants 'for the disappearance of the supermarket or for the effect of that on the other businesses in the shopping centre'.

However, the House of Lords reversed this decision and refused an order of specific performance. It applied the principle that a mandatory injunction which required a defendant to carry on a business would not be granted (**Attorney General v Colchester Corporation**

[6] Note that we are avoiding the temptation to write about equitable remedies in general but instead we are always coming back to the theme of discretion.

[7] Note how we have used one case to illustrate a number of points. It is often better to really know a few cases well and to use them to illustrate a number of points rather than glide superficially over a number of cases.

[8] This is one case where you will add to your marks by not only looking at the decision of the highest court (the House of Lords here) but also the Court of Appeal, and contrasting the differing approaches of the two courts.

[1955] 2 QB 207 HC), and applied this to the decision on whether to grant the remedy of specific performance, which would have the same effect here as a mandatory injunction.[9]

In one area, that of the remedial constructive trust, it has indeed been argued that equity does have a very general discretion.[10] Lord Denning MR sought to develop what he called 'a constructive trust of a new model' (*Eves* v *Eves* [1975] 3 All ER 768 CA). The existence of a fiduciary relationship was not required to found such a trust: instead one would be imposed 'whenever justice and good conscience require it . . . it is an equitable remedy by which the court can enable an aggrieved party to obtain restitution' (Denning MR in *Hussey* v *Palmer* [1972] 3 All ER 744 CA). However, this very broad principle has not found favour in more recent years and in *Lonrho plc* v *Al-Fayed (No 2)* [1992] 1 WLR 1 HC Millett J observed that although equity must be flexible 'its intervention must be based on principle'.

However, discretion is not a feature of equitable remedies in every situation and sometimes there is no room for discretion at all.[11] One example is where a trustee has wrongly parted with trust property by, for example, placing trust money into his own bank account and then taking that money out and perhaps buying a yacht with the proceeds. The courts can impose a constructive trust on that person to enable the beneficiaries to trace their claim into the yacht and sell it to recover their property. In this case there is no discretion.

The essential point is that there are no rigid rules governing the grant of equitable remedies[12] but on the other hand the grant of equitable remedies is not just at the whim of each judge. Instead, as we have shown, the exercise of discretion is based on recognised principles.

[9] There is no need at this point to go into detail on discretion in the issue of injunctions. There would be nothing actually wrong in this but why not instead make an unexpected point, as we do in the next paragraph?

[10] This is an especially good area to mention as most students will forget that it is considered a remedy and so ignore it.

[11] Once again we are casting our net widely and going beyond the traditional examples based on, for instance, specific performance and injunctions. It would be possible to give many more examples of how equitable remedies are not completely discretionary but you have now made your point.

[12] You are returning to the point of the question at the end – always essential.

✓ Make your answer stand out

■ The term 'discretion' needs some explanation so do not just plunge into the cases and forget to explain.

■ Do not be afraid of dealing with less obvious areas such as the remedial constructive trust.

■ Read and refer to articles such as Luxton (1998) on *Co-operative Insurance Society Ltd* v *Argyll Stores (Holdings) Ltd* and Dowling (2011) on *Matila Ltd v Lisheen Properties Ltd.*

❓ Question 2

Advise John, who owns a medium-sized hotel, on the following matters:

(a) He has engaged Fred on a self-employed basis for three months from 1 February to redesign the business's website and to assist with marketing the hotel for the summer season. Fred had worked on this project for two months but on 1 April he rang John and told him that he was not going to continue any longer as he had obtained a 'very lucrative job' in Germany which he felt that he could not turn down. John feels that it is too near to the summer season to engage anyone else and he wishes to obtain a court order to compel Fred to work for the remaining month.

(b) John is owed £10,000 by Rosemary, a guest who stayed at the hotel for a long time. He intends to bring proceedings against her to claim this sum but has learned that, very shortly, she intends to sell her stamp collection which he believes is her main asset. If it is sold then, even if John wins the case, Rosemary is likely to have no assets to satisfy the judgment. Is there any action which he can take to prevent the sale of the stamp collection?

Answer plan

→ Explain the general principles of equity which apply to enforcement of a contract for personal services.

→ Go on to link this to the point that equitable remedies are discretionary.

→ Apply these to the question and briefly mention the question of damages.

→ Explain the idea behind freezing orders.

→ Apply the guidelines for the grant of these orders to the question and in the process decide if one is likely to be granted in this case.

Diagram plan

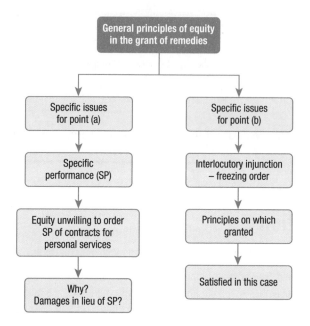

A printable version of this diagram plan is available from **www.pearsoned.co.uk/lawexpressqa**

Answer

[1] Note the overlap between the two remedies. Later on in the answer you can develop this point and it will certainly earn extra marks.

[2] This is more of an employment law point than an equity one, but it flows from the point that, as all law students know, the label which the parties attach to their relationship is not decisive. It is certainly an excellent point for this answer.

(a)   The contract which Fred has with John is one for personal services. We are told that John has engaged Fred on a 'self-employed basis', which means that Fred is not an employee but is an independent contractor. John wishes to obtain a court order to compel Fred to work for the remaining month of his contract and this means that he is seeking either an order of specific performance to directly compel performance of the contract or possibly a mandatory injunction to restrain its breach which would have the same effect.[1] Section 236 of the Trade Union and Labour Relations (Consolidation) Act 1992 prohibits the courts from enforcing performance of contracts of employment either by specific performance or injunction but this will not apply to Fred as he is not an employee, unless the court finds on the facts that despite the description of Fred as self-employed, he is in fact an employee.[2] If Fred is self-employed, this means that the matter is governed by equity alone.

[3] This is an important general point which you should always include in any question on equitable remedies.

The remedies of specific performance and injunction are equitable, and equitable remedies are discretionary. This means that although the court has a discretion in the grant of a remedy, its discretion is guided by certain principles.[3] In this case the principle is that equity has always refused to grant an order which would compel performance of a contract for personal services.

[4] Although we are simply asked to advise John on whether he can obtain an order against Fred, it will add depth to your answer if you can explain the reasons why such an order cannot be obtained.

This is based on a number of factors:[4] the difficulty of supervision, the undesirability of one person being compelled to submit to the orders of another and the difficulty of deciding whether an employee was actually performing his contract. Thus, as Megarry J observed in *Giles (CH) & Co Ltd v Morris* [1972] 1 WLR 307 HC: 'if a singer sang flat, or sharp, or too fast, or too slowly . . . who could say whether the imperfections of performance were natural or self-induced?'

It is true that in some situations equity has appeared to enforce a contract for personal services where an injunction is sought by the employee to restrain dismissal by the employer, as in *Irani* v *Southampton and South West Hampshire Health Authority* [1985] ICR 590 HC, where an injunction restrained implementation of a dismissal notice until a disputes procedure had been complied with. However, in this case it was not sought to enforce the contract, so that, for example, his employers would not be expected to actually employ Irani.[5] In addition, here the order is sought by the employer and not the employee. Also in *Posner* v *Scott Lewis* [1987] Ch 25 HC specific performance was indeed granted of a contract to employ a resident porter at a block of flats; however, this was not strictly enforcement against the porter but enforcement of a contract to employ a porter.

[5] This is the vital point. Do not be misled by a superficial glance at the cases into thinking that here equity literally enforced contracts for personal services.

The conclusion must be that John cannot obtain an order enforcing this contract. Section 2 of the Chancery Amendment Act 1858 (Lord Cairns Act) allows the court to grant damages in substitution for an order of specific performance but as the remedy of specific performance is not available in this case it seems likely that damages cannot be awarded under this Act. However, there is no reason why John cannot seek damages at common law against Fred for breach of his contract.

(b) The other question is whether John can take action to prevent the sale of Rosemary's stamp collection so that it is available to satisfy any damages which may be awarded against her for her breach of contract in failing to pay her hotel bill.

The appropriate remedy here is a freezing order, which is an interlocutory injunction designed to prevent the defendant from disposing of assets which would otherwise be available to meet the claimants' claim or removing them from the courts' jurisdiction. It was originally known as a Mareva order, from the case where it was first used: **Mareva Compania Naviera v International Bulk Carriers SA** [1975] 2 Lloyd's Rep 509 CA. The order is normally granted without notice to the other party (the previous term, still often used in practice, was *ex parte*) because of the need for speed and because if the other party knew that the order was being sought they would dissipate the assets.

John will need to check whether he can satisfy the guidelines, suggested by Lord Denning MR in the **Mareva** case, which the courts apply for the issue of a freezing order. The relevant ones[6] are:

(i) The claimant must have a good arguable case. The court will therefore need to form a provisional view on the final outcome of the case on the evidence before it and where there are substantial disputes of fact the requirement of a 'good arguable case' will be difficult to meet. Here John will need to check if there are any possible grounds on which Rosemary might dispute liability to pay the bill. One possibility would be if she had complained about the standard of service and/or accommodation at the hotel.[7]

(ii) The claimant should make full and frank disclosure of all material matters (see **Brinks-MAT Ltd v Elcombe** [1988] 3 All ER 188 HC), together with full particulars of his claim and its amount and should state fairly the points made against it by the defendant. Thus John would need to produce any letter of complaint from Rosemary.

(iii) John, as the claimant, should normally give grounds for believing that the defendants have assets (here the stamp collection) in the jurisdiction.

[6] It is vital that you stress that you are only mentioning the *relevant* guidelines. You could waste time and valuable marks to list them all.

[7] Notice how we have not only stated the guidelines but also applied them to the specific facts of the question. This is what an examiner wants to see.

(iv) The claimant should normally give grounds for believing either that the assets will be removed from the jurisdiction before the claim is satisfied or that in some way they might be dissipated so that there will be a real risk that a judgment in the claimant's favour will not be satisfied (see ***Babanaft International Co SA v Bassatne*** [1988] 1 All ER 433 HC). Thus, John will have to bring evidence that Rosemary intends to sell the stamp collection and that it is her main asset.

[8] This is one of those areas where you need to decide which of a long list of points to mention. There would be no point in setting out all the guidelines, as if you did you would have no time to relate them to the question and so you would lose marks.

There are other guidelines,[8] such as the fact that the court should exercise caution before granting an order which would bring the defendant's business to a standstill, but they are not relevant here. What is clear is that John has no automatic right to a freezing order and that, in order to obtain it, he will need to collect evidence to satisfy the court on all the above points.

✓ Make your answer stand out

- Mention the idea behind an interlocutory injunction and the general principles which decide if it will be granted: *American Cyanamid Co v Ethicon Ltd* [1975] AC 396 HL.
- Mention other cases where the court has considered the question of possible enforcement of an employment contract: *Gunton v Richmond-upon-Thames LBC* [1981] Ch 448 HC.
- Consider whether there are sufficient safeguards for the defendant in an application for the grant of a freezing order. This will add some depth to your answer, although of course you will not have much time to consider this in detail.

! Don't be tempted to . . .

- Just say in the first part of the question that the contract cannot be enforced. Although this may be the conclusion in the end, you should consider the law fully.
- Forget to mention the possibility of damages where specific performance is not granted.
- Be too dogmatic and think of the guidelines for the grant of a freezing order as absolute rules.

❓ Question 3

Fred and Elsie jointly own their house, 12 High Road Westview. Fred also owns a building business which he wishes to expand. He asks his bank manager, Oliver, for a loan of £100,000 and Oliver says that this will be possible but only if the mortgage on the house is extended to provide security. Oliver tells Fred that Elsie will have to agree to this and, knowing that she will not be keen on the idea, Fred tells her that the loan is only for 'no more than £5,000' to cover some extensions to his workshop. Oliver says that Elsie can only sign once she has had advice from a solicitor and that Oliver's own son, Jake, can do this. Elsie almost always takes Fred's advice on financial matters and so, when Jake says 'There's nothing to worry about, love', she willingly signs the mortgage deed.

Fred is now bankrupt and the bank is seeking to enforce its security.

Advise Elsie on whether she has any grounds to resist this.

Answer plan

→ Consider whether Elsie's signature was procured by undue influence.

→ Then move on to ask if it could also have been procured by misrepresentation.

→ If it was procured by either of these methods, then ask if the bank could be affected by this and apply the principles in *Barclays Bank* v *O'Brien* and *Royal Bank of Scotland* v *Etridge*.

→ Conclude by considering the effect on the bank if it was so affected.

Diagram plan

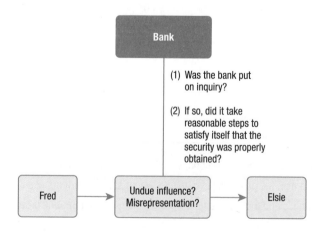

A printable version of this diagram plan is available from **www.pearsoned.co.uk/lawexpressqa**

Answer

The first question is whether Fred used either undue influence or misrepresentation to procure Elsie's signature on the mortgage deed.[1]

Undue influence is a doctrine that, by its nature, is difficult to define precisely but in essence it aims to prevent the vulnerable from exploitation. It is really directed at the manner in which a transaction is entered into. In ***Royal Bank of Scotland v Etridge (No 2)*** [2001] UKHL 44 Lord Nicholls held that there is a distinction between:

(a) Cases of actual coercion.

(b) Cases where the undue influence arises from a particular relationship.

In (b) there is a subdivision between:

(i) Cases where there is a relationship of trust and confidence between two people. If it is established that there has been a transaction which calls for some explanation then the burden shifts to the person seeking to uphold the transaction to produce evidence to counter the inference of undue influence.

(ii) Certain types of relationship where one party has acquired influence over another who is vulnerable and dependent and by whom substantial gifts are not normally to be expected (e.g. parent and child, trustee and beneficiary and medical adviser and patient). In these cases there is a presumption of undue influence by the stronger party over the weaker. The effect is that, if (b) applies, it is for Fred, as the party seeking to uphold the transaction, to show that there was no undue influence because if there is undue influence then Elsie may not be bound and so the whole liability will fall on him.[2]

[2] It is vital to stress the significance of deciding into which category the particular type of undue influence falls. This does not decide if there has been undue influence or not but how it is proved. Make this clear.

In this situation it is impossible on the facts to show that there was actual coercion exercised by Fred over Elsie and so we need to ask if either of the situations in (b) applies. All that we know is that Elsie usually takes Fred's advice on financial matters but this does not really show a relationship of trust and confidence as in (b)(i) above, nor is there any evidence that Elsie is vulnerable and dependent on Fred as in (b)(ii).[3] The conclusion must be that, if she is to rely on undue influence, Elsie will need to prove it as it will fall under the first category of actual coercion. On the facts there is no evidence of this.

[3] Link your conclusions clearly to Lord Nicholls's categories.

She may, however, be able to show that her signature was procured by the misrepresentation of Fred. Misrepresentation is an untrue statement of fact which induces a person to enter into a transaction and here Fred told Elsie that the amount which he was borrowing was 'no more than £5,000'. This is clearly untrue, as it was £100,000.

However, proving that Fred was guilty of misrepresentation will only enable Elsie to avoid the transaction as against Fred himself, but the document which she signed was in favour of the bank. Thus Elsie will need to show that the bank had notice of Fred's undue influence under the principles first laid down in **Barclays Bank plc v O'Brien** [1995] 1 All ER 438 HL, which have now been clarified by the House of Lords in **Royal Bank of Scotland v Etridge (No 2)**.[4]

[4] Be careful not to use the law as set out in *O'Brien:* much of the detail has now been superseded by that in *Etridge.*

Here Lord Nicholls said that a lender, the bank in this case, is put on inquiry when one person offers to stand surety for the debts of:

(a)   his or her spouse;

(b)   a person involved in a non-commercial relationship with the surety and the lender is aware of this;

(c)   any company in which any of the above hold shares.

[5] This is a crucial point, as if Elsie also owned the business, the bank would not be under this duty.

In this case it is clear that (a) applies, as Elsie is standing surety for Fred's debts as the business does not belong to her.[5]

The House of Lords in **Etridge** then clarified the steps[6] which the creditor should reasonably be expected to take in satisfying itself that the security has been properly obtained:

[6] You must put this in the correct order. First decide if the bank is put on inquiry and only if it is do you need to consider the steps which it should take to satisfy itself that the security has been properly obtained.

(a)   The lender must contact the surety and request that it nominate a solicitor.

(b)   The surety must reply nominating a solicitor.

(c)   The lender must, with the consent of the surety, disclose to the solicitor all relevant information – both the debtor's financial position and the details of the proposed loan.

(d)   The solicitor must advise the surety in a face-to-face meeting at which the debtor is not present. The advice must cover an explanation of the documentation, the risks to the surety in signing and emphasise that the surety must decide whether to proceed.

(e) The solicitor must, if satisfied that the surety wishes to proceed, send written confirmation to the lender that the solicitor has explained the nature of the documents and their implications for the surety.

In this case the lender has not requested the surety, Elsie, to nominate a solicitor to advise but instead the lender in the person of the bank manager, Oliver, has himself nominated his own son, Jake.[7] In addition, there is no evidence that the lender has disclosed all relevant information to the solicitor. Moreover, it is not clear whether Jake advised Elsie when the debtor, Fred, was not present and it is obvious that Jake did not explain the risks to Elsie as all that he said was: 'There's nothing to worry about, love.' Finally, it appears that Jake did not send written confirmation to the lender that he has explained the nature of the documents and their implications for Elsie. In a later decision,[8] **National Westminster Bank plc v Amin** [2002] UKHL 9, it was held that the solicitor must be expressly instructed to advise the surety on the nature and effect of the transaction and clearly this has not happened here.

In view of this, it is suggested that as the bank was 'put on inquiry' and it has failed to take steps to ensure that the security has been properly obtained,[9] it cannot enforce the security against Elsie, although of course it can do so against Fred. This will mean that the bank will be able to enforce its security against Fred's beneficial interest in the property but not that of Elsie and it may apply for a sale of the property.

Finally, there has been some discussion as to whether the surety should still be liable for the amount to which she consented, in this case, £5,000. In **TSB v Camfield** [1995] 1 WLR 340 HC, it was held that the mortgage so far as the surety is concerned should be entirely set aside. The question is probably whether Elsie agreed voluntarily to some liability and on the facts it is doubtful if she did.

[7] The failure of the bank on this point alone is probably enough to make it impossible for it to enforce the security against Elsie but you should go through all the other points to pick up marks.

[8] Students often quote the guidelines in *Etridge* and no more. Although these must of course be the main focus of your answer, it will add to your marks if you can quote a post-*Etridge* case.

[9] When you are coming to a conclusion on this point try to come back to the phrases used by Lord Nicholls to set out what the lender must do: 'put on inquiry', 'take reasonable steps'.

✓ **Make your answer stand out**

- Clear explanation of the *O'Brien* principle.
- Read Andrews (2002). This looks at the decision in *Royal Bank of Scotland* v *Etridge (No 2)*.
- Read Thompson (2003). This gives a clear account of the law and of how it has developed, which many textbooks do not do.
- A brief reference to the possibility of the bank being able to force a sale of the property and the relevant provisions of the Insolvency Act 1986.

! Don't be tempted to . . .

- Assume that there has been undue influence. Check the facts of the question.
- Assume that just because the parties are married, this means that Elsie has trust and confidence in Fred so that undue influence is presumed.
- Talk of the lender 'having notice' of undue influence or misrepresentation. This term was used in *O'Brien* but not in *Etridge,* which talked of being 'put on inquiry'. The term 'notice' could lead to confusion with 'notice' in other areas.

www.pearsoned.co.uk/lawexpressqa

Go online to access more revision support including additional essay and problem questions with diagram plans, You be the marker questions, and download all diagrams from the book.

The three certainties

▨ Before you begin

It's a good idea to consider the following key themes of the three certainties before tackling a question on this topic.

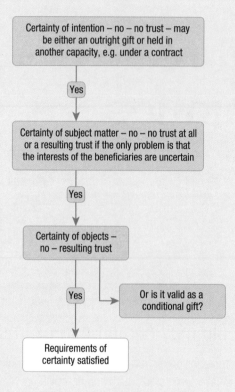

A printable version of this diagram is available from **www.pearsoned.co.uk/lawexpressqa**

🢂 Question 1

Paul died in March 2015, leaving a will dated 7 April 2010 containing the following bequests:

(a) £50,000 to Tom, and it is my wish that he will hold this sum to provide a reasonable amount out of it to enable my girlfriend Eileen to keep up her present standard of living, and generally 'keep up appearances'.

(b) £1 million to my trustees Josephine and Maureen to distribute in their absolute discretion to any inhabitant of the County of Herefordshire who has attained the age of 21 years at the date of my death or any child of such an inhabitant on reaching the age of 21 years.

Advise on the validity of these gifts.

Would your answer differ if the will had been dated 5 April 2010?

Diagram plan

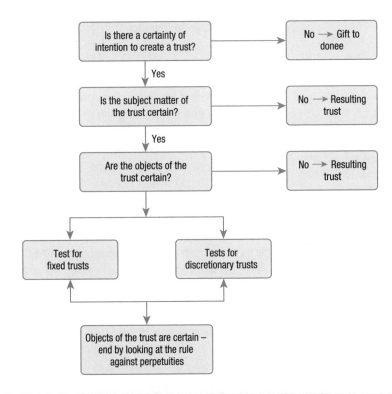

A printable version of this diagram plan is available from **www.pearsoned.co.uk/lawexpressqa**

Answer plan

→ In each part of the question you should check that the following are present and apply the relevant law:

Certainty of intention

Certainty of subject matter

Certainty of objects.

→ Then consider the possible application of the rules against perpetuities.

→ If you decide that the gifts are not valid and will not go to the intended beneficiaries then you must decide where the property contained in the gifts will go – always find a home for the property.

Answer

(a) The first question is whether there is certainty of intention to create a trust or just a request which Tom can comply with or ignore as he wishes. In **Re Hamilton** [1895] 2 Ch 370 CA Lindley LJ said that the courts must look at all the words used by the testator or settlor to see if, on their true construction in the context of the particular gift, a trust was intended.[1] The test asks what the actual intentions of the person were, looking at the words as a whole, rather than concentrating only on particular words. Here the gift is 'to Tom, and it is my wish that he will hold this sum to provide Eileen'.[2] It is suggested that the words 'it is my wish' do not imply any intention by Paul to place Tom under an obligation to hold the £10,000 on trust for Eileen. However, it is important to look at the gift as a whole[3] (**Comiskey v Bowring-Hanbury** [1905] AC 84) and here the will goes on to say that Tom is to 'hold this sum' which looks like the language of trusts. This can be contrasted with **Suggitt v Suggitt** [2011] EWHC 903 (Ch) where the words used were: 'And I express the wish (without imposing a trust).' It was quite clear looking at all the words, that no trust was intended.

The next question is whether there is certainty of subject matter as it appears that Tom is to take some of the £50,000 as a gift and that he only has to allocate a sum out of this to provide a reasonable amount out of it[4] to enable the girlfriend Eileen to keep up her present standard of living, and generally 'keep up appearances'. Is the phrase 'a reasonable amount' certain

[1] A mention of this general principle is an excellent way to begin an answer in certainties.

[2] There is no need at this stage to set out the terms of the bequest – this will waste time as you will come to this later. Just concentrate on the intention point.

[3] This point is always worth making – analyse the exact words of the gift and look at it as a whole and you will boost your marks!

[4] See how very close reading of the words of the question pays off: the key words are 'a reasonable amount out of it' and not the entire sum to be held for Eileen.

enough? In *Anthony* v *Donges* [1998] 2 FLR 775 HC a widow was left 'such minimal part of (the) estate as she might be entitled to . . . for maintenance purposes'. This was held to be too uncertain as no such minimal entitlement exists.

Where the trustees are given discretion this may enable the court to declare that there is certainty of subject matter. This seems to be the explanation of *Re Golay* [1965] 1 WLR 969 HC where the testator directed that a Mrs Bridgewater should 'enjoy one of my flats during her lifetime' and 'receive a reasonable income from my other properties'. It was held that the word 'reasonable' provided a sufficiently objective standard to enable the court if necessary to quantify the amount. The case must be regarded as borderline as there was no further assistance given in the will to guide the trustees or the court.[5] In this case Paul has also added the words 'and generally to keep up appearances'. This sounds very informal and may distinguish it from *Re Golay* and mean that there is no certainty. If the court finds that there is no certainty of subject matter at all and so the whole trust fails then the property will also be held on a resulting trust for Paul's estate.

[5] It is important to clarify this point. Too many students see the words 'reasonable income' etc. in a question and automatically apply *Re Golay* without any explanation.

(b) The gift of '£1 million to my trustees Josephine and Maureen' obviously satisfies the test of certainty of intention as the word 'trustees' is used and certainty of subject matter as the gift is of £1 million. The problem is with certainty of objects. The words 'to distribute in their absolute discretion'[6] indicate a discretionary trust, and the test for certainty of objects was laid down in *McPhail* v *Doulton* [1971] AC 424 HL where Lord Wilberforce in the House of Lords held that the test was: 'Can it be said with certainty that any given individual is or is not a member of the class?' (This is often known as the individual ascertainability test.) Thus it is open to anyone to come forward and show that they are an inhabitant of the County of Herefordshire.

[6] If you see these words remember that they indicate a discretionary trust and so if the question involves certainty of objects then you will have to apply *McPhail* v *Doulton*.

Lord Wilberforce in *McPhail* v *Doulton* pointed out that trustees should not approach their duties in a narrow way but 'ought to make such a survey of the range of objects or possible beneficiaries as will enable them to carry out their fiduciary duty'. In *Re Baden's Deed Trusts (No 2)* [1973] Ch 9 CA Sachs LJ said that the trustees must assess the size of the problem in 'a

[7] Add to your marks by not just mentioning *McPhail* v *Doulton* but this point too.

[8] There is some debate on whether this is actually a separate point or not but most textbooks treat it separately and you would be unwise not to mention it.

[9] The perpetuity point is often missed: you should always mention it in a certainties question.

[10] Check in any question exactly when the will was executed.

[11] It is an (almost) infallible rule that if a question says: 'would your answer differ' then it will, but it may not so do not assume this! However, here it does.

[12] You could mention that the gift could have specified a period of 80 years but in fact it did not.

businesslike way'. In *Re Hay's Settlement Trust* [1982] 1 WLR 202 HC Megarry V-C said that a trustee should first appreciate the 'width of the field' and the 'size of the problem' before considering whether a grant was appropriate in individual cases.[7]

The other point is that there are nearly 200,000 inhabitants of the County of Herefordshire and in *McPhail* v *Doulton* Lord Wilberforce said that even though a description of beneficiaries complied with the test he had laid down it might be 'so hopelessly wide as not to form anything like a class', and gave as an example 'all the residents of Greater London'. This principle was applied in *R* v *District Auditor ex parte West Yorkshire Metropolitan County Council* [1986] RVR 24 HC where a trust set up for the inhabitants of the County of West Yorkshire, of which there were about 2,500,000, was held void for administrative unworkability.[8] Lloyd LJ held that 'A trust with as many as 2½ million potential beneficiaries is . . . quite simply unworkable.' If the court decides that the trust is administratively unworkable then it will fail. As there is certainty of intention and subject matter the trustees cannot treat the £1 million as an absolute gift but will hold it on a resulting trust for Paul's estate.

Assuming that there is a valid trust there is also the question of whether it complies with the rule against perpetuities.[9] There are two perpetuity rules and the applicable one here concerns remoteness of vesting of interests. Section 5 of the Perpetuities and Accumulations Act 2009 provides that in these cases there shall be a perpetuity period of 125 years but by section 5A the new period will not apply to a will executed before the 2009 Act comes into force, which was on 6 April 2010. Here the will is dated 7 April 2010 and so the 2009 Act will apply.[10] In the cases of the trusts for individuals this period will clearly be satisfied but in the case of the trust for the inhabitants of the County of Herefordshire the trustees must distribute the funds within 125 years. Any funds remaining will be held on a resulting trust for those entitled under Paul's estate.

If the will had been dated 5 April 2010 then my answer would differ[11] as the old law on perpetuities would apply and the gift would have to vest within lives or lives in being plus 21 years.[12] Here the lives in being will be the inhabitants of the County of

Herefordshire who have attained the age of 21 at the date of Paul's death and any child of such an inhabitant who clearly must reach the age of 21 years within 21 years of the date of their parents' death. Thus the gift satisfies the perpetuity period.

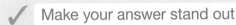

✓ Make your answer stand out

- Work your way through the three certainties, taking one at a time, and analysing the exact words of the question.
- Discussion of why the courts impose the requirements of certainty.
- Discussion of *McPhail* v *Doulton* and reference to academic criticism, e.g. Matthews (1984).
- Is there any need for the 'administratively unworkable' principle at all? See McKay (1974) who feels that this principle has no satisfactory basis. In *Re Manisty's Settlement* [1974] Ch 17 HC, Templeman J held that Lord Wilberforce's example of a class consisting of all the residents of Greater London showed that the settlor/testator had no sensible intention and was 'capricious'. However, in the West Yorkshire case there was no question of capriciousness and so the administrative unworkability principle may add something to the law.

❗ Don't be tempted to . . .

- Omit to mention in each case each of the three certainties even if it is obvious that there is certainty. If so a brief mention will suffice.
- Fail to recall accurately *exactly* what Lord Wilberforce laid down in *McPhail* v *Doulton* on the requirement of certainty of objects in discretionary trusts.
- Miss the perpetuity point.
- Apply the decision in *Re Golay* uncritically.

❓ Question 2

Matt, who has just died, left the following bequests in his will. You are asked to advise the trustees, Tim and Tom, on their validity.

(a) £20,000 to my daughter Mary and I wish her to use part of it for herself and I am confident that she will hold the remaining part for all my cousins.

(b) My collection of rare plants in my garden to be held to enable any work colleague of mine or friend who wishes to buy one. [Matt worked at a local college.]

(c) £10,000 to the landlord of the Black Bush public house to distribute at his discretion among my old drinking pals. He knows who they are.

Diagram plan

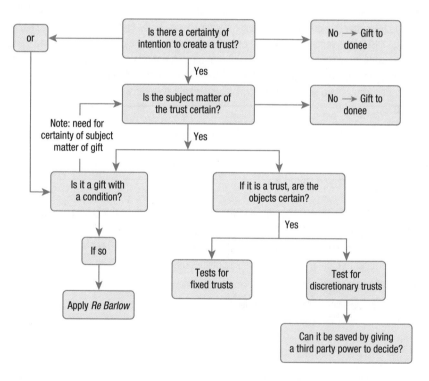

A printable version of this diagram plan is available from **www.pearsoned.co.uk/lawexpressqa**

Answer plan

→ Analyse exactly what the words of each bequest mean.

→ Then go on to analyse each bequest to see if there is certainty of intention, subject matter and objects.

→ Is there a gift with a condition rather than a trust in any of these cases?

→ If any of the certainties are not present, identify what the consequences will be and apply the relevant law.

→ Is it possible to save the gifts in any way?

→ If the gifts are not valid and will not go to the intended beneficiaries then identify where the property contained in the gifts will go.

Answer

[1] An excellent start and a sure way to pick up marks: you can see at once that the terms of this gift need analysis.

(a) We first need to clarify the terms of this bequest.[1] There is an initial gift of '£20,000 to my daughter Mary' with the intention that she is to use 'part of it for herself' and then there is a further and apparently separate part where the testator says that she is 'confident' that Mary 'will hold the remaining part for all my cousins'. There is no doubt that there is an initial gift to Mary but the question is whether the separate part imposes a trust on Mary for the benefit of her cousins or whether this is just a request to Mary which she can comply with or ignore it and can keep this as a gift also.

First, we must decide if there is certainty of intention to create a trust. In **Re Hamilton** [1895] 2 Ch 370 CA, Lindley LJ said that the courts must look at all the words used by the testator or settlor to see if, on their true construction in the context of the particular gift, a trust was intended. The word 'confident' may not indicate a trust as in **Re Adams and the Kensington Vestry** (1884) 27 Ch D 394 HC, where a testator left his property to his wife absolutely 'in full confidence that she will do what is right as to the disposal thereof between my children . . . '. It was held that no trust was created but there was only a moral obligation on her to provide for the children. Such a case is often known as a gift with a motive. However, it is important to look at the gift as a whole and here the word 'hold' is used which could indicate a trust.[2] Thus, in **Comiskey v Bowring-Hanbury** [1905] AC 84

[2] This point is always worth making – analyse the exact words of the gift and look at it as a whole and you will boost your marks!

HL a testator also left his property to his wife 'in full confidence that she will make such use of it as I would myself and that at my death she will devise it to such one or more of the nieces as she may think fit and in default of any disposition by her thereof by will or testament I hereby direct that all my estate and property acquired by her under this my will shall at her death be divided among my said nieces'. The language is clearly intended to create a binding obligation. As Halsbury LC observed, one significant phrase is 'I hereby direct' and this can be compared to 'hold' in this case.

If there is certainty of intention then is there certainty of subject matter? This is doubtful, as the words used are 'the remaining part' as in **Sprange v Barnard** (1789) 2 Bro CC 585, where the will gave property to the testatrix's husband 'for his sole use' and then provided that 'the remaining part of what is left, that he does not want . . . to be divided between' members of his family. As the term 'remaining part' was uncertain, the husband took absolutely. It is suggested that the same will apply here and, although the objects (the cousins)[3] seem to be certain, the lack of certainty of subject matter will cause this trust to fail. Thus, as Mary was intended to take part anyway as a gift and we do not know what part was to be held on trust, she will take all as a gift.

(b) The next gift is of 'my collection of rare plants in my garden' and evidence would be needed on whether the actual rare plants can be identified. If not, the gift will fail for lack of certainty of subject matter.[4] If this is certain then we must consider the bequest, which is that they are to be held to enable 'any work colleague of mine or friend who wishes to buy one'. This looks like a gift with a condition precedent attached, as the rare plants can only be bought by a work colleague or friend. In **Re Barlow's Will Trusts** [1979] 1 WLR 278 HC a testatrix directed her executor 'to allow any member of my family and any friends of mine who wish to do so' to purchase paintings belonging to her. The court held that the trust was valid, even though the words 'family' and, more particularly, 'friends' may have been uncertain because this was not a discretionary trust, where trustees had to 'survey the field' but merely a case of conditions being attached to individual gifts.[5] Thus a gift to a person who did come within

[3] Extra marks for picking up this small but relevant point.

[4] We cannot decide if there is certainty of subject matter, so take this point as far as you can and then move on to certainty of objects. You will lose marks (a lot of them!) if you just stop at one point and decide that the gift fails there. Instead, go on to consider the possibility that the gift might just be valid. You can then look at the next point and earn more marks.

[5] Note this important distinction and make sure that you can spot it in an exam. It is likely to arise on the type of facts set out here: if there was a gift of £20,000 to be held on trust to be distributed among my friends this would be a discretionary trust, as there are no individual gifts.

the meaning of 'family' or 'friend' would not be invalidated by uncertainty as to whether another person does so. Moreover, the court laid down tests to establish if a person is a friend, such as whether they met socially. On this basis it seems that, as the term 'work colleagues' is probably certain and 'friends' can be made so by applying **Re Barlow**, this gift can be upheld.

(c) The bequest of £10,000 to the landlord of the Black Bush public house to 'distribute among my old drinking pals' probably contains certainty of intention as the words 'to distribute' are used, which implies an obligation, and there is certainty of subject matter – £10,000.[6] The problem is that the term 'old drinking pals' may not satisfy the test for certainty of objects. The words 'to distribute in their absolute discretion' indicate a discretionary trust, and the test for certainty of objects was laid down in **McPhail v Doulton** [1971] AC 424 HL, where Lord Wilberforce in the House of Lords held that it was. 'Can it be said with certainty that any given individual is or is not a member of the class?' (Often known as the individual ascertainability test.) So in this case it is open to anyone to come forward and show that they are an old drinking pal, and the landlord is made the judge of this.

[6] Students sometimes fall into the trap of thinking that there is no certainty of subject matter as we do not know how much each beneficiary is to get. That is not the point: we know the total sum to be held on trust and that is what matters.

Given that the term 'old drinking pals' seems to be conceptually uncertain, does this power given to the landlord to decide assist?[7] It is suggested that it does not. In **Re Tuck's Settlement Trusts** [1978] Ch 49 CA any dispute as to whether a person was of the Jewish faith was to be determined by a Chief Rabbi and that was held to validate the trust, but this was a question of fact and here we have a question on which the landlord will have to exercise judgement. Moreover, as the landlord is not specified, the landlord at the time of making a judgement may not have known Matt. As Jenkins J observed in **Re Coxen** [1948] Ch 747 HC, 'if the testator had insufficiently defined the state of affairs on which the trustees were to form their opinion . . . merely by making their opinion the criteria' would not save the gift.

[7] This point is a bit of a trap for the unwary. Students often just say: 'Well of course he will know who they are as they are his customers.' This approach will lose you marks. Instead, follow through the law as shown here.

It is suggested that this is a case of conceptual uncertainty and so the gift fails. Instead, the trustees will hold the £10,000 on a resulting trust for Matt's residuary legatees or, if there is none, for those entitled on his intestacy.

Make your answer stand out

- Analysis and criticism of the decision in *Re Barlow's Will Trusts* [1979] 1 WLR 278 HC: see Emery (1982).
- Analysis of the idea of conceptual uncertainty.
- Analysis of the reasons why the courts will not be likely to uphold the clause allowing the landlord to decide who the drinking pals are. See also *Re Jones* [1953] Ch 125 HC and *Re Tepper's Will Trusts* [1987] Ch 358 HC. Could either of these decisions be applied to this situation?

! Don't be tempted to . . .

- Plunge straight in without analysing the exact terms of each bequest.
- Mention all three certainties in each question.
- Just mention *Adams and Kensington Vestry* in the first part – contrast it with *Comiskey.*
- Assume in the final part that there is no problem with deciding whether the gift is certain as the landlord can decide.

Question 3

Consider the problems of lack of certainty of subject matter in trusts in contracts for the sale of unascertained goods and intangible property.

Answer plan

→ Set the scene by explaining briefly the problems in these cases.

→ Trace the cases involving possible trusts of goods.

→ Analyse the impact of the Sale of Goods (Amendment) Act 1995.

→ Evaluate both the decision in *Hunter* v *Moss* and the criticisms of it.

→ Round off the answer by looking at how the Supreme Court of New South Wales dealt with the problem in *White* v *Shortall.*

Diagram plan

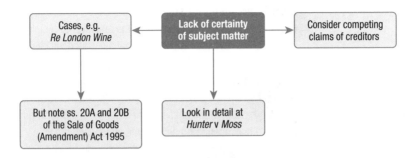

A printable version of this diagram plan is available from **www.pearsoned.co.uk/lawexpressqa**

Answer

[1] In an answer on a detailed theoretical area such as this it always helps to start with a simple example and then, as seen in this paragraph, you can build on it.

Where, for example, a trust is declared by John over 'my Rolls Royce motor car registration number XYZ 123', there is of course no problem of certainty of subject matter.[1] Suppose, however, that John buys 100 bottles of a vintage wine from wine shippers who then go into liquidation. At that moment, John's 100 bottles have not been set apart for him. To whom do the 100 bottles belong? Is it to John or the firm's creditors? Suppose again that John owns 1,000 shares in X Company and declares that he holds 100 of these in trust for Z: the question is, which 100 shares?

The first of the modern cases is **Re London Wine Co (Shippers) Ltd** [1986] PCC 121 HC. Wine was sold to customers but it often remained at the warehouse of the company. It was held that no trust of the wine had been created even though customers received a certificate of title describing them as beneficial owners of particular wine. Nothing had been done to appropriate the wine to individual customers and the existence of the certificates proved little, as in some cases they were issued before the wine had even been ordered by the company. This was followed by **Re Goldcorp Exchange Ltd (in receivership)** [1995] 1 AC 74 PC, where purchasers of bullion for future delivery from Goldcorp received a certificate of ownership, but no bullion was set aside for them, nor was this intended, as the object was to enable the owners to sell it when the price had increased. The court held, as in **Re London Wine,** that title could

[2] Note how in this paragraph we have mentioned three cases and have linked them, as where we said 'as in' the case of . . .

not pass because the bullion was unidentified and so could not be the subject of a private trust.[2] Again, in *Mac-Jordan Construction Ltd* v *Brookmount Erostin Ltd* [1992] BCIC 350 CA there was no trust of a sum of money retained by the employer of a builder which was to be paid over on confirmation that the work done by the builder was satisfactory, as although the employer was called the trustee, no separate fund of this money was set up. However, under sections 20A and 20B of the Sale of Goods (Amendment) Act 1995, purchasers who have paid for unascertained goods which form part of an identified bulk acquire property rights as tenants in common, which means that the decision in *Re Goldcorp* would now be different, as the purchasers would now have rights at common law meaning that they would not need to rely on equity.[3]

[3] An examiner will expect you to mention this point and you need to show how it would have affected the decision. It is often missed by students.

One reason why the courts have been reluctant to hold the existence of a trust where there is a competing claim by creditors was mentioned in *Re Stapylton Fletcher Ltd* [1994] 1 WLR 1181 HC, where the judge said that the court should be 'very cautious in devising equitable interests and remedies which erode the statutory scheme for distribution on intestacy'.[4] Moreover, the courts feel that where chattels such as bottles of wine have not been segregated, there cannot be a trust, as they are not necessarily identical, but is this true when goods are mass produced?

[4] At this stage we have set out the law and, in order to gain a good pass, we need to move on to criticisms and analysis, which is what this sentence sets out to do.

The above cases concerned contests between claimants under a possible trust and creditors. A case which did not is[5] *Hemmens* v *Wilson Browne* [1995] Ch 223 HC: a document which was intended to give a party the right to call on the other for a payment of £100,000 did not create a trust, as there was no identifiable fund.

[5] Note how this answer is being developed – this case illustrates a different area.

[6] This is an absolutely essential case to mention in an essay on trusts of intangible property and your marks will suffer if you do not consider it in detail.

Hunter v *Moss* [1994] 1 WLR 452 CA concerns another area, that of trusts of intangible property, to which the Sale of Goods (Amendment) Act 1995 does not apply. Nor was there a contest with creditors.[6] The defendant was the registered owner of 950 shares in a company and executed a declaration that he held 50 of them on trust for the claimant, who was also an employee. The court upheld the trust even though the shares, which were the subject of the trust, could not be identified.

The decision is usually explained on the basis that the court distinguished between tangible assets such as wine and intangible assets such as shares, although the court simply referred to a distinction

[7] Having mentioned the facts of this case, the examiner will expect you to consider the criticisms of it as it is a controversial decision.

[8] Inclusion of this point will really boost your marks, as you are demonstrating knowledge of another area outside the syllabus in order to explain your criticism.

[9] An examiner will expect balance in an answer and here you are looking at the opposing viewpoint which is that in fact *Hunter* v *Moss* is a good decision.

[10] In this essay we have not concluded by summing up the answer as the discussion of *Hunter* v *Moss* was detailed and any summing up would only have repeated what we have said. Instead, we have gained extra marks by bringing in a case which has considered *Hunter* v *Moss*.

between trusts of chattels and shares.[7] In addition, the court relied on an analogy with gifts of shares in a will. Such a gift is valid even though the shares are part of a larger whole, for example 100 shares out of 1,000 shares of mine in the Hanbury Bank. The problem is that this analogy is false. Although such a gift is valid, the shares are not held by the executors as trustees but as personal representatives until administration of the estate has been completed[8] (***Commissioner of Stamp Duties (Queensland)* v *Livingston*** [1965] AC 694 PC). The result is that beneficiaries in this situation do not have rights as holders of a proprietary interest in the property and so the problems set out above do not apply.

Hunter* v *Moss has been criticised on the basis that the distinction between shares (or intangible property) and chattels (or tangible property) is a distinction without a difference. Even if there is likely to be less difference between individual shares than there is between individual bottles of wine, is this a satisfactory basis on which to found a distinction between which trusts are valid and which are not? In any case, what if some of the shares have been acquired by a forged gratuitous transfer? What is the position if some of the shares have been gambled away? Are they shares belonging to the trust or not? Had a trust been declared of one-nineteenth of the shares, this would have undoubtedly been valid as there would then be certainty of the subject matter. As it is, the uncertainty makes it impossible to hold that there is a trust.

In support of the decision, it has been said that the problem of precisely which shares are subject to the trust can be solved by applying the duty to safeguard the trust property, which means that the trustee is under an immediate duty once the trust is declared to separate those shares which are subject to the trust from the rest of them.[9] If a trustee fails to do this, then she has mixed trust property with other assets and would be liable under the tracing rules. It could be argued, however, that this confuses two distinct issues: the rules on establishing a trust, with which we are concerned here, and the rules which apply once a trust has been established, such as the duties of trustees.

The Supreme Court of New South Wales did not follow the reasoning in ***Hunter* v *Moss*** in their decision in ***White* v *Shortall*** [2006] NSWSC 1379,[10] where there was a declaration of trust over 1,500,000 shares and the claimant was to acquire an equitable interest in 222,000 of them. Instead of holding that there was a trust of the 222,000 shares, it held that the trustees could elect which of the total 1,500,000 shares would count as the 222,000 to be held on trust. Is this a better solution than that reached in **Hunter v Moss**?

 Make your answer stand out

- Structure the answer so that it focuses directly on the difficult theoretical issues (especially those considered in *Hunter* v *Moss*), possibly at the expense of the facts of some cases.
- Consider carefully how the Court of Appeal in *Hunter* v *Moss* distinguished *Re London Wine*.
- Look at Hayton (1994), who is critical of *Hunter* v *Moss*.
- Then look at Martin (1996) for a contrary view.

! Don't be tempted to . . .

- Discuss the law on certainty of subject matter in trusts in general. Focus on the exact area raised in the question.
- Worse still, begin by listing *all* the certainties.
- Fail to explain how the Sale of Goods (Amendment) Act 1995 relates to the case law.

Question 4

'In view of the importance of the discretionary trust today it is vital that the tests for certainty of objects in cases of these trusts are clear and workable'.

Consider why discretionary trusts are important today and whether the present test for certainty is indeed clear and workable.

Answer plan

→ Explain exactly what a discretionary trust is and distinguish it from a fixed trust.

→ Explain with examples why discretionary trusts are used.

→ State and explain the reasons why there needs to be a clear test of certainty of objects in discretionary trusts.

→ Explain the actual decision in *McPhail* v *Doulton* and analyse the judgments.

→ Explain the problem with the words 'is not' as used in the individual ascertainability test in *McPhail* v *Doulton.*

Diagram plan

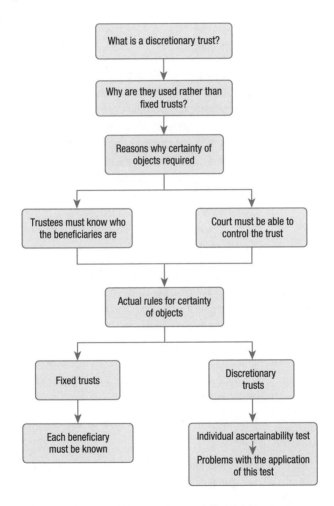

A printable version of this diagram plan is available from **www.pearsoned.co.uk/lawexpressqa**

Answer

A discretionary trust is where the trustees have a discretion as to which beneficiaries shall benefit from a trust and in what proportion.[1] For instance the trust may be for 'such of my five children and in such shares as my trustees shall in their absolute discretion decide'. So where the trustees make a particular distribution of money they have a discretion as to which children shall be the recipients and how much they shall receive. They are distinguished from fixed trusts where the trust instrument specifies the share which each beneficiary is to take (the 'list' principle').

Discretionary trusts are important today in comparison with fixed trusts for three main reasons. First, they are flexible. If we take the above example of a discretionary trust then it may be that one of the children is seriously disabled and will not be able to earn their living whereas the other four will be able to be financially independent. So it may well make sense for the trustees to allocate a larger share of the trust's capital to the disabled child. Secondly, these trusts have advantages when a beneficiary goes bankrupt. As any money beneficiaries might receive from the trust is entirely at the trustees' discretion they have no ascertainable interest that their creditors can seize in repayment of their debts.

[2] You need to be careful here. This is not a tax examination and the examiner will not expect detailed knowledge of tax law. However, what you do say must be accurate. Here we have contented ourselves with a general example.

Thirdly, and probably the most important advantage today, is tax planning.[2] Suppose that James executes his will in 2000 but in 2015 the Government introduces changes to tax laws that mean that as his will stands there is an increased liability to tax. James could make a new will but suppose that he is not interested in doing this or is difficult to contact. However, the trustees, using the discretionary character of the trust, can make sure that any distributions of capital are tax efficient.

[3] In this area the decisions of the courts have been arrived at against a background of fundamental points in trust law about the role of the courts in the administration of trusts. This is why it is vital to begin by stating these clearly and only then go on to look at the cases.

There are two reasons[3] why some degree of certainty of objects is required:

(a) Unless the trustees know who the beneficiaries are, they cannot distribute the trust property.

(b) The court needs to be able to control the trust so that if the trustees come to the court asking for directions as to who the beneficiaries are, it can give them. In ***Morice v Bishop of Durham***

(1804) 10 Ves 522 HC Sir William Grant said: 'There can be no trust over the exercise of which this court will not assume control; for an uncontrollable power of disposition would be ownership, and not trust.' This principle also appears, in the guise of the beneficiary principle, in connection with the linked but not identical principle that a trust must have a beneficiary who can enforce it.[4]

[4] This is a separate, but linked, point and mainly arises in the context of non-charitable purpose trusts. A brief reference to it at this point shows the kind of wider thinking which will bring you extra marks.

The test for certainty of objects in discretionary trusts was laid down in *McPhail v Doulton* [1971] AC 424 HL, where Lord Wilberforce in the House of Lords held that it was. 'Can it be said with certainty that any given individual is or is not a member of the class?'[5] (This is often known as the individual ascertainability test.)

[5] Make sure for the exam that you can memorise these words and, above all, apply them. It will certainly increase your marks. Students often forget the 'or is not' part.

In *McPhail v Doulton* the trustees were directed to apply the net income of a fund in making at their absolute discretion grants to the following beneficiaries: the officers and employees or ex-officers or ex-employees of a company or their relatives or dependants. Under the list principle, the trust would have failed as although a list of the officers and employees of the company could doubtless be drawn up, it would not be possible to do so in the case of relatives and dependants. Should this cause the trust to fail?

Following Lord Wilberforce's statement of the individual ascertainability test, the case was remitted to the Chancery Division to decide if the test was satisfied and it was held that it was: *Re Baden's Deed Trusts (No 2)* [1973] Ch 9.

The problem has been to find a way of reconciling the need for a more relaxed test in discretionary trusts than the 'list' test in fixed trusts, as discretionary trusts by their nature are more flexible, with the need for a test which gives the courts a reasonable yardstick with which to exercise control if need be.

[6] Try to think of examples to illustrate theoretical issues – they will make your essay come alive.

Suppose that in the *McPhail* situation a sister of an employee came to the trustees and said that she was a relative.[6] It could doubtless be proved that she was or was not. But suppose that someone came and said that they were a second cousin twice removed? How could it be said with certainty that she was not a relative? She might be able to show that she probably *was* a relative but how could it be proved that she *was not*?

In *Re Baden* Sachs LJ took a straightforward view: if a person is not proved to be within the class then he is not within it. However, the fact that he cannot be proved to be actually in the class does not mean that he is not, in fact, within it. Proof of a negative does not follow from lack of proof of a positive. Megaw LJ said that the individual ascertainability test was satisfied if 'as regards a substantial number of objects, it can be said with certainty that they fall within the trust', even though it cannot be proved whether others fall within it or not. This test has merit, but it is not the individual ascertainability test of Lord Wilberforce. Stamp LJ[7] sought the aid of the principle in **Re Benjamin** [1902] 1 Ch 723 HC in which trustees, having done their best to find the beneficiaries, can apply to the court to be allowed to distribute the estate to those of whom they have knowledge.

The trouble seems to be the words 'is not'.[8] Why not then omit them and the test would then simply be 'can there be certainty that any given individual is a member of the class?' The problem is that if we omit these words we arrive at the one-person test proposed by Denning MR in **Re Gulbenkian's Settlement Trusts (No 1)** [1970] AC 508 HL and rejected by the House of Lords: is it sufficient if it can be said with certainty that any one person is a member of the class? This is considered to be too narrow, as there might only be one certain member of the class.

The difficulty is that the individual ascertainability test if applied strictly is too near to the 'list' test for fixed trusts.[9] To say that it must be said with certainty if a person is or *is not* a member of the class comes near to saying that we need to know who is and who is not within it, and the best way of doing this is by drawing up a list. The truth is that we do not have a satisfactory test for deciding the objects of a discretionary trust and so we are left with the **McPhail** one.

[7] Note the reference in this paragraph to the views of three judges – it is this kind of detail which makes an answer stand out as it shows that you have gone beyond the facts of the case and looked at the judgments.

[8] This is the point which most students so often miss in this type of question, whether it is an essay or a problem. Make sure that you are clear about it.

[9] This conclusion seeks to draw the discussion to a close by stating the real difficulty: if we abandon the 'list' test for certainty of objects when we have not yet found a replacement. You could come to a different conclusion and say that the decision in *McPhail* v *Doulton* has stood since 1971 and there does not seem to be evidence from the cases that the 'individual ascertainability' test has not worked.

✓ Make your answer stand out

- Contrast powers of appointment and discretionary trusts.
- Discuss with examples the distinction between evidential and conceptual uncertainty.
- Idea of 'administrative unworkability': is this helpful?
- Read and refer to Harris (1971), which analyses *McPhail* v *Doulton*.
- Ask what test will apply to certainty of objects in the cases of valid non-charitable purpose trusts and *Quistclose* trusts.

! Don't be tempted to . . .

- Fail to distinguish between fixed and discretionary trusts.
- Fail to consider the practical advantages of discretionary trusts.
- Just state the law on certainty of objects.
- Begin your answer with a long account of the case law.
- Only provide a superficial analysis of *McPhail* v *Doulton*. You must *really* know this case if you attempt this question!

www.pearsoned.co.uk/lawexpressqa

 Go online to access more revision support including additional essay and problem questions with diagram plans, You be the marker questions, and download all diagrams from the book.

Formalities

4

How this topic may come up in exams

This is not a popular topic for students because the facts of the cases tend to be very complex as they often concern convoluted tax avoidance schemes. Remember that the actual facts are unlikely to reoccur in exams simply because this is not a tax law exam. The vital message is to be absolutely clear on the principles established by the cases and then to recognise how they can arise in exam questions.

(Material in this chapter can arise in other areas such as constitution and certainties and you will find a question of this kind in Chapter 13.)

Before you begin

It's a good idea to consider the following key themes of formalities before tackling a question on this topic.

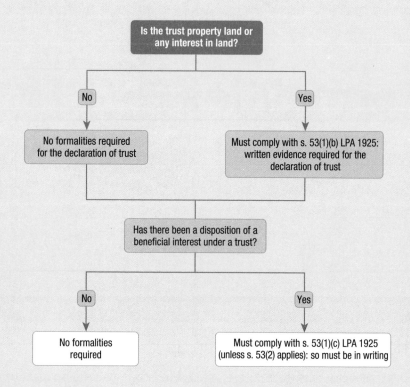

A printable version of this diagram is available from **www.pearsoned.co.uk/lawexpressqa**

❓ Question 1

Nick transferred the freehold house, 'Seaview', which he owned and where he lived with his girlfriend Sally into her name as he was going to work abroad for five years. There was a properly executed deed of transfer but there was no consideration expressed in the transfer deed nor was it expressed to be by gift.

When he was abroad Nick rang Sally and said, 'As you know I have put my house in your name but any remaining interest which I may have in it is to be held for my friend Freda.'

Nick was visited when abroad by his brother Sam and Nick said to Sam: 'You know those shares in the Hanbury Bank that Aunt Agatha made you a trustee of for me? It would be better if all my interest in them went to your son Tom'.

Sally, Freda, Sam and Tom ask your advice on the legal and beneficial ownership of:

(a) 'Seaview'

(b) the shares in the Hanbury Bank.

Answer plan

→ Identify that the transfer of 'Seaview' must comply with section 52(1) of the LPA 1925.

→ Note that the transfer of 'Seaview' by Nick to Sally may create either an express trust or a resulting trust.

→ Set out the formal requirements for an express trust of land in section 53(1)(b) of the LPA 1925 and apply them to the question.

→ Explain how a resulting trust could arise on these facts and explain that there are no formal requirements for this type of trust.

→ Identify where section 53(1)(c) applies as there is a transfer of an equitable interest.

→ Apply the relevant law.

→ Consider the consequences where either of the above requirements are not complied with.

→ Examine whether Nick's beneficial interest in the shares has been disposed of applying section 53(1)(c) and cases.

Diagram plan

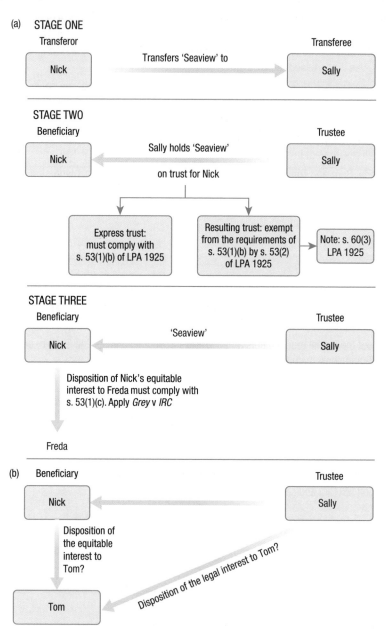

A printable version of this diagram plan is available from **www.pearsoned.co.uk/lawexpressqa**

Answer

(a) The first point is that Nick transferred Seaview to Sally by a properly executed deed of transfer. We are told that it is validly executed and so will satisfy section 52(1) of the LPA 1925.[1] However, the transfer was for no consideration and no words of gift were expressed.

[1] There is no need to set out the requirements of section 52(1) for a valid deed as you are told that the transfer is validly executed, but you will gain credit for picking this issue up at the start.

There are two possibilities here.[2] One is that there was an express trust of 'Seaview'. Although Nick did not actually say to Sally when he transferred the house that it was to be held on trust, he later rang her and said, 'As you know I have put my house in your name but any remaining interest which I may have in it is to be held for my friend Freda.' The reference to 'any remaining interest' and the need to tell Freda of this at all may indicate that the transfer by Nick to Sally was expressly on trust for Freda. If so then the requirements of section 53(1)(b) of the LPA 1925 must be complied with. This provides that 'a declaration of trust concerning land or any interest therein must be manifested and proved by some writing signed by some person who is able to declare the same or by his will' and it is clear that there was no written declaration of trust here.

[2] This is a nice confident start – clearly you know where you are going!

Section 53(1)(b) is silent on the position when these requirements are not complied with[3] but it is accepted that this will not make the trust void but only unenforceable, in line with what was the position under section 40(1) of the LPA (*Gardner* v *Rowe* (1826) 5 Russ 828 HC). Therefore Nick could not enforce the trust against Sally who could thus take 'Seaview' beneficially.

[3] Students generally miss this point entirely – so a mention of it is bound to increase your marks.

The other possibility is that there is a presumed resulting trust.[4] These arise on the basis that the presumed intention of the transferor, Nick in this case, was not to make an outright transfer but to transfer the legal title to the transferee, Sally here, with the intention that Sally should hold on a resulting trust for Nick. Thus in *Re Vinogradoff* [1935] WN 68 HC the testatrix had transferred an £800 War Loan which was in her own name into the joint names of herself and her four-year-old daughter. It was held that the daughter held it on a resulting trust for the testatrix. In this case Nick's later conversation with Sally in which he states that 'any remaining interest which I may have in it is to be held for my friend Freda' does not provide

[4] This shows the importance, when revising for an exam, of making sure that you have a basic understanding of all the main areas as they constantly relate to each other. As you can see here, the provisions of section 53(2) of the LPA 1925 provide a link between formalities and resulting and constructive trusts.

[5] Note how we have analysed these facts to show how there are two possible results: an express or a resulting trust. This is the type of reasoning that really does add to your marks. The trick is very simple: study the exact words used in a question and remember that there might be more than one possible answer!

[6] This is a useful point to mention in order to clarify the position.

[7] Do remember this – it is one of those vital points which, if you get it wrong, could send your answer off in a completely wrong direction.

[8] This point of detail is worth recalling – it is almost universally omitted by students.

[9] Note how the essential point of the case has been emphasised first as this is what you need to recall in formalities questions.

evidence of an express trust but instead supports the presumption of a resulting trust on the basis that Nick may well have regarded himself as having retained some interest in 'Seaview'.[5]

Section 60(3) of the LPA 1925 provides that in a voluntary conveyance, as was the case here, 'a resulting trust for the grantor shall not be implied merely by reason that the property is not expressed to be conveyed for the use or benefit of the grantee.'[6] However, this merely means that just because the transfer to Sally did not expressly state that she was to hold 'Seaview' for her own benefit does not by itself mean that she holds it on a resulting trust. It is submitted, however, that there is sufficient evidence of a resulting trust for Nick by the omission of any words of gift in the transfer and Nick's later reference to Freda.

If there is a resulting trust then the requirements of section 53(1)(b) of the LPA 1925 do not apply[7] and section 53(2) of the LPA 1925 provides that section 53(1)(b) 'does not affect the creation or operation of resulting, implied or constructive trusts'. Therefore there is no need for any written evidence of this trust and the result is that Sally holds the legal title of 'Seaview' but, as she does so on a resulting trust for Nick, Nick has the equitable interest.

However, this analysis means that Nick originally retained the beneficial interest in 'Seaview' under a resulting trust and so when he later said to Sally that he wanted Freda to have 'any remaining interest' that he has in 'Seaview' he was making a disposition of his equitable interest under the trust. As such it must comply with section 53(1)(c) of the LPA 1925 which provides that a disposition of an equitable interest or trust must be in writing signed either by the settlor or by his authorised agent. Failure to comply with section 53(1)(c) makes the disposition void. This has always been accepted as the correct view and this is supported by the word '*must*' in the subsection although, as with section 53(1)(b), the subsection is silent on this point.[8] In this case Nick does not make a direct disposition but directs Sally as trustee to hold on trust for another person, Freda.

In **Grey v IRC** [1960] AC 1 HL it was held that such a transaction was caught by section 53(1)(c) and so required writing.[9] Here the settlor transferred shares to trustees to hold as nominees for him. He then orally directed the trustees to hold the shares on trust for his grandchildren and the trustees later executed a written declaration of trust. However, the actual disposition was by the oral direction and so it was void. It is submitted that the same will apply here and that in consequence Sally will continue to hold on trust for Nick.

(b) Nick was visited when abroad by his brother Sam and Nick said to Sam: 'You know those shares in the Hanbury Bank that Aunt Agatha made you a trustee for me? It would be better if all the rights in them went to your son Tom.'

[10] There is no need to set out section 53(1)(c) again.

[11] This phrase – or something similar – in a question often indicates the possible application of *Vandervell* v *IRC*.

Is this a disposition of Nick's beneficial interest in the shares? If so, it will be caught by section 53(1)(c) of the LPA 1925[10] and, as it is not in writing it will be void so that Nick will still be the trustee. The vital point is that Nick directs 'all the rights' in the shares[11] to be transferred and so it can be argued that he is not transferring a beneficial interest, as there will no longer be any beneficial interest as Tom will own the shares absolutely.

Thus in ***Vandervell v IRC*** [1967] 2 AC 291 HL a bank which held shares on trust for Vandervell as a bare trustee then transferred them, on Vandervell's instructions, to the Royal College of Surgeons. It was held that as the bank's legal title to the shares and Vandervell's equitable interest were both transferred section 53(1)(c) did not apply as there was no equitable interest to dispose of as it had merged with the legal interest. If this

[12] It is Sam as he is the legal owner.

applies here then all that Sam needs to do is transfer the shares to Tom.[12]

Make your answer stand out

■ Look very closely at the exact words used in the question and make a clear distinction between an express and a resulting trust.

■ Be prepared to look beyond the formalities issue and apply the relevant law on certainty of objects to the question.

■ Avoid too much detail on the cases involving formalities and concentrate on the principles which they establish.

■ Read Green (1984) especially at pp. 396–8. It is a really useful and clear explanation of the law on formalities.

Don't be tempted to . . .

- Set out the sections of the LPA 1925 in great detail at the expense of application of the facts.
- Set out facts of cases and not see the underlying point.
- Fail to point out the consequences of failing to comply with the formalities requirements.
- Fail to find a home for the property if the intended trust fails.

Question 2

Critically consider the circumstances in which formal requirements are imposed on the creation of trusts and the transfer of beneficial interests in trusts and the justifications for imposing these. Are these formal requirements justified?

Diagram plan

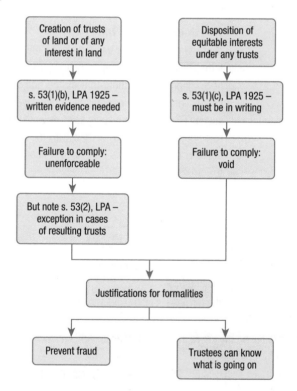

A printable version of this diagram plan is available from **www.pearsoned.co.uk/lawexpressqa**

Answer plan

→ State and explain the formal requirements in section 53(1)(b) and section 53(1)(c) of the LPA 1925.

→ Examine the exception for implied, resulting and constructive trusts in section 53(2).

→ Assess whether the prevention of fraud is an adequate justification for these requirements.

→ How applicable is the alternative justification: to enable the trustees to know what is going on?

→ Consider possible reform in this area as suggested by the Law Commission.

Answer

[1] Although much of the focus in this essay is to be the justification for this area of the law to exist at all the first part asks you to consider what the formal requirements actually are. This is the easier part of the answer and so to gain really good marks you must aim to pick up as many marks here as you can. This means being absolutely accurate as here.

[2] This is the kind of extra detail which will really add to your marks.

Formal requirements are imposed only on the creation of trusts where the trust is of land[1] by section 53(1)(b) of the LPA 1925, which provides that 'a declaration of trust concerning land or any interest therein must be manifested and proved by some writing signed by some person who is able to declare the same or by his will'. The signature of the settlor is needed. That of an agent will not suffice because of the words in section 53(1)(b) 'signed by some person who is able to declare the same'.

However, the actual declaration of trust need not be in writing. The words 'manifested and proved' require only written evidence.[2] Section 53(1)(b) does not specify what written evidence is required but it is likely that the cases on section 40(1) of the LPA 1925 (now repealed) will be a guide here. Section 40(1) required written evidence in cases of contracts for the sale of land (now the actual contract must be in writing), and the courts interpreted this to mean that, provided the main terms of the contract were evidenced by writing, the actual written evidence did not need to be in any particular form. It could be in more than one document, so long as there was evidence to show that they were linked, and the written evidence could have come into existence after the trust was created. In **Gardner v Rowe** (1826) 5 Russ 828 HC a trust of a lease was granted orally but later a deed was executed stating the trusts. This was held valid.

[3] This is a vital point which you must include. Section 53(2) is also important in other areas as it is really the foundation of the law on the family home as here most trusts are not in writing.

An important exception is that the requirement in section 53(1)(b) applies only to express trusts and not to resulting, implied or constructive trusts (s. 53(2) of the LPA 1925).[3] This has enabled the

[4] The detail of these cases would help if you have time but you certainly need to give examples as here.

courts to impose a resulting, implied or constructive trust in many cases where there was no written declaration of trust. Good examples are those involving disputes over the beneficial entitlement to the family home and where it is felt necessary to impose a trust to prevent fraud or unconscionable conduct. Particularly good instances are *Rochefoucauld v Boustead* [1897] 1 Ch 196 CA and *Hodgson v Marks* [1971] 1 Ch 892 CA.[4]

Section 53(1)(b) is silent on the position when these requirements are not complied with but it is accepted that this will not make the trust void but only unenforceable, in line with what was the position under section 40(1) of the LPA (*Gardner v Rowe* (above)). Therefore, it cannot be relied on in any legal proceedings but remains valid unless or until these are brought.

[5] Clarity is vital in this type of essay: so note here how we have contrasted the two relevant subsections. You could mention briefly that although this question only deals with trust law, section 53(1)(c) can surface in other areas: see the leasehold case of *Hardy* v *Haselden* [2011] EWCA Civ 1387.

By contrast to section 53(1)(b), which, as we have seen, only applies to trusts of land, dispositions of equitable interests arising under any trusts are caught by section 53(1)(c) of the LPA 1925,[5] which provides that a disposition of an equitable interest or trust must be in writing signed either by the settlor or by his authorised agent. Unlike the position under section 53(1)(b), the actual disposition must be in writing. Written evidence will not suffice. However, the disposition can be contained in more than one document provided that there is evidence to connect them (*Re Danish Bacon Co Ltd Staff Pension Fund Trusts* [1971] 1 WLR 248 HC).

[6] This is an important point of detail which will gain you extra marks, as most students just assume that section 53(1)(c) actually states that a failure to comply with it makes the disposition void.

The signature of an agent is sufficient in these cases and, as with section 53(1)(b), this subsection does not, by virtue of section 53(2) of the LPA 1925, apply to resulting, implied or constructive trusts. Failure to comply with section 53(1)(c) makes the disposition void. This has always been accepted as correct although, as with section 53(1)(b), the subsection is silent on this point.[6] The accepted view is supported by the word 'must' in the subsection, and also by the fact that the cases, including two decided by the House of Lords (*Grey v IRC* [1960] AC 1 and *Oughtred v IRC* [1960] AC 206), all proceed on the assumption that a failure to comply with this requirement is fatal to the disposition.

There appear to be two justifications for requiring formal requirements. The first is to prevent fraud. The requirement for formalities was first introduced by the Statute of Frauds 1677 when the requirement for written evidence of a contract for the sale of land was first introduced. The word 'fraud' gives the reason: to prevent someone fraudulently alleging that either a trust of land had been created or that an interest under a trust had been transferred.[7] The relevant parts of the Statute of Frauds were repealed in relation to trusts by the LPA 1925 and replaced by section 53(1)(b) and (c). The requirement of written evidence for a contract for the sale of land is now a requirement that the actual contract shall be in writing (s. 2 of the Law of Property (Miscellaneous Provisions) Act 1989).

Although it is obviously sensible to require writing as a safeguard against fraud, there is no doubt that this area of law is ripe for reform. The cases can be extremely complex and the object of the law can be lost sight of entirely. The Law Commission intended to review this topic and a Consultation Paper was expected in 1999 but there has been no progress as the Commission's resources have been concentrated on other topics.[8] Perhaps it is time for it to return to this area.

The other justification only applies to section 53(1)(c) and was suggested in *Vandervell* **v** *IRC* [1967] 2 AC 291 by Lord Upjohn, who said that the policy was to 'prevent hidden oral transactions in equitable interests in fraud of those truly entitled, and making it difficult, if not impossible, for the trustees to ascertain who are in truth the beneficiaries'. In simple terms, the policy is to enable the trustees and beneficiaries to know what is going on. However, it is arguable that the decisions of the courts on section 53(1)(c) do not always bear this policy out.[9] For example, in *Grey* **v** *IRC* it was held that a direction by a beneficiary to trustees that they now to hold on trust for another person required writing, although as the trustees are, by definition, involved here it is difficult to see how this accords with Lord Upjohn's policy reason in *Vandervell* **v** *IRC*.

The conclusion must be that this area of the law is ripe for review.[10] It has generated complex case law and although there may be a rationale for requiring formalities in both the creation of trusts and the disposition of beneficial interests under trusts the details of this area of the law urgently need revising.

[7] Do not stop at the point where you have said that the object is to prevent fraud. For a good mark you need to explain exactly what fraud it is designed to stop.

[8] This research detail will add to your marks. Keep an eye on this area, as the Law Commission may include it in a future programme of reform.

[9] Note that rather than just state what this particular justification is, we have added to our marks by taking a case and including a point of criticism. It would be possible at this stage to give great detail on the facts of this case and those of others but this would take you away from the point.

[10] There are two possible conclusions here: that the law should stay as it is or that it should change. Either is acceptable but you do need one of them.

Make your answer stand out

- Critical discussion of the decision in *Oughtred* v *IRC,* which dealt with whether the doctrine of constructive trusts applies to equitable interests. If it does, then a purchaser of property where the contract has not yet been completed, as was the case in *Oughtred* v *IRC* has an interest in the property in that they have the right to apply for a decree of specific performance to compel completion. The consequence is that the seller stands in the position of a constructive trustee for them. Follow this argument from *Oughtred* v *IRC* to *Neville* v *Wilson* [1997] Ch 144 to the decision of the Australian High Court in *Halloran* v *Minister Administering National Parks and Wildlife Act 1974* (2006) 80 AJLR 519. This case is helpfully considered by Turner (2006). Do make diagrams of the cases as you go along – it will help here a great deal.

- Discussion of *Neville* v *Wilson* in the context of the relationship between section 53(1)(b) and section 53(2) of the LPA 1925 and the article by Nolan (1996). Nolan refers to the 'extreme technicality and artificiality of the case law' in this area, a view with which it is impossible to disagree!

- Discussion of views in academic literature, e.g. Green (1984). Although this is now slightly outdated, it is a useful starting point.

! Don't be tempted to . . .

- Forget to distinguish clearly between section 53(1)(b) and section 53(2) of the LPA 1925.
- Just set out the relevant law and not discuss the justification for it.
- Leave out a mention of the Law Commission's intention to review this area.

www.pearsoned.co.uk/lawexpressqa

 Go online to access more revision support including additional essay and problem questions with diagram plans, You be the marker questions, and download all diagrams from the book.

Constitution of trusts

How this topic may come up in exams

This is a frequent topic for problem questions where you may also find that the question includes material on certainties and/or formalities and so you need to make sure that you are confident in these areas as well before you tackle a constitution question. You need to adopt an extremely structured approach to problems as there are many marks to be picked up by a detailed, thorough approach. There is also material for essay questions, especially as there have been fairly recent cases on the application of the principles in *Milroy* v *Lord* and on *donationes mortis causa*.

Before you begin

It's a good idea to consider the following key themes of constitution of trusts before tackling a question on this topic.

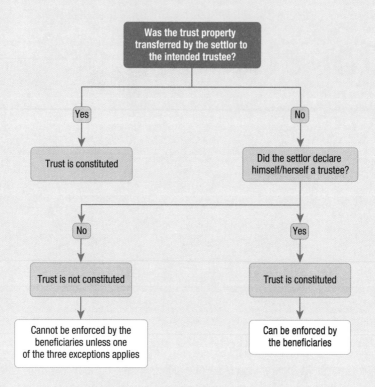

A printable version of this diagram is available from **www.pearsoned.co.uk/lawexpressqa**

❓ Question 1

John lived in a nursing home but still owned a cottage, 'Rosemount'. In April 2014 he thought that he had not long to live and so he wrote to his favourite granddaughter, Amanda: 'I would like you to have Rosemount when I die. You have been so kind to me and you have done so much work in helping me to renovate the cottage.' John then took the title deeds of 'Rosemount' and wrote: 'These deeds and all that they refer to I give to Amanda Jones from this time forth.' He then put the deeds back in their box which he kept.

In August 2014 John recovered sufficiently to leave the nursing home and returned to live at 'Rosemount' with live-in carers. In January 2015, still at 'Rosemount', John died from a stroke. John's will appoints Anita, Amanda's mother, as his executor and leaves Anita all his property.

Advise Amanda whether she has any claim to 'Rosemount'.

Answer plan

→ Examine why the actual transfer by John was invalid.

→ Explain methods one and two of constitution of a trust/gift.

→ Apply these to the question to see if the gift by John of 'Rosemount' can be upheld.

→ Look at possible ways in which equity may intervene even though the methods of constitution were not complied with: *donatio mortis causa* and estoppel.

Diagram plan

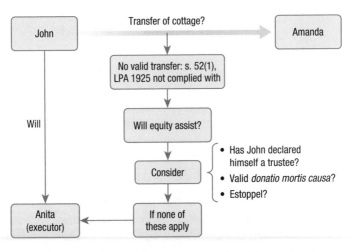

A printable version of this diagram plan is available from **www.pearsoned.co.uk/lawexpressqa**

Answer

The first question is whether there has been a valid transfer using the correct formalities, of 'Rosemount' from John to Amanda.[1] Legal estates in land must be transferred by deed (s. 52(1), LPA 1925) and, if title is registrable, then the requirements of the Land Registration Act 2002 must be observed.[2] It is clear that this has not happened and so we must ask if equity will assist.

John appears to have made an attempted gift[3] of the cottage to Amanda and, as Lord Eldon put it in *Ellison* v *Ellison* (1802) 31 ER 1243 HC: 'Equity will not assist a volunteer.' Thus in principle Amanda cannot compel John, by the equitable remedy of specific performance, to transfer the cottage to her nor can she seek damages at common law as she has not provided consideration.

However, Amanda may try to argue that John has, by his words and actions, made himself a trustee of the cottage for her. A trust of land requires written evidence (s. 53(1)(b), LPA 1925) and John has written that he would like Amanda to have the house when he dies although he has kept the keys to the deed box. Thus there is written evidence of what John has done but, and this is the crucial question, is it written evidence of a trust?

In *Milroy* v *Lord* (1862) 4 De GF & J 264 HC Turner LJ indicated that a trust will be completely constituted when either:

(a) the settlor has vested the legal title to the trust property in the trustee(s) (Method One); *or*

(b) the settlor has declared that he now holds the property as trustee (Method Two).[4] Clearly, John did not transfer the cottage to a trustee to hold on trust for Amanda but Amanda may argue that John has made himself a trustee of the cottage for her and so constituted a trust. In effect, a transfer which has failed to comply with the statutory formalities will be rescued by a finding that there is a trust.[5] But is there a trust?

In fact the courts have not been willing to impose the duties of a trustee on a person such as John without clear evidence that a trust was intended.

A decision which is very similar on its facts to this one is **Richards v Delbridge** (1874) LR 18 Eq 11 HC: Delbridge was tenant of premises and shortly before his death, he wrote and signed the following memorandum on the lease: 'This deed and all thereto belonging I give to Edward Bennetto Richards, from this time forth, with all the stock-in-trade.' Edward was his grandson. Delbridge then gave the document to Edward's mother to hold for him. On Delbridge's death there was no mention of the property.

The court held that there was no effective transfer of the lease because there was no declaration of trust. Jessell MR observed that 'for a man to make himself trustee there must be an expression of intention to become a trustee'.[6] This was not so as an outright gift was intended and here it is suggested that the same will apply. John put the deeds in a box whereas in **Richards v Delbridge** they were given to the intended donee's mother, and this seems even stronger evidence that no trust was intended.[7]

There are two other possibilities. One is whether there is a valid *donatio mortis causa* of the cottage. In **Sen v Headley** [1991] 2 WLR 1308 CA it was held that there can be a valid *donatio* of land but are the conditions for one fulfilled?[8]

The first is that the donor must have contemplated death in the near future. In **Vallee v Birchwood** [2013] EWHC 1449 (Ch) it was held that: 'the gift must be made in contemplation, although not necessarily in expectation, of impending death'. When he made the gift John thought that he had not long to live and, although he does not seem to have been terminally ill at this point, it is suggested that he clearly contemplated death and this is sufficient.

The second is that the subject matter of the gift must be delivered to the donee in the lifetime of the donor with the intention of parting with dominion over it. In **Sen v Hedley** dominion of land was parted with when the donor handed the donee the keys to the house and a key to a box containing the title deeds. Here John did not hand over the deeds to Amanda but kept them himself in a box. It is doubtful if this would suffice. Moreover there was a gap of nine months between the statement by John that he would leave Amanda the house and his death and in that time he had moved back to the house. In **Vallee v Birchwood** the fact that the donor continued to live in the house for

[6] This is an example of a useful quote which will add to your marks.

[7] Note the close comparison between the facts of the case and those of the problem: always the sign of a good answer.

[8] As a general rule, you should go through all three conditions for a valid *donatio* as it is likely that the answer as to whether there is a valid *donatio* will not be certain.

[9] Note the close analysis of the facts of the case and of the problem: this is what gains you marks.

[10] Make it a habit to check for this point in questions on *donationes* of land. If you are in doubt about whether title is registered or not then do not worry – this is not a land law exam – but answer on the basis of both.

[11] Estoppel is of course a topic on its own, so in this type of question concentrate on the essential conditions for estoppel to apply.

[12] The reference to a decision of the House of Lords will boost your marks rather than the alternative of a bald mention of the need for a representation.

[13] Notice that this conclusion sums up the process by which we arrived at the answer: first the lack of a valid transfer, then an examination of how equity might assist and finally, on the basis that equity could not assist, the identification of a destination for the property.

four months after the *donatio* was not, surprisingly, held to affect the fact that he had parted with dominion over it but here John actually moves back into the cottage after the purported gift to Amanda.[9] It seems that title to 'Rosemount' was unregistered or not as John has the title deeds.[10] As title was unregistered then as in **Sen v Hedley** and **Vallee v Birchwood** a *donatio* is possible although as dominion of the land was not parted with then it is suggested that there is in fact no *donatio*.

The final condition is that the gift must be conditional on death but John may have intended Amanda to have the cottage as an outright gift, as it is not clear whether at the time of the gift John intended to return there. In any event as there was no parting with dominion there is no valid *donatio*.

The other possibility is estoppel.[11] John says to Amanda that he would like to give her the cottage for two reasons: she has been kind to him and she has helped him to renovate it. Helping to renovate the cottage may amount to detrimental reliance by Amanda on a representation by John that he would leave her the cottage but although in **Thorner v Major** [2009] UKHL 18[12] the House of Lords was prepared to accept various hints and remarks made by one party to the other over the years as amounting to an estoppel, there is no evidence of even these here. Nor do we know the extent to which Amanda did help John: trivial acts will not be enough.

In conclusion, as there was no valid transfer of the cottage by John to Amanda and as none of the ways in which equity might assist Amanda applies, when John died the cottage formed part of his estate and so will pass to Anita.[13]

 Make your answer stand out

- Make reference to academic discussion, e.g. Baker (1993) on *donationes* where the decision in *Sen v Headley* is considered.
- Refer to the article on *Vallee v Birchwood*: Panesar (2013).
- Include further discussion of *Thorner v Major* – see e.g. Dixon (2009).

■ Consider other cases on constitution, e.g. *Jones* v *Lock* [1865] 1 Ch App 25 HC, which you can compare with *Richards* v *Delbridge*.

■ Mention that if title to land is registered then the Singapore High Court held in *Koh Cheong Heng* v *Ho Yee Fong* [2011] SGHC 48 that a *donatio* is possible.

! Don't be tempted to . . .

■ Start the answer without checking first whether there has been an invalid transfer. It is very likely that there will have been, but you will lose marks if you miss this out.

■ Forget to distinguish between the two methods of constitution.

■ Mention *donationes* or estoppel unless you have first satisfied yourself that the trust/gift has not been constituted.

■ Go into great detail on estoppel.

? Question 2

Luke died intestate last month. He was not married and had no children. His niece and nephew, Babs and Norman, are his administrators and, together with 26 other nieces and nephews, are entitled to all the estate. You are asked to advise on the following claims against the estate:

(a) Babs tells you that Luke allowed her to borrow his car while she was a student at Newtown University. At the time, he said that he would transfer the car into her name but later, after Babs went to study for a year abroad, Luke started using the car again himself. Babs now finds that, whilst Luke filled out the vehicle registration documents, he did not send them off to the Vehicle Licensing Authority.

(b) Dan tells you that the day before Luke's death, he visited him and Luke said: 'I'm done for and will never leave this room again. Take this key to my strong box and you will have a nice surprise.' Dan took the key and, on opening the strong box, he found a jewellery box containing a diamond ring, Luke's car keys and a cheque for £1,000 made out to Dan.

Answer plan

→ Consider the possible application of *Strong* v *Bird* to the intended gift of the car.

→ If *Strong* v *Bird* is inapplicable then move on to consider the *Re Rose* principle and how the law stands now in view of *Pennington* v *Waine* to see if this can validate the transfer.

➜ Next consider whether there is a valid *donatio mortis causa* by Luke to Dan of the diamond ring, car keys and cheque.

➜ Remember to decide what will happen to the property in each case if the intended gifts cannot be upheld.

Diagram plan

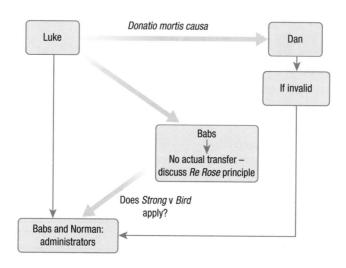

A printable version of this diagram plan is available from **www.pearsoned.co.uk/lawexpressqa**

Answer

[1] As it is always vital to find a home for the property, you can usefully make this point here.

The question is whether in any of these cases there is a valid transfer of the property from Luke to the intended transferees. If not, the property will form part of Luke's estate on his death and will pass to those entitled on his intestacy.[1]

[2] If an intended transferee is also an executor/administrator then almost certainly you should mention and apply *Strong* v *Bird*.

(a) Luke allowed Babs to borrow his car while she was a student at Newtown University. At the time, he said that he would transfer the car into her name but did not do so. Later, after Babs went to study for a year abroad, Luke started using the car again himself. As Babs is one of the administrators under Luke's will, she may try to use the rule in **Strong v Bird** (1874) LR 18 Eq 315 HC to claim the car.[2] The rule states that if an incomplete gift is

QUESTION 2

made during the donor's lifetime and the donor has appointed the donee his executor, then the vesting of the property in the donee completes the gift.

The rule may be said to rest upon the donor's intention but Babs was not appointed executor but administrator[3] and this is an important difference, as an executor is appointed by the testator but an administrator is appointed by the court. Thus there can be no question of Luke appointing Babs as administrator in order to perfect the gift to her. In **Re James** [1935] Ch 449 HC the rule was extended to administrators. In **Strong v Bird** (1874) itself the rule was said to apply only to an executor and in **Re Gonin** [1979] Ch 16 Walton J would only have followed **Re James** with the greatest reluctance. If the rule does apply to administrators then the fact that Norman was also appointed administrator will not affect Babs's claim as the whole estate vests in each administrator (**Re Stewart** [1908] 2 Ch 251 HC). However, what will be fatal to Babs's claim under **Strong v Bird** is that after Babs went to study for a year abroad, Luke started using the car again.[4] This is because the rule only applies where the donor has a continuing intention to make an immediate gift (**Re Gonin**) and here the fact that he starts to use the car again shows that he does not.

The other point is that Babs now finds that whilst Luke filled out the vehicle registration documents, he did not send them off to the Vehicle Licensing Authority.[5] In **Re Rose** [1952] Ch 499 CA Evershed MR added a kind of gloss on the principle in **Milroy v Lord** that, in order to constitute a trust the settlor must have done all in his power to vest the legal interest in the property in the donee. Obviously, Luke did not as he did not send the documents off. However, in **Pennington v Waine** [2002] EWCA Civ 227 this rule seemed to be relaxed.[6] Mrs Crampton, a shareholder in a private company, told Pennington, a partner in a firm who acted for the company, that she wished to transfer some of her shares to her nephew, and she later signed a share transfer form to this effect and gave it to Pennington. He took no further action and the question was whether, on her death, the shares had been transferred to the nephew.[7]

[3] Watch for this point in exams but note that there is some doubt as to whether the rule in *Strong* v *Bird* can apply where there is an administrator rather than an executor.

[4] This is a very common exam point – watch for it as it means that the rule in *Strong* v *Bird* will not apply and you will have to look elsewhere to see if the gift can be saved.

[5] This is a good example of how to earn extra marks: the question obviously involved *Strong* v *Bird* and most students will probably spot this. However, the extra information concerning Luke's failure to send the documents off to the Vehicle Licensing Authority does not seem to affect the application of *Strong* v *Bird* as we have *already* decided that it will not apply. Therefore, this information must relate to something else.

[6] In cases involving the *Re Rose* principle you must now always follow *Re Rose* with this case and explain how the reasoning in it differs from that in *Re Rose*.

[7] We have given fairly full details of the facts of this case. This is because it involves the question of whether conduct was unconscionable and this often turns on the details of each case.

[8] This is the kind of detail which impresses examiners as it shows that you have read the judgments in the case. It was the reasoning of Clarke LJ which differed although he concurred with the result.

The Court of Appeal held that they had, although the reasonings in the two main judgments differ.[8] Arden LJ upheld **Re Rose** but also held that the fact that there was clear evidence that Mrs Crampton intended an immediate gift of the shares amounted to an assignment of them to the nephew anyway. She held that, on the facts, it would be unconscionable to allow Mrs Crampton, in view of all that she had done to transfer the shares to the nephew, to then turn round and change her mind and say that they were not his. Thus, it may be that in this case the court could hold that it would be unconscionable for Luke to have said that the car still belonged to him but this is very doubtful as he started using it again, showing that he may well have changed his mind about giving it to Babs and there really does not seem to be any evidence that it would actually be unconscionable if the car went to Babs and not to the estate.

(b) The question is whether there is a valid *donatio mortis causa* by Luke to Dan of the diamond ring, car keys and cheque. The cheque can be eliminated now, as it cannot pass by a *donatio*.[9] The reason for the exclusion of cheques is that the donor's death terminates the bank's authority to pay on it (**Re Beaumont** [1902] 1 Ch 889 HC). A holder for value may sue, but in this case there will, by definition, have been a contract and the rules on *donatio* will be inapplicable. A possible exception to this rule is where a cheque is paid immediately after death before the banker has been told of the death and closed the account (**Tate v Hilbert** (1793) 30 ER 548 HC). In this case there would be a *donatio* of the money represented by the cheque and not of the cheque itself. So Dan should be quick![10] The ring and car can pass by *donatio* provided that the conditions are satisfied.

[9] In a problem question on *donatio* watch for a cheque appearing. If so, you can eliminate *donatio* at once.

[10] This extra discussion should bring a bonus in marks as it shows the examiner that you know exactly why there cannot normally be a *donatio* of a cheque.

[11] When you get a problem question involving a *donatio mortis causa* you should apply each point in turn to the question as marks will be allocated to knowledge of each.

The first is that the donor must have contemplated death in the near future.[11] In **Vallee v Birchwood** [2013] EWHC 1449 (Ch) it was held that the test is not whether the donor expected death but whether he or she contemplated it. This seems to be the case as Dan visited Luke the day before his death and Luke said: 'I am done for and will never leave this room again.'

Secondly, the subject matter of the gift must be delivered to the donee in the lifetime of the donor with the intention of parting with dominion over it. In **Woodard v Woodard** [1995] 3 All

ER 580 CA a donor gave his son the keys to his car and said to him: 'You can keep the keys. I won't be driving it anymore.' Even though he retained another set of keys, it was held that these words indicated that he intended to part with dominion over the car. Here the keys are in a strong box to which Dan is given the keys and this should be sufficient delivery of both the car and the ring.

[12] This point often arises: the donor does not say that the gift is conditional but in these circumstances this can be inferred. Be confident in your advice here.

[13] Note that we always need to decide where the property will go.

Finally, the gift must be conditional on death in that the donor intends to keep the gift if he recovers. The courts may infer an intention where there are no words indicating a gift and the gift is made when the donor is *in extremis* (**Re Lillingston** [1952] 2 All ER 184) and it is suggested that this would be the case here.[12] Thus it is submitted that there is a valid *donatio* of the ring and of the car but the money represented by the cheque remains in Luke's estate and will pass to those entitled on his intestacy.[13]

✓ Make your answer stand out

■ Reference to Kodilinye (1982). There is little published on *Strong* v *Bird* and you will find this research should add to your marks.

■ Look in more detail at *Re Gonin* – this decision deals with a number of areas.

■ Read and refer to Doggett (2003), who examines the decision in *Re Rose* in the light of *Pennington* v *Waine*.

■ Look at the discussion on parting with dominion of land in cases of *donationes mortis causa* in *Vallee v Birchwood*. Although the case concerned land it also considers what dominon means in general.

■ Articles on recent cases on *donatio* – there were a number on *Sen* v *Headley*, e.g. Baker (1993).

! Don't be tempted to . . .

■ *Assume* that the rule in *Strong* v *Bird* can apply to administrators.

■ Apply *Re Rose* without also discussing *Pennington* v *Waine*.

■ Neglect to go through all the conditions for a valid *donatio*.

■ Say that a cheque can pass by *donatio*.

Question 3

In *Curtis* v *Pulbrook* [2011] EWHC 167 (Ch), Bridge J stated that he reached his conclusion 'without any great comfort that the existing rules about the circumstances when equity will and will not perfect an apparently imperfect gift of shares serve any clearly identifiable or rational policy objective'.

Critically consider this statement.

Answer plan

→ Explain the decision in *Curtis* v *Pulbrook* in the context of this case.

→ Explain what 'gift' and 'imperfect' mean.

→ Set out the rules in *Milroy* v *Lord* and show relevance to this situation.

→ Distinguish between gifts and trusts.

→ Look at the three situations identified by Arden LJ in *Pennington* v *Waine* where equity will perfect an imperfect gift.

→ Conclusion: is the present law justified?

Diagram plan

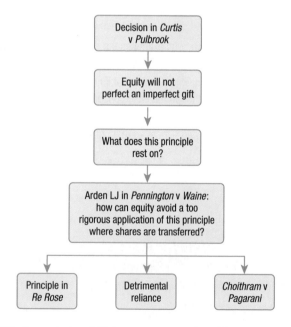

A printable version of this diagram plan is available from **www.pearsoned.co.uk/lawexpressqa**

Answer

Although Bridge J was commenting on the whole area of law dealing with when equity will and will not perfect an apparently imperfect gift of shares we should start with the actual decision in **Curtis v Pulbrook** [2011] EWHC 167 (Ch) to see what prompted this remark.[1] Pulbrook made two deeds of gift of shares in a company that he controlled effected by the execution of new share certificates and an entry in the company's share register. However, neither his daughter nor wife received a stock transfer form. Pulbrook had misappropriated money from the bank account of T, his financial adviser, in payment of personal legal fees and T sought a charging order over the shares. However, Pulbrook contended that they were no longer his, legal title having passed to his wife and daughter.

There was no question that Pulbrook intended to make a gift of the shares but, and this is what prompted the remark of Briggs J, his intention might be defeated by a failure to comply with the formalities. In fact, Pulbrook's claim had no real merit to it and in any event the court granted T an order setting aside the gifts pursuant to the Insolvency Act 1986, section 423(3).[2]

[2] This topic is often dealt with in Land Law courses and appears in *Law Express Q&A: Land Law* (Chapter 3). There is no need to discuss it here in detail as it is not relevant to this answer.

[3] Go back to basic principles and show the examiner that you are clear on them.

[4] A failure to appreciate this distinction often confuses students.

In this case Pulbrook's transfers fell foul of the rule that equity will not perfect an imperfect gift. There are two vital terms: gift and imperfect.[3] First we are concerned with outright gifts and not declarations of trust.[4] Equity, and the common law, places great importance on consideration for the enforcement of contracts. Equity, in the words of the old maxim, 'follows the law' although its definition of consideration is wider as it includes marriage consideration. Where a person has not provided consideration for a promise they are volunteers and, as Lord Eldon said in **Ellison v Ellison** (1802) 31 ER 1243: 'Equity will not assist a volunteer.'

Thus where there is a gift but the formalities have not been complied with, and which is therefore imperfect, equity will not aid in its enforcement as to do so would assist a volunteer.

However, difficulties arise where equity has tried to avoid what Briggs J in **Curtis v Pulbrook** called 'the rigorous application of the principle that equity will not compel the completion of an imperfect gift, in the absence of a valid declaration of trust'. He adopted the classification of Arden LJ in **Pennington v Waine** [2002] EWCA

5 Keep the focus on this
area and do not stray into
a general discussion of
constitution of trusts. We
have used the classification
of Arden LJ as a basis for
our answer but you could
use other formulations of
the cases where equity may
perfect an imperfect gift.

6 It is important to make the
connection between the basic
rule in *Milroy* v *Lord* and what
the court said in *Re Rose*.

7 Note that we have once
again made the distinction
between gifts and trusts.

8 There was a choice here
of which case to mention in
more detail. *Zeital* v *Kaye*
won as it is more recent and also
as it illustrates a different
point of law: transfers of the
beneficial interests rather than
the legal one as in *Mascall*.

9 We could have used another
case to illustrate this point but
why? The facts of *Re Rose*
have already been given and
so it saves time to mention
this one. You can then use
this time to mention an extra
point and earn those valuable
extra marks!

Civ 227 who identified three ways where there is a defective voluntary transfer of shares[5] but equity might, as she put it, 'temper the wind to the shorn lamb'.

The first derives from **Re Rose** [1952] Ch 499 CA where Evershed MR added a kind of gloss on the principle in **Milroy v Lord** (1862) 4 De GF & J 264 CA.[6] In **Milroy v Lord** itself Turner LJ indicated that a trust will be completely constituted when either:

(a) the settlor has vested the legal title to the trust property in the trustee(s); *or*

(b) the settlor has declared that he now holds the property as trustee.

On the basis that neither of these has occurred, the principle in **Re Rose** is that in order to constitute a trust, or to perfect a gift in this context,[7] the settlor must have done all in his power to vest the legal interest in the property in the donee. The word donee reminds us that this principle can apply to trusts, where the intended trustee will be a donee, or to outright gifts. This case concerned possible liability to estate duty at the time when a transfer of shares was complete and it was held that the transfer was complete when the transferor executed the transfer as there was no more that the transferor could do. The principle was applied to land registration in **Mascall v Mascall** (1984) 50 P&CR 119 HC and in **Zeital v Kaye** [2010] EWCA Civ 159 it was applied to an attempted transfer of a beneficial interest in shares where on the facts the transferor had not done all in his power.[8]

The second is where, as Arden LJ put it, 'some detrimental reliance by the donee upon an apparent although ineffective gift may so bind the conscience of the donor to justify the imposition of a constructive trust.' This applied in **Re Rose**[9] so that the beneficial interest in shares passed when the share transfers were delivered to the transferee, and thus the transferor was a trustee of the legal estate in the shares from that date.

The third is where in Arden LJ's phrase by 'a benevolent construction an effective gift or implied declaration of trust may be teased out of the words used'. In **Choithram (T) International SA v Pagarani** [2001] 2 All ER 492 Mr Pagarani, in his last illness, executed a trust

[10] You do need to set the facts of this case out in some detail as there were two issues in this case and so you need to give sufficient detail of the facts to make the decision on each point understandable.

deed establishing a foundation which would act as an umbrella for four charities which he had established.[10] Immediately after he had signed, he stated that all his wealth, including shares in a number of companies, would now belong to the trust. He himself was one of the trustees. He told his accountant to transfer all his money to the trust but he failed to sign the necessary forms and the companies in which he held shares duly registered the trustees of the foundation as shareholders. After Pagarani died, his family claimed that he had not effectively transferred his wealth to the foundation, which accordingly belonged to them. The Privy Council's decision that the trust was constituted rested on two points:

(a) Pagarani had made a declaration of trust. He did not use the word 'trust' and his actual words appeared to indicate a gift but the context of the words clearly indicated a trust: he intended to give to the foundation and this body was a trust.

(b) It did not matter that the trust property was not vested in the other trustees as Pagarani had executed a solemn declaration of trust and it would be unconscionable to allow him to go back from this promise.

[11] Come back to the issue raised in the question at the end: what, if any, is the rationale for this area of the law?

One can see a tension in these cases[11] between trying to give effect to the wishes of testators and settlors, which clearly influenced the court in Pagarani, and trying to adhere to the principle that 'equity does not assist a volunteer' which itself seems to derive merely from a desire by equity to follow the law. Beyond this, as Arden LJ observed in **Pennington v Waine**, 'the cases to which counsel have referred us do not reveal any, or any consistent single policy consideration behind the rule that the court will not perfect an imperfect gift'. The statement by Briggs J appears to be justified.

✓ Make your answer stand out

- Ensure that your answer is grounded on basic principles: What is meant by an imperfect gift? How is a trust constituted?
- Refer to the facts of *Curtis* v *Pulbrook* but make sure that you do so in relation to the question. ▶

- Paragraph 62 of Arden LJ's judgment in *Pennington* v *Waine* [2002] EWCA Civ 227 goes into more detail on the possible rationales for the rule that equity will not perfect an imperfect gift.
- Doggett (2003), Halliwell (2003) and Garton (2003) discuss the two cases which are the main subject of this question. Make sure that you read and refer to at least one of them.

 Don't be tempted to . . .

- Just set out the facts of the cases without any discussion of the principles.
- Discuss the cases without first setting out the basic law on constitution in *Milroy* v *Lord*.
- Discuss *Pennington* v *Waine* without first setting out the *ratio* of *Re Rose*.

📝 Question 4

Critically consider the circumstances in which a *donatio mortis causa* will be upheld by the courts and assess whether there is any justification today for these types of gifts to be held valid.

Diagram plan

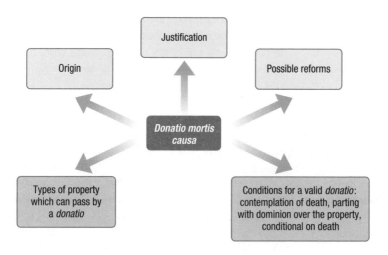

A printable version of this diagram plan is available from **www.pearsoned.co.uk/lawexpressqa**

Answer plan

→ Describe the origin of the *donatio mortis causa* principle.

→ Outline the conditions which must be satisfied for a valid *donatio*.

→ Identify the special cases of property which either cannot be left by *donatio* or could not in the past.

→ Consider possible justifications for *donationes* to continue to exist.

→ Outline possible reforms which would make this area of law fairer and more workable.

Answer

[1] The origin of *donatio mortis causa* is interesting and you will gain marks by briefly mentioning it.

[2] The plural of *donatio* is *donationes*.

[3] Short, memorable quotes such as these always add marks to your answer provided that you integrate them into it as we have done here.

Gifts in contemplation of death were recognised by Roman law, and the principle that such a gift could validly dispose of property was recognised by English law soon after the passage of the Statute of Frauds 1677, which introduced strict rules for the validity of oral wills and effectively ended them.[1] Thus, *donationes*[2] mortis causa became the way to leave property informally. However, they are an anomaly in English law, as they enable property to be transferred without formalities and so their continued existence needs to be justified. In addition, as Baker (2002) has observed, the rules on *donatio* have 'characteristically developed slowly and haphazardly'[3] and, as a result, the richness of the case law has led to unnecessary complexity. Nor is their continued existence an academic question, as there have been a number of important cases involving *donationes* in the last 20 years: **Sen v Headley** [1991] 2 WLR 1308 CA, **Woodard v Woodard** [1995] 3 All ER 580 CA and **Vallee v Birchwood** [2013] EWHC 1449 (Ch).

There are three requirements for a valid *donatio*.

(a) The donor must have contemplated death in the near future and what matters is the donor's state of mind and not whether death is imminent. In **Vallee v Birchwood** it was held that the question is not whether death was expected but whether it was contemplated, a lesser test. However, in **Thompson v Mechan** [1958] OR 357 HC the court held that contemplation of death from the ordinary risks of air travel was not enough as this was a cause that 'exists only in his [the donor's] fancy'.[4] The extent to which the courts can apply an objective test to the belief is

[4] The point here which you need to stress is that the case law is, as the quote above says, haphazard.

thus uncertain. When the gift is made in contemplation of death then this requirement is satisfied even though death occurs from another cause. In **Wilkes v Allington** [1931] 2 Ch 104 HC a donor transferred the mortgage deeds to a farm to his nieces when suffering from cancer but in fact died from pneumonia. It was held valid. Whether a valid *donatio* can be made when the donor intends to commit suicide is uncertain.

(b) The subject matter of the gift must be delivered to the donee in the lifetime of the donor with the intention of parting with dominion over it. When the subject matter is a chose in action actual delivery may not be possible and therefore some document which constitutes the essential *indica* of title must be delivered. In **Re Weston** [1902] 1 Ch 680 HC a dying man handed his fiancée the keys to a drawer where there were some share certificates and his Post Office savings book and told her to take them. This was held to be sufficient. What if the donor gives keys but retains a duplicate set? In **Re Craven's Estate** [1937] Ch 423 HC it was held that this could indicate that the donee was not given exclusive control of the property. But in **Woodard v Woodard** the donor gave his son the keys to his car and said to him: 'You can keep the keys. I won't be driving it anymore.' Even though he retained another set of keys, it was held that these words indicated that he intended to part with dominion over the car.[5] It is arguable that the concept of parting with dominion was stretched to its limits both in **Woodard v Woodard** and in **Vallee v Birchwood** where it was held that the donor had parted with dominion over his house even though he continued to live there.

(c) The gift must be intended to be conditional on death. An immediate unconditional gift cannot be the subject of a valid *donatio*. The courts may infer an intention where there are no words indicating a gift and the gift is made when the donor is *in extremis*: **Re Lillingston** [1952] 2 All ER 184 HC.

Any property can be comprised in a *donatio*, although the following types need special treatment.

(a) It was thought that land could not be the subject of a *donatio* following Lord Eldon in **Duffield v Elwes** (1827) 4 ER 959 HL when he appeared to say, *obiter,* that land cannot be, possibly

[5] You will see that this answer is using a large number of cases. This is because there are only three main principles (the conditions for a valid *donatio*) and this subject gains its richness and complexity from the cases. As you can see, a good answer will indicate that sometimes the cases do seem to conflict.

⁶ *Sen* v *Headley* is the most important recent case on *donatio* and an examiner will definitely expect you to have a good knowledge of it.

because it is not possible to hand over dominion of it. However, in ***Sen v Headley*** [1991] 2 WLR 1308 the Court of Appeal held that there can be a *donatio* of land.[6] The deceased was visited in hospital by the claimant, with whom he had had a close relationship for many years. He apparently dropped the keys of the deed box into her bag and then said to her: 'The house is yours Margaret. You have the keys. They are in your bag.' This was held to be enough for a *donatio* of a large house.

⁷ This important point needs explaining carefully.

(b) In principle, a cheque cannot be the subject of a *donatio,* as cheques do not effectively give money but are only orders to a bank to pay the donee and the mandate is revoked on the drawer's death.[7] They could be effective *donationes* if the bank pays on the cheque before it is told of the drawer's (i.e. the donor's) death.

(c) Shares in companies are probably capable of passing by a *donatio* although the cases are old and conflicting. See ***Ward v Turner*** (1752) 1 Dick 170 HC and also ***Re Weston*** (above), where building society shares were held incapable of passing by *donatio*. Surely, this is an example of where the law needs clarifying?[8]

⁸ Here is a short point of criticism which, however, does add to your marks. Look at the cases on *donationes* and see if you have any other ideas about how the law could be made less haphazard.

It should be noted that *donationes* only take effect on death, like wills, and, as with wills, a *donatio* fails if the donee predeceases the donor (***Tate v Hilbert*** (1793) 30 ER 548 HC).[9] Also, a *donatio* can be revoked, as can a will, although the methods are different: by the donor recovering from the illness or by simply recovering dominion over the subject matter.

⁹ This is an example of adding to your marks by doing some research and familiarising yourself with some principles of succession law.

The justification is that *donationes* provide a means of disposing of property when donors are very ill and for whom making a will could pose serious difficulties. Yet it is odd that in ***Sen v Headley*** a large house was disposed of so informally.[10] What of proof? In ***Sen*** there appeared to be no independent witnesses of what was said. Roman law required five witnesses for certain types of *donatio* and surely English law should require at least one. Should *donationes* be retained with a presumption that there can be no *donatio* unless it can be shown that there was no reasonable alternative means in the circumstances of disposing of the property? Or should there be an upper limit on the value of property transferable by a *donatio*?

¹⁰ This is an example of where an answer which could be pedestrian is lifted out of the ordinary, even if only in a small way. Having mentioned a justification for the present law, you immediately mention a case which appears to show difficulties with the law.

When the law on *donatio* was originally developed in the seventeenth century, the doctrine of proprietary estoppel did not exist, certainly in its modern form, nor did the modern law of constructive trusts. Both of these might have been appropriate in a case such as **Sen v Headley**. Perhaps we should abolish *donatio* altogether and rely on these other doctrines to act where the operation of formality requirements in areas covered by *donatio* would have wrought injustice.

 Make your answer stand out

- Do some research on the law of succession so that you are familiar with basic principles and can use them in this essay.
- Do some research in the cases – they are usefully collected in Borkowski (1999). You could then either add them to this answer or, preferably, substitute those which you consider more appropriate for those mentioned here.
- Look at articles on recent cases – there were a number on *Sen* v *Headley,* e.g. Baker (1993). This will help you to appreciate the modern application of *donatio.*
- Explain how a constructive trust arises on a *donatio* of land and refer to Nourse LJ in *Sen* v *Headley.*

! Don't be tempted to . . .

- Just go through the requirements for a valid *donatio.*
- Spend too long on individual cases without drawing out the actual point which was decided. It is easy to get immersed in the facts of cases in this area, as many of them are memorable.
- Neglect to explain the idea behind allowing *donationes* in the first place.
- Forget to mention some practical ideas for possible changes in the law.

www.pearsoned.co.uk/lawexpressqa

 Go online to access more revision support including additional essay and problem questions with diagram plans, You be the marker questions, and download all diagrams from the book.

Secret and half-secret trusts; mutual wills

6

How this topic may come up in exams

This is often a problem question topic where there is a mix of fundamental points which all students should get and less obvious ones which give you an opportunity to spot them and gain those vital extra marks. There can also be an essay question on why secret trusts exist at all. In addition, as secret trusts can be considered constructive, a question on constructive trusts will also require you to mention secret trusts. Finally, you may get a question on mutual wills which has generated a number of recent cases and which also provides material for a discussion of constructive trusts.

Before you begin

It's a good idea to consider the following key themes of secret and half-secret trusts before tackling a question on this topic.

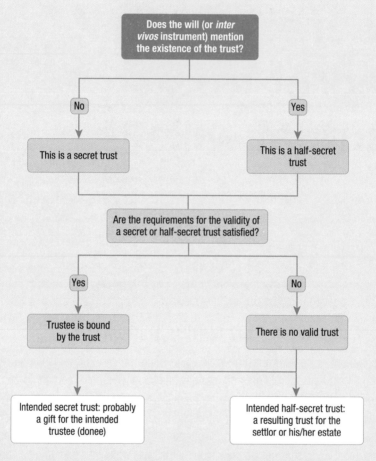

A printable version of this diagram is available from **www.pearsoned.co.uk/lawexpressqa**

? Question 1

Colin, a married man, was due to enter hospital for an operation and asked his friends, Ted and Sam, if they could help him over a 'private matter'. He told them that he had been married before, to Alice, but had never disclosed this to his present wife, Margaret, as he felt that she would disapprove. He wanted Alice to have something to remember him by and asked them if they would help. Ted said 'of course' but Sam just smiled.

The next day Colin executed his will which left £20,000 to Ted and Sam 'for the purpose which we have discussed' and £5,000 to Janet, a long-standing friend, absolutely. Sam witnessed the will.

Colin then wrote to Ted and Sam 'confirming what we have agreed – all to Alice'.

Colin then wrote to Janet asking her to hold the £5,000 'for the benefit of such people as shall be specified in a letter to be found in the top drawer of my desk'. He added, 'if you do not reply within a week I shall assume that you agree to this'.

Colin has now died. Janet has found a letter in his desk specifying that the £5,000 is to be divided, at Janet's discretion, among Colin's 'immediate family'.

Advise Steve, Colin's executor, on who is entitled to the gifts in Colin's will.

Diagram plan

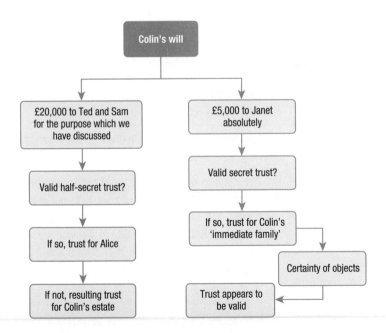

A printable version of this diagram plan is available from **www.pearsoned.co.uk/lawexpressqa**

Answer plan

→ Identify that the bequest to Ted and Sam is a half-secret trust.

→ State and apply the requirements for the validity of a half-secret trust.

→ Explain the significance, if any, of the fact that Sam witnessed the will.

→ Identify that the bequest to Janet is a secret trust.

→ State and apply the requirements for the validity of a secret trust.

→ Consider the certainty of objects point as applied to the bequest to Janet.

Answer

[1] Unless you are given any information to indicate otherwise, you should assume that the will is valid. Do not waste marks which you could get elsewhere by ploughing through the rules on formalities for making a will and capacity to make a will.

We can assume that Colin's will is valid[1] and so the question is whether the gifts to those actually mentioned in it will take effect or whether a trust will be imposed on Ted, Sam and Janet.

[2] The applicable law for each situation in a secret trusts question will be different, so it is best to deal separately with each.

Taking the bequest to Ted and Sam first,[2] Colin's will[3] states that he has left £20,000 to Ted and Sam 'for the purpose which we have discussed'. This looks like a half-secret trust, which arises where property is left by will to a beneficiary but although the will states that the beneficiary is to hold on trust, the terms of the trust are not declared in the will but are agreed between the testator and beneficiary. Therefore, the will mentions the existence of a trust but not the terms of the trust. Here the word 'trust' is not actually mentioned but the words 'purposes we have discussed' are similar to those used in ***Blackwell v Blackwell*** [1929] AC 318 HL.[4] So here there is a potential half-secret trust.

[3] Always go to the words of the will first in a secret trusts question as this will tell you if the trust is secret or half-secret.

[4] You will gain marks in a question on half-secret trusts if you spend time asking what the actual words used by the testator mean: trust or not?

In ***Ottaway v Norman*** [1972] Ch 698 HC, Brightman J held that the following requirements must be proved:

(i) The intention of the testator to subject the primary donee (i.e. the intended trustee) to an obligation in favour of the secondary donee (i.e. the intended beneficiary). In ***Kasperbauer v Griffith*** [2000] WTLR 333 HC, Peter Gibson J emphasised that all three certainties must be satisfied. Here Colin asked Ted and Sam if they could help him over a 'private matter' and told them that he had been married before to Alice but had never disclosed this to his present wife, Margaret, as he felt that she would disapprove. He wanted Alice to have something to remember him by and asked them if they would help.[5] These words do not by

[5] Note how information in the first paragraph has been used and analysed: often students ignore this first paragraph and so lose marks.

themselves indicate any certainty of intention to create a trust, but Colin's will states that the £20,000 is left to them for 'the purposes we have discussed' and so their conversation might have been more specific. Later, Colin wrote to Ted and Sam 'confirming what we have agreed – all to Alice'. This looks more like certainty of intention. There is certainty of subject matter (the £20,000) and objects (Alice).

(ii) The second requirement is communication of that intention to the primary donee. Where the trust is half-secret then the probable rule is that communication must occur before or at the time of the making of the will (**Re Keen** [1937] Ch 236 CA). In the conversation between Colin and Ted and Sam, communication seems tentative, and only after the execution of the will did Colin become explicit and say 'all to Alice'. However, he also uses the word 'confirming' indicating that at an earlier stage this intention had been communicated. Another explanation of the decision in **Re Keen**[6] is that communication must be in accordance with the terms of the will. Colin's will says 'for the purpose which we *have* discussed' so this means that any communication must be *before* the will, but here it is not clear if this is so.

[6] You will gain extra marks if you also mention this alternative means of communication.

(iii) The final requirement is acceptance[7] of the obligation by the primary donee either expressly or by acquiescence. We are told that Ted said 'of course' but Sam just smiled, and so Ted has accepted expressly and Sam by acquiescence.

[7] Do not forget to mention acceptance – it is easily overlooked.

[8] There is clearly some doubt as to whether the trust is valid or not but it *could* be. This means that it is time to move on and gain more marks from another point, in this case the question of the witnessing of the will.

If we assume that all three requirements were satisfied, the other issue is that Sam witnessed the will.[8] Attestation of a will by a trustee of a half-secret trust should not affect the validity of the legacy, and therefore of the trust, because he is not a beneficiary on the face of the will (**Cresswell v Cresswell** (1868) LR 6 Eq 69 HC) and so the trust in favour of Alice will be valid.

[9] Do remember to find a home for the property to round off your answer.

[10] This mention of an unresolved point of law shows your confidence in handling the subject matter.

If the trust fails then the trustee cannot take beneficially.[9] Unlike secret trusts (see **Wallgrave v Tebbs** (1855) 20 JP 84 HC), the trustee of a half-secret trust cannot take beneficially if the trust fails. As Ted and Sam have been named as trustees, they will hold on a resulting trust for the testator's estate. An interesting but as yet unresolved issue is the position where the trustee is himself the residuary legatee.[10]

The second possible trust results from the bequest of £5,000 to Janet absolutely.[11] This will be a secret trust as this arises where a will states that property is left to a beneficiary as an absolute gift, but the testator has agreed with the beneficiary that the beneficiary is to hold the property as trustee. There is therefore no mention in the will of any trust.

[12] It is important to stress this, as it saves you having to set out the rules again. But remember where they do differ!

There are the same basic requirements for the validity of a secret trust as for a half-secret trust.[12] Colin asked Janet to hold the £5,000 'for the benefit of such people as shall be specified in a letter to be found in the top drawer of my desk' and after Colin died, Janet found a letter in his desk specifying that the £5,000 is to be divided at Janet's discretion, among Colin's 'immediate family'.[13] Although there seems to be certainty of intention with the words 'hold for the benefit of' and the subject matter of £5,000 is certain, there is a problem with certainty of objects: who are Colin's 'immediate family'? This is a discretionary trust as indicated by the word 'discretion' in the gift and so the test for certainty of objects is that laid down in *McPhail v Doulton* [1971] AC 424 HL: can it be said with certainty if a person is or is not a beneficiary? It is submitted that evidence could be brought to show who Colin's immediate family are.

[13] Here is an excellent chance to earn extra marks, as there is a certainty of objects point. You do not need to answer it in the same detail as you would if this was a certainties question but you must deal with it.

If so, the question is then whether there has been communication. Where the trust is secret, communication must take place and the details of the trust must be communicated to the legatee before the testator's death (*Wallgrave v Tebbs* (above)). It does not matter whether communication is before or after the will.

However, it also appears that the secret trust can be enforced if the legatee is not actually told its details *before* the testator's death but is told where to find them *after* his death (*Re Keen* (above)) and this is what seems to have happened here as Colin then wrote to Janet asking her to hold the £5,000 'for the benefit of such people as shall be specified in a letter to be found in the top drawer of my desk' and this is where she found the letter with details of the trust.

[14] Again, do not ignore acceptance.

Finally, although Janet did not expressly accept the trust, she did so by implication[14] in that she complied with his statement that 'if you do not reply within a week I shall assume that you agree to this'.

It is suggested that this trust is valid.

✓ **Make your answer stand out**

- Discussion of the standard of proof required for the existence of a secret trust: see Megarry VC in *Re Snowden* [1979] Ch 528 HC. This is only a short point but it is a practical one and can easily be integrated into your answer.
- A brief mention of whether the law should actually enforce half-secret trusts at all. The reason is that if they were *not* enforced then there would still be no question of the trustees committing a fraud as they could not take beneficially because a trust had been declared in the will.

❗ **Don't be tempted to . . .**

- Just set out the rules on the validity of secret and half-secret trusts and not apply them.
- Ignore the certainties points.
- Only mention one rule on communication of a half-secret trust.
- Fail to mention what happens to the property if the trust fails.

Question 2

On 13 March 2014, Agatha met her friends Frank and Margaret at a party at the 'Eventide Home for the Elderly' where they all lived. She said to them, 'I am going to see my solicitor tomorrow to execute my will. In it you are left £30,000. Half is for you and I wish you to hold the other half on trust for my two grandsons, Peter and Sam. I also want you to hold my house "The Laurels" on trust for my niece Mary.'

Frank said, 'Whatever you wish dear, we'll do what we can.' Margaret did not hear as she is deaf.

Agatha executed her will on 14 March 2014. It left £30,000 and 'The Laurels' to Frank and Margaret absolutely. The will was witnessed by Sam and also by Edith and Cecilia, two other residents of the home.

Peter died on 17 March 2014. Agatha died on 1 September 2014.

Advise Paul, who is the executor under Agatha's will, on who is entitled to the gifts in it.

Answer plan

→ Identify that the bequest to Frank and Margaret is a secret trust.

→ State and explain the requirements for the validity of a secret trust.

→ Identify the certainty of intention point in this part of the question and explain how it could affect the outcome.

→ Apply the rule in *Re Stead*.

→ Note that the will was witnessed by a beneficiary.

→ Note that a beneficiary predeceased the testator.

→ Note that it is a trust of land and explain how this could affect its validity.

Diagram plan

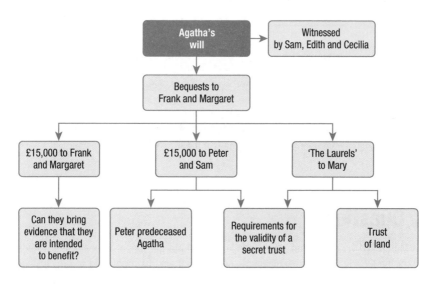

A printable version of this diagram plan is available from **www.pearsoned.co.uk/lawexpressqa**

[1] There is no evidence that the will is *not* valid and it would be unusual to have to deal with the validity of wills in a trusts exam as this is part of the law of succession.

[2] The word 'absolutely' in a question like this indicates a secret trust as there is no evidence of who the intended beneficiaries are and so it appears on the face of the will that there is a secret trust.

Answer

We can assume that Agatha's will is valid[1] and so the question is whether the gifts to those actually mentioned in it will take effect or whether a trust will be imposed on Frank and Margaret.

Agatha's will states that she has left £30,000 and 'The Laurels' to Frank and Margaret 'absolutely'.[2] This will be a secret trust as this arises where a will states that property is left to a beneficiary as an absolute gift, but the testator has agreed with the beneficiary that the beneficiary is to hold the property as trustee. There is therefore no mention in the will of any trust. This is so here.

In **Ottaway v Norman** [1972] Ch 698 HC, Brightman J held that the following requirements must be proved:

(i) The intention of the testator to subject the primary donee (i.e. the intended trustee) to an obligation in favour of the secondary donee (i.e. the intended beneficiary). In **Kasperbauer v Griffith** [2000] WTLR 333 HC, Peter Gibson J emphasised that all three certainties must be satisfied. Here Agatha said to Frank and Margaret: 'In [my will] you are left £30,000. Half is for you and I wish you to hold the other half on trust for my two grandsons, Peter and Sam. I also want you to hold my house "The Laurels" on trust for my niece Mary.'

The problem is with the words 'I wish you to hold' in the gift to Peter and Sam.[3] The word 'wish' may not indicate a trust as in **Suggitt v Suggitt** [2011] EWHC 903 (Ch) where the words used were: 'And I express the wish (without imposing a trust)'. However, it is important to look at the gift as a whole (see **Comiskey v Bowring-Hanbury** [1905] AC 84) and here the word 'trust' is used later and so it is clear that there is an intention to create a trust of the £30,000. There seems no problem with the intended trust of 'The Laurels' as the wording is clear: I want you to hold on trust. There is certainty of subject matter – £30,000 and 'The Laurels'.[4] The objects of the trust are Peter and Sam, who are to receive half, and Frank and Margaret themselves. Mary is the object of the trust of the house.

Can Frank and Margaret bring evidence that they were intended to be beneficiaries as any evidence will be extrinsic to the will?[5] In **Re Rees' Will Trusts** [1950] Ch 204 HC the court refused to allow extrinsic evidence to be admitted that the trustees were intended, after certain payments had been made, to hold any surplus for themselves, but here there is a straightforward gift. Moreover, in **Re Tyler's Fund Trusts** [1967] 1 WLR 269 HC while finding on the facts that no beneficial gift was intended, Pennycuick J confessed that he found difficulty with **Re Rees** and it is suggested that there is no reason why Frank and Margaret cannot bring evidence that they were intended to be beneficiaries.[6]

---

[3] This is a good example of how a certainties point can appear in a secret trusts question. Make sure that you address it. Note how a recent decision has been used as an authority. This always impresses an examiner.

[4] This point is straightforward but you do need to mention it, otherwise you will lose marks, but you need to do it quickly.

[5] Always check if the gifts under the secret or half-secret trust include ones to the trustees – if so, you will need to mention these cases.

[6] This clear and confident conclusion on a difficult area will impress the examiner.

(ii) Communication of that intention to the primary donee. Where the trust is secret, as here, communication must take place and the details of the trust must be communicated to the legatee before the testator's death (**Wallgrave v Tebbs** (1855) 20 JP 84 HC). The problem is that Frank heard the details of the trust but Margaret is deaf and did not hear. The question of whether Margaret is bound depends on the application of **Re Stead**. This provides that[7] communication to one joint tenant before the execution of the will binds the other. Frank and Margaret are joint tenants as there are no words of severance[8] in the gift in the will to them and communication appears to have been made to Frank before the execution of the will. Therefore it is submitted that Margaret is bound as well as Frank.

(iii) Acceptance of the obligation by the primary donee either expressly or by acquiescence. We are told that Frank said: 'Whatever you wish dear, we'll do what we can', and so he seems to have agreed to act as a trustee and Margaret is bound on the basis of **Re Stead** (above).

Although the trust therefore appears valid there are three other points. [9] The first is that Sam, as a beneficiary under the secret trust, witnessed the will although there were two other witnesses, Edith and Cecilia, residents of the home. In **Re Young** [1951] Ch 344 HC the beneficiary under a half-secret trust had witnessed the will in which the existence of the trust was declared. The rule that a witness to a will cannot normally take a legacy (Wills Act 1837, s. 15) was held not to apply here because the beneficiary did not take by virtue of the gift in the will but by virtue of the half-secret trust. The result would of course have been the same had the trust been secret, and so Sam can still take a benefit. In addition as there were two other witnesses it would be possible to disregard the signature of Sam.[10] This is because section 15 of the Wills Act, which provides that a witness cannot take a benefit under a will which either the witness or his/her spouse or civil partner attested, as amended provides that where there are more than two witnesses then the signature of the witness who is a beneficiary is ignored.

The second point is that Peter has predeceased Agatha the testator. In **Re Gardner (No 2)** [1923] 2 Ch 230 HC one of the beneficiaries

[7] Note how in this answer we have only mentioned the relevant part of the decision in *Re Stead*: resist the temptation to set it out in great detail regardless of whether all of the decision is relevant to the question!

[8] It is likely that in a trusts exam this point will not be a difficult one: the existence or lack of existence of words of severance will be made fairly clear and marks will not be gained by a detailed discussion of this point.

[9] Leave these points until you have established that the trust satisfies the requirements for its validity.

[10] Strictly speaking this point need not be mentioned as you have already established that the bequest is valid but as the question mentions it so you must deal with it to gain those extra marks.

under a secret trust predeceased the testatrix but it was held that the share of the deceased beneficiary did not lapse but passed to her personal representative. This decision has been doubted in most of the leading textbooks and thus it is doubtful if *Re Gardner* would be followed. If it is not, then Peter's share would pass to Agatha's estate.[11]

[11] It is extremely unusual to have to say this in an answer but here the decision in *Re Gardner* is so generally disapproved that you need to mention this otherwise you will lose marks.

[12] Make it a habit to check at the start of any question on secret or half-secret trusts if land is involved. If so, you will have to mention this point.

Finally, as this is a trust of land the question is whether the trust of 'The Laurels' is required to be in writing to satisfy section 53(1)(b) of the LPA 1925[12] which requires a declaration of trust of land to be evidenced by writing. However, constructive trusts are exempted from this requirement by section 53(2) and secret trusts are generally regarded as constructive. Thus writing is not required for this trust to be valid.

✓ Make your answer stand out

- Discussion of whether the rule in *Re Stead* should represent the law and what should be the rule instead: see Perrins (1972).
- Discussion of why the questionable decision in *Re Gardner* was actually reached.
- Discussion of whether secret and half-secret trusts are express or constructive. For one view see Perrins (1985) at p. 253.
- Mention that *Re Young* may illustrate the point that secret trusts operate *dehors* the will – or do they?

! Don't be tempted to . . .

- Spend time discussing whether the will is valid when there is nothing in the facts to suggest that it is not.
- Set out the rules for the validity of these types of trusts in a lengthy fashion without applying the law.
- Miss the certainty of intention point.
- Miss the point that one trust concerns land.

Question 3

Critically examine the proposition that on grounds of both legal principle and public policy there is little justification for the existence of secret trusts and still less for the existence of half-secret trusts.

Answer plan

→ Account for the origin of secret and half-secret trusts.

→ Consider each type separately.

→ Explain one possible basis of secret trusts: prevention of fraud.

→ Then go on to look at another basis: valid declaration of an *inter vivos* trust.

→ How can half-secret trusts be justified?

→ Consider their practical use – is this a sufficient justification by itself?

→ Do they fulfil a social need?

→ Possible alternative: letters of wishes?

Diagram plan

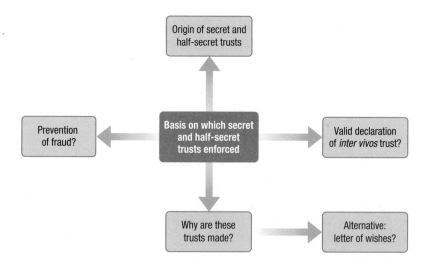

A printable version of this diagram plan is available from **www.pearsoned.co.uk/lawexpressqa**

Answer

The origin of secret trusts can be traced to immediately after the passage of the Statute of Frauds in 1677, but the recognition of half-secret trusts came much later and their complete recognition can be said to date from ***Blackwell v Blackwell*** [1929] AC 318 HL. This is important as it means that the justification for both types need to be considered separately.[1]

A secret trust arises[2] where a will states that property is left to a beneficiary as an absolute gift, but the testator has agreed with the beneficiary that the beneficiary is to hold the property as trustee. There is therefore no mention in the will of any trust. The original justification for them was to avoid fraud which could occur where statutory provisions were not complied with, and so they are an example of the maxim that equity 'will not allow a statute to be an engine of fraud'. The Statute of Frauds 1677 imposed formal requirements even on oral wills of more than £3 in value and also on declarations of trust of land and very soon after testators began to avoid these provisions by leaving property to a particular person but imposing a trust on them to hold it for the benefit of others. The first reported case is ***Thynn v Thynn*** (1684) 1 Vern 296.[3] The present law on the formal requirements for a will is contained in the Wills Act 1837 and specifically in section 9.[4]

The clearest statement of the principle is found in the speech of Lord Westbury in ***McCormick v Grogan*** (1869) 4 App Cas 82 HL: 'the jurisdiction which is involved here is founded altogether on personal fraud'. Thus, if John, the testator, says to Susan,[5] 'I will leave you £1,000 absolutely in my will but you are to hold this sum on trust for my daughter Mary' then it would be a fraud on John if Susan were to disregard this and keep the money for herself.

The problem with this principle[6] is that a jurisdiction based on fraud is indeed a reason why the intended trustee should not take beneficially but is not by itself a reason why the secret trust should be enforced in favour of the beneficiaries. A resulting trust in favour of the testator's estate would achieve the desired result.[7] A possible way round the difficulty is to give the word fraud a wider meaning as fraud on the beneficiaries through their not receiving their entitlement under the trust. The point seems to have been recognised by Lord Buckmaster in ***Blackwell v***

---

[1] This is an excellent opening as it shows the examiner that you have a clear structure for your answer, based on looking at secret and half-secret trusts separately.

[2] You do need to state clearly what a secret trusts is, but do this concisely and do not fall into the temptation of writing a general essay on them!

[3] The reason for mentioning this case is its date, as it shows that in 1684, not long after the passage of the Statute of Frauds, the courts of equity were enforcing secret trusts.

[4] It is important to make this clear now, as you will be discussing the Wills Act later.

[5] An example here does really help to clarify this point so do not be afraid to use it!

[6] This is where you start to climb out of the average zone and earn those extra marks: an average student would stop at the end of the previous paragraph!

[7] More marks gained: you have not only criticised the law but suggested a solution.

Blackwell [1929] AC 318 HL: 'the trustee is not at liberty to suppress the evidence of the trust . . . in fraud of the beneficiaries'.

The modern view is that secret trusts are enforced simply because the testator validly declared an *inter vivos* trust[8] and on the testator's death this trust became completely constituted by the property vesting in the trustee. Their essence is therefore the acceptance by the legatee of a personal obligation. Thus, Lord Warrington in ***Blackwell v Blackwell*** said: 'what is enforced is not a trust imposed by the will but one arising from the acceptance by the legatee of a trust communicated to him by the testator on the faith of which acceptance the will was made or left unrevoked'. This principle is often expressed by saying that secret trusts operate '*dehors* [outside] the will'. However, the theory does not account for not imposing a resulting trust[9] because the effect of this would usually be that the testator's family received the property which, if the testator had intended to benefit a mistress or an illegitimate child, would run counter to the obligations imposed on the legatee. Critchley (1999) argues that the '*dehors* the will' theory is wrong and points out that section 1 of the Wills Act 1837 provides that its provisions apply to 'any testamentary disposition' and she argues that this can include a secret trust.[10]

Critchley concludes that the fraud theory is still a possible justification for the enforcement of fully secret trusts if certain conditions are met but cannot explain the enforcement of half-secret trusts. Why is this so?[11]

A half-secret trust arises where property is left by will to a beneficiary but although the will states that the beneficiary is to hold on trust, the terms of the trust are not declared in the will but are agreed between the testator and beneficiary. The result is that because their existence is declared in the will, there is no possibility of the intended trustee taking beneficially. The will states that he is a trustee. By the time that the validity of half-secret trusts was accepted in ***Blackwell v Blackwell*** in 1929 the fraud theory had long been established and so clearly this could not be their rationale. Thus the only possible justification for half-secret trusts can be that the testator has declared a valid *inter vivos* trust.

A quite different rationale for both types is that in fact they do fulfil a social need.[12] Both types of trusts have traditionally been used where a testator does not wish his family to know who is to benefit from his will, a familiar example being where a man wished to leave property to a mistress of whom his wife was unaware as in ***Re Keen*** [1937] Ch

---

[8] Do remember what this means: a declaration of trust between the living (*inter vivos*) as distinct from a declaration of trust in a will.

[9] The phrase '*dehors* the will' is a well-known explanation of secret trusts and you need to mention it. Note also that you have followed your statement of the theory by also criticising it – this is a sure way to increase your marks.

[10] Although you will not, of course, be able to quote academic authorities at length in an answer it will help your marks a great deal if you can incorporate ideas from them as here.

[11] Here is where you look at half-secret trusts separately. Note again that we have briefly said what they are but without unnecessary detail.

[12] Here we break away from technical legal arguments to practical issues. This point, and the research which accompanies it, will certainly gain marks.

236 CA). There are other considerations too as illustrated by Rowena Meager (2003) in an article based on a postal survey in 2001 of solicitors specialising in wills and probate. This shows that 35% of respondents had clients who had asked them about 'a secret testamentary bequest'. The article lists a number of reasons why these trusts are made, one being where a gentleman wished to make a gift to 'a lady friend' without causing her any embarrassment as she was in 'reduced circumstances'. This may be acceptable but what of another instance where a secret trust was suggested 'to make a gift for the benefit of a handicapped child on state-funded support so as not to break the personal asset threshold'. This brings us back to the fundamental question: should secret trusts be allowed as the element of secrecy can allow a beneficiary to profit in a way which would not be possible were the gift made publicly. Is this right?

[13] In this conclusion we are going to another area of trusts law and making a comparison. Try to think like this as in practice different areas are not pigeonholed and it certainly adds to your marks.

The question ultimately rests on whether or not we see the importance of the wishes of the testator being carried out as paramount, even if it means disregarding statutory formalities. However, we should remember that there were good reasons for requiring formalities in the first place. Moreover, now that the courts are upholding letters of wishes[13] we could ask if these could replace secret and half-secret trusts as vehicles for wishes that testators wish to be kept out of the will. The disadvantage of this is that the courts may, as in ***Breakspear v Ackland*** [2008] EWHC 220 (Ch), order that the letters should be disclosed. In the end, why should testators have anything to hide anyway?

✓ Make your answer stand out

- Make more use of statistics from Meager (2003) to show the continued usefulness of secret trusts.
- Greater use of Critchley (1999) and her views of the theoretical basis of secret trusts.
- Explain another possible justification for secret and half-secret trusts: that they are a species of remedial constructive trust (see Chapter 8). This will help you to add depth to your answer by explaining exactly why the idea of a remedial constructive trust could be a possible basis for secret trusts.
- Look further into letters of wishes as a possible alternative to secret and half-secret trusts. These are considered in Chapter 11.
- Consider the issue from another angle: what if it is the testator who seeks to change the will and so disappoint the (secret) beneficiary? This is considered by Pawlowski and Brown (2004).

> **!** **Don't be tempted to . . .**
>
> - Fail to set these trusts in their historical context.
> - Just state the law on what secret trusts are – this question is about the underlying principles behind them.
> - Fail to subject the theories which you mention to critical examination.
> - Forget to distinguish between secret and half-secret trusts – the trusts are different and so the reasons for enforcing them will also differ.
> - State theories and not test them against the evidence.

? Question 4

Mike and his wife Mary are happily discussing the future. They have two children, Bob and Sue. Mary says to Mike: 'I wonder which of us will die first?' Mike says: 'I don't know but now that you mention it I would like to make a will leaving all of my property to you for life and then after your death it will go to Bob and Sue. Then I think that you should do the same so that if you die first then all will go to Bob and Sue in the end.' Mary says: 'That is a good idea – let's do it soon. You never know what is round the corner.' Their house is in Mike's name and they have savings in a number of accounts, some held jointly. In addition, Mary has a large sum invested in shares which formed part of the estate of her late Aunt Maud and which she has inherited.

Mike and Mary come to you for advice on what the legal effect will be if they put into effect what they have agreed to. Advise them.

Diagram plan

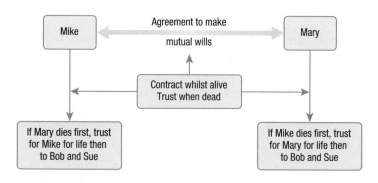

A printable version of this diagram plan is available from **www.pearsoned.co.uk/lawexpressqa**

Answer plan

→ Explanation of exactly what a mutual will is.

→ Explain the position where one party, Mike or Mary in this case, breaks the agreement to have mutual wills by revoking the will they have made, and consider the remedies and when they are available.

→ Mention that any will made can be revoked.

→ Then consider the position where the first spouse dies. Look at the part played by equity in holding that a constructive trust comes into existence and the problems which this causes.

→ End by advising Mike and Mary of alternative ways of putting their wishes into effect.

Answer

[1] Try for a clear and confident start like this. In these two opening sentences we have first answered the question directly by explaining that Mike and Mary should make mutual wills and then defined exactly what a mutual will is. In the process, we have gained a lot of marks for relatively few words.

The best way for Mike and Mary to put their wishes into effect would be for them to make mutual wills. These are where two people, having mutually agreed that the same person(s) should have their property after they are both dead, make separate wills, usually in which they leave property to each other, but which have the essential characteristic that there is a gift to the same agreed beneficiary and it is mutually agreed that the trust which arises cannot be revoked by the survivor.[1] Although each party's will is often in similar terms, as is intended to be the case here, there seems no reason why this should always be so in order for the doctrine of mutual wills to apply. In this case they both wish each other to benefit during their lives and the property to go to their children, Bob and Sue, after they have died. What is essential is that the agreement must make it clear that the wills are to be mutually binding and both are clear as to what making mutual wills involves (*Re Oldham* [1925] Ch 75 HC). It seems that the conversation between Mike and Mary may satisfy this requirement but this is not clear.[2] In *Re Oldham* the parties made wills in similar form but did not agree that they should be irrevocable and so they were not mutual wills. However, as part of the property concerns land[3] as Mike owns the house, that part of the agreement at least must be evidenced in writing to satisfy section 2 of the Law of Property (Miscellaneous) Provisions Act 1989 (*Healey v Brown* [2002] All ER (D) 249 (April) HC). It would, of course, be better if the whole agreement was then in writing.

[2] This is a vital point, which you must stress: if the parties have not agreed to make mutual wills then there cannot be mutual wills.

[3] This point often arises in mutual wills questions.

The first question is what will happen if, while Mike and Mary are still alive, one of them revokes this agreement and makes a will in different terms? No action can be brought to restrain the actual revocation of the mutual will because wills are always revocable (**Re Hey's Estate** [1914] P 192 HC). However, under the law of contract the revocation by either of them without notice to the other of a mutual will made in pursuance of the agreement will be a breach of contract, and damages will be payable by the party in breach.[4] An action could probably also be brought by Bob and Sue as beneficiaries under the Contracts (Rights of Third Parties) Act 1999. This Act can apply as the agreement was entered into after 11 May 2000 but it will only apply if the agreement can be construed as conferring a benefit on them as third parties.[5] The oral agreement mentioned in the question certainly shows an intention that they should benefit and it is suggested that any written agreement should be made in the same terms so that they can sue for breach.

[4] Note how this question requires knowledge of the law of wills and then the law of contract. Equity comes later.

[5] Do not *assume* that any third party can sue using this Act.

[6] This is a good practical point and worth making.

[7] This is a separate point and must be considered separately.

[8] Note the point where equity intervenes and make this clear in an answer.

However, until the party in breach has died it is likely that any damages for breach of contract would not be substantial as at this stage it is impossible to quantify the loss.[6] For example, if Mike made another will leaving all his property to Sarah then if Mary sued him at this stage it would be impossible to tell what the value of Mike's property would be at the date of his death and thus what loss Mary has suffered. The only case where there would be no right of action would be if Mike's will was revoked by operation of law (**Robinson v Ommanney** (1883) 23 Ch D 285 HC), as where he and Mary divorced and he then remarried.

The same applies if the breach consists of a refusal by a party to make a will.[7] If, for example, it was only found after Mike's death that he has not left a will in accordance with the agreement, then damages can be recovered from his estate as in **Robinson v Ommanney** (above). Here also it is not clear how damages would be calculated in these cases. In **Re Parkin** [1892] 3 Ch 510 HC, Stirling J referred to the possibility also of an action for specific performance to complete the transfer of the property.

Suppose, though, that Mike dies and Mary inherits his property under the terms of his will but then breaks the agreement for mutual wills by revoking her will so that Bob and Sue are no longer beneficiaries. Here equity intervenes,[8] as on the death of Mike, Mary holds the

[9] Do keep this point in mind: although the making of a will may be in breach of the agreement, the will itself can still be valid. What you have to do is then explain how equity resolves this. Note also that we have said 'if that will is valid', as if for some other reason it is not then the agreement is not broken as there is no will. This type of small but possibly significant point impresses examiners.

[10] This is an important and difficult issue. The law is by no means certain and you will gain marks by recognising this and setting out the possibilities.

[11] Although you may not have time to say much on this point, you will gain marks by showing that you are aware that it is a potential problem.

[12] This is a good way to end: it brings you back to the actual question and it is a practical point.

property on a constructive trust for Bob and Sue. However, as under the law of wills Mary is entitled to make another will then, if that will is valid,[9] any property will be held by the executors under that will under a constructive trust for Bob and Sue.

What property is the subject matter of this trust?[10] This will primarily be determined by the agreement and obviously includes the property of Mike which means that the house held in his name and any property in an account in his own name will be held on trust by Mary. The question is the extent to which Mary's own property will be held on trust. In **Re Hagger** [1930] 2 Ch 190 HC it was held that the trust attaches to all the property which was held by the survivor, Mary, at her death. This means that any disposition by Mary would be in breach of trust. What then of property acquired by Mary after the agreement to make mutual wills? If the trust applies to this also then Mary is a life tenant of all the property standing in her name and is entitled to enjoy the income but the capital must be preserved for the beneficiaries. However, in **Re Cleaver** [1981] 1 WLR 939 HC it was held by Nourse J that the survivor can enjoy the property as an absolute owner in her lifetime subject to a fiduciary duty which 'crystallised' on death. He held that a person in Mary's position was only disabled from making dispositions which were calculated to defeat the whole agreement, which in this case could mean selling the house, and that she could make gifts of small value. The problem then is that the actual subject matter of the trust is not certain.[11]

The final point is that, in view of the complications involved with making mutual wills, Mike and Mary might well be better advised not to make one and instead make joint wills which take effect as separate wills which can be revoked by either of them at any time.[12]

 Make your answer stand out

- Mention that in *Healey* v *Brown* it was suggested that if an agreement to make mutual wills involving land was not in writing then it would be unconscionable for the party in breach to rely on this.
- Note that by section 7(1) of the Contracts (Rights of Third Parties) Act 1999 the operation of this Act does not affect any other rights or remedies. This means that it is possible to use the trust basis as a means of enforcement also. ▶

- Mention the theoretical basis of the enforcement of mutual wills: the prevention of fraud because any revocation of the mutual will after the death of the first to die would be a fraud by the survivor.

- Consider possible alternative ways of enforcing these obligations. One would be to use the reasoning in *Beswick* v *Beswick* [1968] AC 58 HL but this was not accepted in *Re Dale* [1994] Ch 31 HC.

- Mention that the constructive trust may not be the best solution: Hodkinson (1982) suggested that a floating charge could be imposed over the assets of the first to die.

! Don't be tempted to . . .

- Mix up the contractual, succession and equity issues. Make sure that you are clear where each arises.

- Begin before you have clearly explained what a mutual will is.

- Use this question as an excuse to write all that you know about mutual wills. Link your answer to the facts of the question.

- Omit any discussion of the problems in deciding what the subject matter of the trust is.

www.pearsoned.co.uk/lawexpressqa

Go online to access more revision support including additional essay and problem questions with diagram plans, You be the marker questions, and download all diagrams from the book.

Resulting trusts

7

How this topic may come up in exams

One area which is a favourite of examiners is the actual basis on which the courts impose a resulting trust. This requires you to be familiar with a number of theories and is a good opportunity for students who have done their homework on this to really shine. Another favourite is the extent to which presumptions play a part in deciding if there is a resulting trust or not and another is the *Quistclose* trust. In addition, a clear understanding of when resulting trusts can arise and of how they operate is essential in many other areas, one important one being when an unincorporated association is dissolved (which is considered in Chapter 10).

■ Before you begin

It's a good idea to consider the following key themes of resulting trusts before tackling a question on this topic.

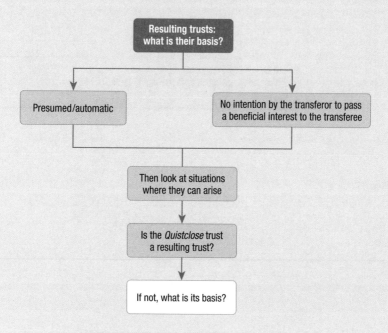

A printable version of this diagram is available from **www.pearsoned.co.uk/lawexpressqa**

 Question 1

'A man does not cease to own property simply by saying "I don't want it." If he tries to give it away the question must always be, has he succeeded in doing so or not? If he has not succeeded in giving it away, it still belongs to him, even if he does not want it; and that, I think, is really the position here.'

Comment critically on this view of the basis of resulting trusts expressed by Plowman J in *Vandervell* v *IRC* [1966] Ch 261 at 275.

Diagram plan

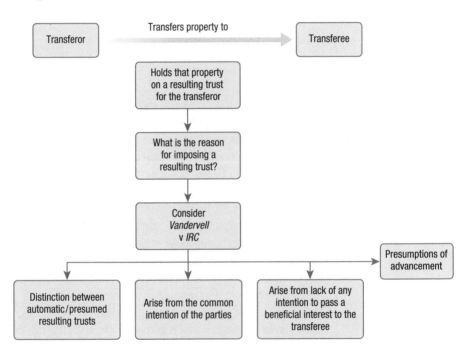

A printable version of this diagram plan is available from **www.pearsoned.co.uk/lawexpressqa**

Answer plan

→ Identify the main issue: what is the basis on which resulting trusts are imposed, when are they imposed and why?

→ Critically consider the classification of Megarry J in *Re Vandervell's Trusts* [1974] Ch 269 HC and the views of Lord Browne-Wilkinson in *Westdeutsche Landesbank Girozentrale* v *Islington BC* [1996] AC 669 HL.

→ Look at the theory of Chambers (1997) that resulting trusts arise from the absence of an intention by the transferor to pass any beneficial interest to the transferee.

→ Refer to the part played by presumptions in the law of resulting trusts.

→ Conclude by looking at another debated area: the beneficial interest under a resulting trust, and then come back to the question.

Answer

[1] Resulting trusts, and when they occur, can be a complex area so why not start with a straightforward example.

[2] Note how we are applying the words of Plowman J in the question to the situation. It really does help if you anchor your answer right at the start to the words of the question.

This view of the basis of resulting trusts put forward by Plowman J in ***Vandervell v IRC*** [1966] Ch 261 offers a clear explanation of what happens when a resulting trust arises. Suppose that Debbie transfers her house, 'Lilac Cottage', into the name of her sister Moyra.[1] There is no consideration and there is no mention that it is by way of gift. In this case Debbie has clearly said that she does not want 'Lilac Cottage' but, as Plowman J put it, the question is always, has she given it away or not? If she has not, then 'Lilac Cottage' will still belong to her.[2] Yet of course it does not belong to her in law as the legal title has been transferred to Moyra, and this is where equity comes in – by holding that in certain cases the legal title will be held by the transferee, Moyra here, for Debbie on a resulting trust. Thus when there is a resulting trust the trust 'springs back' (from the Latin *resilare*), so that the beneficiary under the resulting trust is the person who made the transfer of rights in the property (Debbie here), Moyra is the trustee, and that property is now the subject matter of the trust.

[3] Although not essential it does help if you can refer to the facts of the case from which the reference to the judgment was taken, although you should remember that in some instances the facts will relate to a different point. However, here the facts really do assist.

In ***Vandervell v IRC*** itself[3] Vandervell had given Vandervell Trustees Ltd an option to purchase shares which he had transferred to the Royal College of Surgeons, but had failed to specify the trusts on which the shares were then to be held. There was thus a resulting, or what Lord Wilberforce in the House of Lords called an automatic, trust for Vandervell. The beneficial interest, he said, could not 'remain in the air', therefore 'it remains in the settlor'.

This reference by Lord Wilberforce to an 'automatic resulting trust' tells us that there are some theories of why resulting trusts arise. As Swadling (2008) remarks, 'The most difficult question one can ask about resulting trusts is why they arise'.[4] The circumstances in which resulting trusts occur are reasonably well settled, although there are some disputed areas, but what has never been settled is exactly *why* a resulting trust should arise in these cases. The quotation by Plowman J in the question does not really explain this. It tells us what happens but not why.[5]

Megarry J in *Re Vandervell's Trusts (No 2)* [1974] Ch 269 proposed two types of resulting trust and this for a time became the prevailing orthodoxy.[6] These were:

(a)   Automatic resulting trusts, where there was a resulting trust independent of the intentions of the settlor, as where the settlor has failed to specify the beneficial interests and so there is either a lack of certainty of objects or no objects at all, as in *Vandervell v IRC* (above).

(b)   Presumed resulting trusts, as where a person transferred property to another without consideration but where no words of gift were used. These were considered to arise from the presumed intention of the transferor. Thus in *Re Vinogradoff* [1935] WN 68 HC[7] the testatrix had transferred an £800 War Loan which was in her own name into the joint names of herself and her four-year-old daughter. It was held that the daughter held it on a resulting trust for the testatrix. This would also apply in the example of Debbie and Moyra in the question.

This view clearly distinguishes between two factual situations which are indeed different. In the case of the automatic resulting trust there is an intention by the settlor, such as Vandervell, to create a trust, but a failure to specify who shall receive the benefit. Where there is a presumed resulting trust there is doubt whether a trust is intended at all, as in *Re Vinogradoff*.

This classification was disapproved of by Lord Browne-Wilkinson in *Westdeutsche Landesbank Girozentrale v Islington BC* [1996] AC 669 HL[8] who suggested *obiter* that resulting trusts were 'traditionally regarded as arising from the common intention of the parties'. Yet this cannot explain all cases of resulting trusts. For

[4] This kind of quotation is really useful – but do read the rest of the article!

[5] This is an important paragraph: it takes us from a discussion of the quotation in the question to a wider look at the basis on which resulting trusts arise.

[6] This classification of resulting trusts is not the end of the story but it is a good place to start. It is also useful as you are able to give some actual examples of resulting trusts to illustrate these categories, and this helps to anchor your answer to factual situations rather than becoming too theoretical.

[7] You will notice that this case and *Re Vandervell* are used throughout this essay to illustrate how the resulting trust can apply in different circumstances. This use of the same cases can help to clarify your thinking, as different theories are applied to the same set of facts.

[8] What is essential in an essay in this area is to recognise that the law is not settled and to test a number of theories against each other.

example in **Re Vinogradoff** the transferor could not have intended that the granddaughter should be the trustee.

A different test suggested by Chambers in *Resulting Trusts* (1997)[9] is that all resulting trusts should be considered as arising from the presumption of the *lack of* any intention by the transferor to pass any beneficial interest to the transferee when the transferee has not provided the entire consideration for the property. Thus, as Chambers points out, the resulting trust operates to return specific property to the transferor because he/she did *not* intend to benefit the transferee. One example would be in a case where the objects of the trust were not sufficiently certain and so the trustee holds the trust property on a resulting trust for the settlor *precisely because* the settlor cannot have intended the trustee to benefit, as in **Vandervell v IRC**. The advantage of this theory is that it fits all the cases where a resulting trust has been imposed because the one certain fact is that in none of them was the transferee intended to benefit.[10] Its effect is to give presumptions a greater role than in Megarry J's classification as on the basis of this theory they operate in all cases of resulting trusts whereas Megarry J's classification saw no place for them where the trust was automatic.

In certain situations equity used to hold that there is a presumption of advancement[11] (or gift) which displaces the presumption of resulting trust. One example was the presumption of advancement where a transfer is made from a husband to a wife but it does not apply vice versa. Presumptions of advancement were felt to contravene Article 5 of Protocol 7 of the European Convention on Human Rights, providing for equality between the spouses, and were abolished by section 199 of the Equality Act 2010, but this is not yet in force and is not retrospective and so presumptions of advancement will be relevant for some time as litigation can occur years after a gift.

The final point is the debated one of what happens to the beneficial interest in the property.[12] Lord Reid in **Vandervell v IRC** [1967] argued that this remains with the transferor throughout and so equity is simply recognising a fact. This view is now no longer generally held and instead it is considered by, for example, Chambers, that, on any transfer, only the legal interest passes to the transferor and where the resulting trust arises from that transfer a new equitable interest then

[9] It is vital to recognise that there is more than one explanation of when a resulting trust arises.

[10] This is a vital – and straightforward – point to emphasise.

[11] Although these are not so important as perhaps they once were, you should mention them as if a presumption of advancement applies then there is the opposite result from where there is a resulting trust.

[12] You have just shown that the actual application of the law on resulting trusts is reasonably certain, but why not end with another debatable point which leads you naturally to your conclusion?

arises which is held for the transferor on the basis that otherwise the transferee would be unjustly enriched.

[13] Here we are returning to the words of the question and summing up our argument.

Thus the quotation from Plowman J in the question is a useful starting point. However, it does not explain exactly why resulting trusts arise and in fact this is by no means settled.[13]

✓ **Make your answer stand out**

- A clear recognition of exactly what a resulting trust is and what it does.
- Engage with the different theories of the basis of resulting trusts and recognise that there is no certain answer.
- Look at the suggestion of Lord Browne-Wilkinson in *Westdeutsche Landesbank Girozentrale* v *Islington BC* that a resulting trust should not arise until the conscience of the trustee is affected. Note the criticism of Chambers (1997) that this makes the imposition of a resulting trust depend on notice. What, he asks, is the position *until* the trustee has notice of the trust?
- Look carefully at Swadling (2008) who has a number of criticisms of the use of the term 'presumption' by Chambers, and who remarks that 'Before any progress can be made in the search for an explanation of resulting trusts, a secure understanding of presumptions is required.'

❗ **Don't be tempted to . . .**

- Just set out cases on, for example, the presumption of advancement. Instead you must first set out the theoretical basis for resulting trusts.
- Come to a very definite conclusion about the basis of resulting trusts. There is no theory which is very generally accepted and you will lose marks if you give the impression that there is.
- Spend all of your time discussing the theories behind resulting trusts and none on how they operate. Give your essay balance.

❓ Question 2

Fritz runs a business supplying frozen food to the catering trade and receives an order for frozen foods costing £100,000 from the Swell Hotel, which has just opened.

Rudolf, the owner of the Swell Hotel, tells Fritz that he can only pay him when he receives a payment for a large conference which the hotel is hosting but that it will be made within a week of delivery. Fritz is somewhat reluctant but his own business has been going through financial difficulties and he is reluctant to turn down such a large order.

However, Fritz is still concerned but then Walter, Rudolf's father, agrees to lend the Swell Hotel £100,000 so that it can obtain the food from Fritz and so host the conference and establish the hotel.

Fritz delivers the food but before the conference is held and despite Walter's loan the Swell Hotel goes into liquidation. The liquidator has taken over all its assets.

Walter has agreed with Fritz that if he can recover the £100,000 from the liquidator he will pay it to him.

(a) Advise Fritz on his chances of success in the action for breach of contract against the Swell Hotel.

(b) Advise Walter on his chances of success in an action to recover the £100,000, explaining the relevant law fully.

Diagram plan

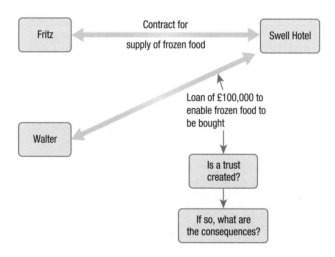

A printable version of this diagram plan is available from **www.pearsoned.co.uk/lawexpressqa**

Answer plan

→ Deal with Fritz's chances of success in an action for breach of contract against the Swell Hotel.

→ Then move on to look at a possible action by Walter based on the principle in *Barclays Bank v Quistclose Investments Ltd*.

→ Look carefully at the facts of this problem and compare them to those in *Re EVTR*.

→ Move on to analyse the nature of trust which arises in these cases.

→ Conclude by applying both your analysis of the facts and of the nature of the trust to the question.

Answer

[1] It helps your marks by setting the answer off in a confident way if you can begin like this. There is no doubt on the law here, so make this clear.

[2] Do not spend too long on this initial point. The reason why it is included is to make the contrast between contractual rights and those under a trust as in *Quistclose*.

[3] It would be a mistake at this point to commit yourself and say that Walter 'will' be able to recover the money.

[4] You need to set out the facts of this case in sufficient detail to make any discussion which follows understandable.

(a) Fritz can certainly bring an action against the liquidator of the Swell Hotel for breach of contract as the food supplied by him was not paid for.[1] The problem is that, although there seems to be a clear breach of contract, Fritz only has rights as a debtor, and there is considerable doubt as to whether he will recover either payment or indeed his legal costs as the Swell Hotel is in liquidation and so Fritz will rank with the other trade creditors. Moreover, as he will almost certainly not be able to recover his legal costs, he will end up worse off than before.[2]

(b) The position of Walter is different, as he has agreed to lend the Swell Hotel the sum of £100,000 so that it can obtain the food. This means that Walter may be able to claim[3] the return of the £100,000 under the principle in **Barclays Bank Ltd v Quistclose Investments Ltd** [1970] AC 567 HL.[4] Rolls Razor was in financial difficulties and declared a dividend on its shares but did not have the money to pay it and so Quistclose made a contract to make it a loan for the express purpose of enabling it to pay this dividend. The money was paid into a separate account at Barclays Bank and it was agreed with the bank that the account would 'only be used to meet the dividend due on July 24th 1964'. Before the dividend was paid, Rolls Razor went into liquidation and the question was whether Barclays Bank could set the sum in the account off against Rolls Razor's overdraft or whether they held it on trust for Quistclose.

The House of Lords held that there was a trust for Quistclose, as the letter clearly indicated that the money was to be used to pay the dividend and for no other purpose. It followed that if, for any reason, the money could not be used for this purpose then it had to be returned to Quistclose. Accordingly, it was held by Rolls Razor on trust for Quistclose.

As Watt (2004) has observed: 'there is something beguiling about the **Quistclose** trust. It has the seemingly magical ability to turn a lender's personal rights under a loan for a specific purpose into proprietary rights under a trust.'[5]

[5] Even if you cannot recall the exact words of this quotation, do try to remember the essential idea of contractual rights then apparently turning into rights under a trust.

The lending of money to purchase equipment, bearing in mind that in this context food counts as equipment, can create a **Quistclose** trust.[6] In **Re EVTR** [1987] BCLC 646 CA the appellant lent £60,000 to a company to assist it in purchasing new equipment. The company made an agreement to purchase this, and temporary equipment was delivered, but the company then went into liquidation before the actual new equipment was due for delivery. The court held that the **Quistclose** principle applied and that the £60,000, less agreed deductions, should be held on a resulting trust for the appellant. Had the contract for the purchase of the equipment been completed and the money entirely spent then, as Dillon LJ observed, no trust would have arisen and the appellant would have merely been an unsecured creditor.

[6] This is a crucial link in your answer. You need to make the connection between payments of money so that dividends can be paid, as in *Quistclose* itself, and payments of money to purchase goods as here and then go on to quote the relevant authority.

In principle the decision in **Barclays Bank Ltd v Quistclose** can apply here. As Lord Millett put it in **Twinsectra v Yardley** [2002] UKHL 12: 'The question in every case is whether the parties intended the money to be at the free disposal of the recipient.' In this case it is clear that this was not so, as Walter lent the £100,000 so that the Swell Hotel could 'obtain the food from Fritz and so host the conference and establish the hotel'.

If this actual purpose has failed then the £100,000 will be held on trust for Walter. In fact, the food was delivered but was not used for the conference as the Swell Hotel then went into liquidation. One could argue that there were two purposes here: the obtaining of the food and its actual use at the conference and only the second purpose failed due to the liquidation of the Swell Hotel.[7] In **Re EVTR** the actual

[7] This is one of those problem questions where you really do increase your marks by looking closely at the words of the question and then analysing them.

equipment was not delivered but the temporary equipment was. On this basis it could be argued that the **Quistclose** principle applied when only one purpose, the delivery of the temporary equipment, was carried out, and the same applies here as only one purpose, the delivery of the food was carried out. The other argument is that in practice there was only one purpose: supply and use of the food, and that this failed. Thus on either view it seems that the **Quistclose** principle does apply and if so Walter will hold the £100,000 on trust for Fritz and will not have to queue, as it were, for payment with the creditors. If it does not apply, he will be just a creditor.

[8] Notice from the words of the question that you are asked to 'explain the relevant law fully'. This is a hint from the examiner that you are expected to explain in detail the law which relates to your answer and this is what we are about to do. However, it is not an invitation to write a general essay on this subject.

The issue of the failure of the purpose takes us on to the nature of the **Quistclose** trust itself.[8] If, indeed, the purpose of the loan has failed then the borrower, the Swell Hotel, will be a trustee for the lender, Walter, but what will be the nature of the trust? In **Barclays Bank Ltd v Quistclose** Lord Wilberforce analysed the trust as a primary trust in favour of the creditors and a secondary one in favour of the lender if in that case the purpose failed and the dividend could not be paid. It is difficult to find a primary trust here and indeed there have been doubts expressed as to whether a primary trust exists at all in this type of case but in **Re EVTR** Dillon LJ held that the trust for the lender could be 'a resulting or constructive trust'. The view of Chambers (1997) is that it is a resulting trust rather than a constructive trust which is imposed. Chambers suggests that the resulting trust arises when the purpose of the loan fails. However, in **Twinsectra v Yardley** Lord Millett analysed the position differently as one where an express trust arises for the lender, Walter in this case, *as soon as* the £100,000 was transferred to the borrower, the Swell Hotel, but subject to the right of the borrower to apply it for the purpose for which it was lent. In this case if it was not applied for that purpose then the express trust takes over.

[9] Note how this conclusion achieves two objects: it provides a conclusion on the facts and it uses the reasoning on the nature of the *Quistclose* trust, as explained by Lord Millett, to explain how this happens.

In conclusion it is suggested that, on the analysis of Lord Millett in **Twinsectra v Yardley**, the £100,000 advanced by Walter to the Swell Hotel was held on an express trust for him as soon as he transferred it and that as the purposes for which it was lent were not carried out in full this trust for Walter now takes effect.[9]

Make your answer stand out

- Mention the case of *Bieber and others* v *Teathers Ltd (in liquidation)* [2012] EWCA Civ 1466 where there was no *Quistclose* trust as the money paid to the defendant under an investment scheme, to be used to invest in TV productions, formed partnership assets.

- Do read and refer to Watt (2004). It is not a long article and really does give you some useful insights into this area.

- Look at a recent article surveying both case law and academic literature in this area: Chan (2013).

- Consider if the *Quistclose*-type trust could be a non-charitable purpose trust.

- Mention, perhaps in the conclusion, this view of Lord Millett in a foreword to Swadling (2004): 'From a commercial point of view . . . the trust is simply a mechanism . . . The commercial need for such a mechanism is obvious.'

- Consider in more detail where the beneficial interest lies in a *Quistclose* trust: does, as suggested by Chambers (1997), the borrower retain a beneficial interest in the money throughout the transaction? Note that this is at variance with the views of Lord Millett in *Twinsectra* v *Yardley* mentioned in the answer.

- Does it help to draw an analogy with non-charitable purpose trusts? Megarry V-C in *Re Northern Developments (Holdings) Ltd* (1978) (unreported, Ch D) felt that in both instances the beneficial interests are in suspense. However, this view conflicts with that of Lord Millett (above) and it is arguable that it is wrong.

! Don't be tempted to . . .

- Confuse rights under a contract with rights under a trust. Make this distinction clear.

- Just quote the *Quistclose* case and fail to analyse it in connection with the facts of the problem.

- Just say that a trust arises in these types of cases without considering what type of trust it may be.

- Set out one point of view on the basis of the *Quistclose*-type trusts and not mention others.

www.pearsoned.co.uk/lawexpressqa

 Go online to access more revision support including additional essay and problem questions with diagram plans, You be the marker questions, and download all diagrams from the book.

Constructive trusts and estoppel

How this topic may come up in exams

This topic is an absolute *must* for your revision as it comes up right across an equity exam. You may get essay questions on constructive trusts, the nature of a fiduciary, estoppel and on the particular area of the remedial constructive trust. Problem questions can deal with unauthorised profits made by a fiduciary, trusts of the home, estoppel and other topics. Moreover, knowledge of this area may be relevant in questions on the nature of equity, trustees, secret trusts, resulting trusts, breach of trust and really any area of equity.

■ Before you begin

It's a good idea to consider the following key themes of constructive trusts and estoppel before tackling a question on this topic.

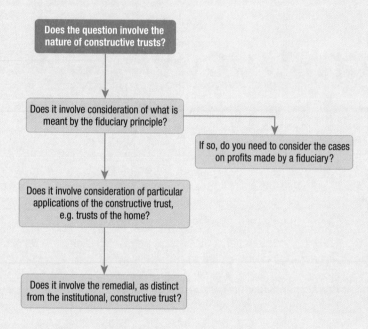

A printable version of this diagram is available from **www.pearsoned.co.uk/lawexpressqa**

 Question 1

'A constructive trust arises by operation of law rather than by the intention of the parties and it can arise in a wide variety of circumstances. But there is little agreement amongst the judiciary or academic writers as to when a constructive trust will be recognised and why it should be recognised.' (Maudsley, in Burn and Virgo (eds), 2008, p. 278)

Critically consider the above statement and the various circumstances in which a constructive trust is recognised by the courts.

Diagram plan

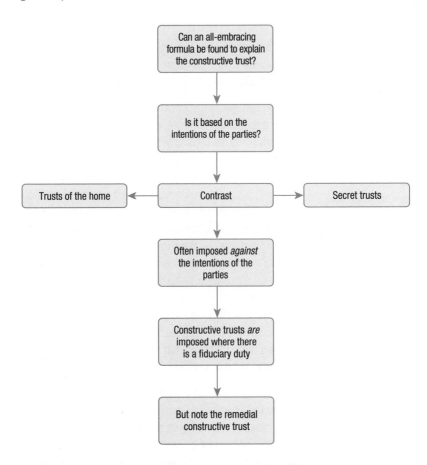

A printable version of this diagram plan is available from **www.pearsoned.co.uk/lawexpressqa**

Answer plan

→ Start by mentioning the idea of an all-embracing formula, explaining the existence of constructive trusts, and say that you intend to see if there is one.

→ Look at the part played by intention: can this be a basis for the constructive trust?

→ Discuss the concept of the fiduciary. Is this a satisfactory basis? Mention cases on receipt of bribes.

→ Look briefly at the idea of the remedial constructive trust.

→ Conclude by returning to the question.

[1] This start will catch the eye of the examiner as it shows that you have considered the issues and that you have a clear structure for your answer. Ensure you keep this in mind throughout the answer.

[2] Although, as we shall see, not all constructive trusts can be explained on this basis you do need to mention the situations where intention can play a part.

[3] Note how this essay is not stopping at the word 'intention' but is asking precisely what it means. Adopt this approach for extra marks.

[4] If mentioning *Stack* v *Dowden* in an essay of this type then you must also mention *Jones* v *Kernott* as this carries the law a stage further.

[5] This is an interesting example and its inclusion shows lateral thinking in using a trust from a different area.

[6] Making clear direct comparisons always helps to 'lift' an answer.

[7] There is no need to look at the circumstances in which 'knowing receipt liability' is imposed as this is irrelevant.

Answer

In this essay we will look at the law on constructive trusts to see if it is possible to identify an all-embracing formula to describe the circumstances in which these trusts are imposed.[1]

Can it be said that constructive trusts are based on the parties' intentions?[2] It is true that in cases involving the beneficial ownership of the family home the constructive trust has been said to be based on the intentions of the parties. In **Stack v Dowden** [2007] UKHL 17, Lady Hale said that 'The search is to ascertain the parties' shared intentions, actual, inferred or imputed, with respect to the property in the light of their whole course of conduct in relation to it.' However, it will be noted that intention is given a wide meaning[3] and the idea of an imputed intention takes us right away from actual intention and amounts to saying that the courts will themselves decide what the parties' intentions were. In the more recent case of **Jones v Kernott** [2011] UKSC 53[4] Lord Wilson seemed to recognise this when he said: 'Where equity is driven to impute the common intention, how can it do so other than by a search for the result which the court itself considers fair?' Thus he based the imposition of a constructive trust on fairness and not intention.

One example where the imposition of a constructive trust does seem to be based on intention is a secret trust.[5] Where a will contains a bequest of property from X to Y 'absolutely' but X has told Y to hold this on trust for Z, then equity can impose a secret trust and this is clearly based on X's intention that Y shall hold the property on trust for Z. However, we could contrast this[6] with the situation where a person knowingly receives[7] trust property. Suppose that

X as a trustee transfers trust property to Y who knows that it is trust property. In this case it is said that Y becomes a constructive trustee of it for the beneficiaries, but here of course becoming a constructive trustee is the last thing on Y's mind; he wants to keep the property for himself. Thus intention cannot explain the imposition of constructive trusts.

[8] It is vital to stress this point: express trusts give effect to the intentions of the parties but constructive trusts are generally imposed against their intentions.

Indeed, in all other cases it is clear that constructive trusts are in fact imposed against the intentions of the parties.[8] Thus in ***Keech v Sandford*** (1726) Eq Cas Abr 741 HC a trustee (X) of a lease of a market was granted a renewal of the lease in his own name because the landlord did not wish to renew it on trust as the beneficiary was a minor who could not be bound by the usual covenants. It was held that X held the renewed lease on trust for the minor. The basis of the decision was stated in ***Bray v Ford*** [1896] AC 44 HL by Lord Herschell thus: 'It is an inflexible rule of a Court of Equity that a person in a fiduciary position . . . is not, unless expressly authorised, entitled to make a profit; he is not allowed to put himself in a position where duty and interest conflict.'

[9] Note how we have developed this answer. A mediocre answer would just have said that constructive trusts are imposed on fiduciaries. Asking who a fiduciary is and coming up with a recent case adds value to our answer!

[10] Examples such as this one do help, not least because they avoid you having to give perhaps lengthy accounts of cases in order to make your point.

[11] Note the link to the words of the question.

What we can say is that English courts have imposed a constructive trust in circumstances where a fiduciary duty can be identified as, for example, in ***Keech v Sandford*** and ***Boardman v Phipps*** [1967] AC 46 HL. However, this only takes us a step backwards as constructive trusts are not always imposed on fiduciaries.[9] Suppose that an employee (Z) is given a sum of money by a firm (X) bidding for a contract with her firm (Y) so that she will place the contract with X? This is a bribe, but although Z may have received the money as a fiduciary does she hold it on trust for her employer (Y)? There is no doubt that Y can recover the sum of money from Z, but suppose that Z is insolvent? If so, Y may wish to trace the amount into Z's assets and impose a constructive trust. But did Z receive the money as a constructive trustee?[10] The courts have reached different conclusions and here we see the truth of the statement in the question that there has been little agreement among the judiciary in this area.[11]

In ***Lister & Co v Stubbs*** (1890) 45 Ch D 1 CA it was held that a bribe received by a fiduciary from a third party was not held on trust for the principal. The reasoning was that proprietary claims (i.e. those founded on trust) were only available where the principal seeks to recover property which belonged to him *before* the breach of fiduciary duty. A bribe, by contrast, is not the property of the principal but is property held by the fiduciary in breach of fiduciary obligation. However, this principle was reversed in **Attorney General for Hong Kong v Reid** [1994] 1 AC 324 PC [12] which held that benefits obtained from a third party in breach of fiduciary obligation, such as bribes, belong in equity to the principal from the moment of receipt. This was in itself reversed in **Sinclair Investments (UK) Ltd v Versailles Trade Finance (In Administration)** [2011] EWCA Civ 347, [13] which has changed the position back to what it was before Reid, and so **Lister v Stubbs** became again good law. However, in the latest case, **FHR European Ventures LLP v Mankarious** [2013] EWCA Civ 17 the court was not happy with the principle in **Sinclair**, which it managed to distinguish, and invited the Supreme Court to consider 'whether **Sinclair Investments** was right to decide that **Lister** is to be preferred to **Reid**'.

[12] In any question on bribes and fiduciaries you should still refer to this decision. Although it has been overruled it is a decision of the Privy Council and it may be restored in future.

[13] We do not need the facts of these cases – it would take too long and divert us from our main theme.

Finally, all of the above situations are examples of what is known as an institutional constructive trust, which arises where the facts of the dispute fall within an existing category of cases where a constructive trust has previously been recognised. However, there is another category, that of the remedial constructive trust. In **Beatty v Guggenheim Exploration Co** (1919) 225 NY 380, Cardozo J said that 'A constructive trust is the formula through which the conscience of equity finds expression' and this approach led to the idea of the remedial constructive trust[14] which would be imposed 'whenever justice and good conscience require it . . . it is an equitable remedy by which the court can enable an aggrieved party to obtain restitution' (Denning MR in **Hussey v Palmer** [1972] 3 All ER 744). However, the idea of the remedial constructive trust has not in general found favour with the courts, as shown by **Re Polly Peck International plc (In Administration) (No 2)** [1998] 3 All ER 812, although in **Thorner v Major** [2009] UKHL 18 Lord Scott did raise the possibility of one existing in some cases of proprietary estoppel.[15]

[14] Although the idea of a remedial constructive trust is not in favour among the judiciary at the moment you do need to mention it as it has played a significant part in the thinking about constructive trusts.

[15] An interesting point to expand if you have time.

In conclusion it is suggested that it is impossible to find any coherent theme which links all types of constructive trusts together. One argument is that constructive trusts are imposed where there has been wrongdoing but even this analysis breaks down in the case of trusts of the family home where the issue is not wrongdoing but an attempt to find a just solution, however it is based.[16]

[16] Note how, in the conclusion, we have briefly raised a new issue which avoids a very lame conclusion along the lines of 'we just don't know'.

Make your answer stand out

- Keep your mind on what the question is asking you and do not just give an account of the cases on constructive trusts. Engage with the question!

- Look at other examples of the constructive trust, such as secret trusts, and see how they fit into an analysis of constructive trusts.

- Consider arguments about the true basis of the constructive trust and refer to them in your answer, such as the argument that certain types of constructive trusts can be analysed as correcting a loss suffered in reliance on the undertaking of another. See Gardner (2010).

- Read and refer to the article by Chambers (2013) on *FHR European Ventures LLP* v *Mankarious.*

- Give more thought to the remedial constructive trust and look for instance at the Court of Appeal decision in *Halifax Building Society* v *Thomas* [1996] Ch 217.

! Don't be tempted to . . .

- Simply write all that you know about constructive trusts with masses of cases and no connecting theme.

- Leave out a mention of the remedial constructive trust.

- Ignore recent cases in this area.

❓ Question 2

Frankie is trustee of a small trust which provides short breaks for ten named people with disabilities aged 18 and over. There are three other trustees, Dave, Jack and Fiona.

The trust owns a house which provides residential accommodation and some farm buildings. Frankie's daughter, Liz, needs a home quickly and Frankie asks at a trustees' meeting if the other trustees will agree to him buying one of the farm buildings so that he can convert it into accommodation for Liz. Frankie leaves the meeting whilst they are considering this. The other trustees unanimously agree.

The trust has a partnership with the local college and through this connection Frankie learns of an opportunity to buy another building from the college which is already equipped as a sensory room and to run it himself as a separate venture. He told the trustees after he had acquired it and they agreed that they would not have wished to buy it even had they had the chance.

Anne has just been appointed as a trustee and she is concerned about these events. She asks you for advice on whether either of the transactions were in accord with Frankie's duties as a trustee.

Answer plan

→ Explain the responsibilities of trustees and how this relates to the question.

→ State and explain the 'self-dealing' rule and how it can apply to the purchase of trust property by Frankie.

→ Then move on to consider the remedies available to the beneficiaries if the purchase by Frankie was in breach of trust.

→ Consider the 'no conflict of interest rule' in relation to the purchase of the building by Frankie.

→ Finally, apply the rule that a trustee must not set up a competing business to this situation.

Diagram plan

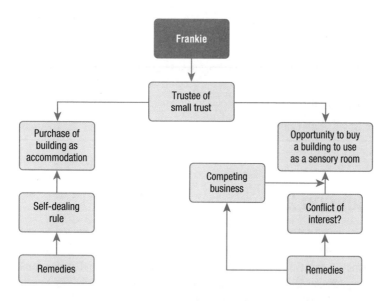

A printable version of this diagram plan is available from **www.pearsoned.co.uk/lawexpressqa**

Answer

There are two issues in this question. The first is the purchase by Frankie personally of a farm building which is trust property.

[1] You should set out this fundamental principle first in any discussion about trustees' duties and then look at particular aspects of this duty.

Trustees are fiduciaries and are subject to the 'distinguishing obligation of a fiduciary' which is 'the obligation of loyalty'.[1] (Millett LJ in **Bristol and West Building Society v Mothew** [1998] Ch 1). Thus, fiduciaries must not act in situations where there is a conflict between their duty as fiduciaries and their personal interest.

[2] You are now relating the general principle set out in the first paragraph to the particular application of this principle to the facts of this case. In this way you are giving your answer a clear structure.

As a result of this principle there is a general rule that a trustee must not purchase trust property because to do so can conflict with his duty as a trustee.[2] This is known as the 'self-dealing rule' and in **Tito v Waddell (No 2)** [1977] Ch 106 CA, Megarry V-C said that in such a case the sale is voidable at the instance of any beneficiary 'however fair the transaction'. The honesty of the trustee is irrelevant and the rule is based on the trustee's status as a trustee. The rule applies even where the price is fixed by a third party as in **Wright v Morgan** [1926] AC 788 CA, where the price was fixed by a valuer. A modern illustration is **Kane v Radley-Kane** [1999] Ch 274 HC.[3]

[3] The facts of this case do not really help in your answer but it does no harm to show the examiner that you are aware of it.

A trustee can, however, purchase if the court allows it, or the beneficiaries, all being of full age and capacity, agree, or the trust instrument permits it. In addition, the trustee must have made full disclosure of all material facts (**Newgate Stud Co v Penfold** [2008] 1 BCLC 46 HC). In this case the beneficiaries of the trust will probably be all those who are likely to use it and even though we are told that they are ten adults, it might be difficult to obtain the consent of all of them and in addition there might be questions of capacity. Although Frankie left the meeting whilst the decision was being made, this does not affect the matter as the point is simply that the sale is voidable however it was arrived at.

[4] It is in this paragraph that you can earn those extra marks. Most students will probably spot that the purchase of trust property by a trustee is in breach of the trustee's fiduciary duties but many students will stop at that.

Any action should be taken by the beneficiaries and not by the trustees such as Anne, who has brought this to our notice.[4] As the property has not been re-sold as it is intended as a home for Frankie's daughter, Liz, they can insist that the property is transferred back to the trust or they can insist that the property is offered for sale again and if this results in a higher price being offered than that paid by the trustee, Frankie, then the property must be sold at that price. It is very unlikely that the property will be sold, as any buyer would be advised that the title of Frankie was defective, but if a resale did take place, the beneficiaries could insist on any profit being paid to them or they could take steps to avoid the sale as it could be argued that the purchaser had knowingly received trust property. In **BCCI (Overseas)**

Ltd v *Akindele* [2001] Ch 437 CA, Nourse LJ held that the test was if 'the recipient's state of knowledge . . . make it unconscionable for him to retain the benefit of the receipt'[5] and it is suggested that on this test a purchaser would be liable.

Finally, this does not look like a charitable trust, as it exists for the benefit of ten named people and so there is a lack of public benefit. However, if it does happen to have charitable status then the matter of the sale should be reported by Anne to the Charity Commission who can take action.[6]

The other issue is the purchase by Frankie of another building from the local college in order to run it as a sensory centre. It is not quite clear whether Frankie came by the information about the building which is equipped as a sensory room in his capacity as a trustee.[7] The question merely says that he learnt of the opportunity to buy it as the trust has a partnership with the local college and he learnt of it through this connection. This is a crucial point, as persons in a fiduciary position such as Frankie must not use that position to make an unauthorised profit for themselves. If they do so, they will be a constructive trustee of those profits (***Keech v Sandford*** (1726) 2 Eq Cas Abr HC).[8]

A parallel case to this one is ***Boardman v Phipps*** [1967] AC 46 HL. The trust owned a substantial holding of shares in a company and the appellant, a solicitor to the trust, and one of the beneficiaries were dissatisfied with its performance.[9] They obtained information, through this connection with the trust, about the company's affairs and so they decided to obtain control of it by purchasing the remainder of its shares. They reorganised it and made considerable profits for themselves. The appellants were held liable to account to the trust for the profits made because they were constructive trustees, as they had used the trust shareholding to acquire the necessary information about the company and in addition the respondent beneficiary had not been kept fully informed of the situation.

Lord Cohen held that the liability of the appellants rested on the fact that they came by the information which led to them purchasing the shares when acting for the trust and it could be argued that Frankie is in the same position if he came by the information about the centre in his capacity as a trustee. The fact that the trustees decided that they would not have bought it does not affect Frankie's liability as

---

[5] You should not spend long on this point as otherwise you will get right away from the question, but it is worth a mention.

[6] This is a really excellent extra point to include in your answer. It shows that you are looking at all the possibilities as a good lawyer should.

[7] This apparent vagueness on the part of the examiner is of course deliberate, as you are expected to discuss this point. The effect is that you will lose marks if you just say that Frankie will be liable.

[8] You could give the facts of this case but those of *Boardman* v *Phipps* are more relevant to this situation. However, you should mention that the principle seems to originate from *Keech* v *Sandford*.

[9] This is not an easy case to summarise and the facts are very relevant to those in the problem and this is why it has been set out in some detail.

in **Boardman v Phipps** the trust had decided that it did not wish to acquire the shares. Thus, Frankie can be liable to hold the sensory centre on a constructive trust for the trust which he chairs and account for any profits made.

¹⁰ If you mention the decision in *Boardman* v *Phipps* then you should try to include a reference to the dissenting speeches as whether this decision was correct is still debated.

It is worth mentioning that Lord Upjohn dissented in **Boardman v Phipps**[10] and observed that 'the appellants have bought for themselves and with their own money shares which the trustees never contemplated buying and they did so in circumstances fully known and approved of by the trustees'. This could be said to be the case here too.

¹¹ Here is another example of where you can pick up extra marks by thinking clearly about the question.

The other point is that if the sensory centre competes for the business of the trust then Frankie will be in breach of the rule which states that a trustee must not carry on a business in competition with the trust.[11] In **Re Thompson** [1934] Ch 342 HC the executors of a will carried on the testator's business of a yacht broker and one executor wished to set up a competing business. He was restrained by injunction from doing so.

✓ Make your answer stand out

- Consider the argument that the decision in *Boardman* v *Phipps* was wrong as information cannot be trust property and so cannot be made the subject of a trust.
- Look at the remarks in *Murad* v *Al-Saraj* [2005] WTLR 1573, where the Court of Appeal suggested *obiter* that the rule as applied in *Keech* v *Sandford* and *Boardman* v *Phipps* might be looked at again where the fiduciary has acted in good faith with no concealment. Was this the case here?
- Ask what remedy was used in *Boardman* v *Phipps*. Was it liability to account or was it a personal remedy? It is arguable that the courts did not make this clear.

! Don't be tempted to . . .

- Forget to stress that this question is primarily about the duties of fiduciaries and that you need to be clear on what the duties of fiduciaries are.
- Deal with liability but not consider the remedies.
- Set out the facts of *Boardman* v *Phipps* in great detail but not apply them clearly to the question.

Question 3

In *Boardman* v *Phipps* (1967) Lord Upjohn referred to the 'fundamental rule of equity that a person in a fiduciary capacity must not make a profit out of his trust which is part of the wider rule that a trustee must not place himself in a position where his duty and interest may conflict'.

Critically consider in relation to this statement what a fiduciary relationship is and the extent of its core obligations.

Diagram plan

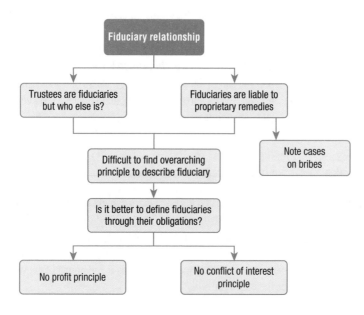

A printable version of this diagram plan is available from **www.pearsoned.co.uk/lawexpressqa**

Answer plan

→ Explain and evaluate the core meaning of the term 'fiduciary'.

→ Outline the well-recognised categories of fiduciary relationships and then give instances of where the courts have held relationships to be fiduciary in more controversial cases.

→ Identify and analyse the core fiduciary obligations: the 'no profit rule' and 'no conflict of interest rule'.

→ Are they two rules or one? Does this matter?

→ Conclusion – link the idea of a concept of a fiduciary to the principles on which fiduciary obligations rest.

Answer

There are two issues in this question: the nature of a fiduciary[1] and, given that a person is a fiduciary, the extent of their core obligations not to make a profit and not to allow a conflict of interest between their duty as a fiduciary and their other interests.

The origin of the word fiduciary is the Latin *fides* meaning trust. Thus, obviously, trustees are fiduciaries but who else is?[2] In **Bristol and West Building Society v Mothew** [1998] Ch 1 CA at 18, Millett LJ said that a 'fiduciary is someone who has undertaken to act for or on behalf of another in circumstances which give rise to a relationship of trust and confidence'. Finn (1992, p. 8)[3] says that all that one can do is to describe a fiduciary but adds that when the fiduciary does act for another he does so 'to the exclusion of his own several interest'. Correct though these statements may be, as Birks points out (1996), attempts at general descriptions of a fiduciary 'have a low predictive value'. That is, they do not get us very far. Indeed Mason (1985) has said that 'The fiduciary relationship is a concept in search of a principle'.

The problem is that there are a number of well-recognised relationships outside that of trustee and beneficiary which can be classed as fiduciary but how far they extend is unclear.[4] In **Lloyds Bank Ltd v Bundy** [1975] QB 326 CA, Denning MR mentioned the following in the context of a presumption of undue influence: 'parent over child, solicitor over client, doctor over patient, spiritual adviser over follower', and there have been a number of cases where the courts have extended the term fiduciary to apply in new situations. In **Norbert v Wynrib** (1992) 92 DLR (4th) 449 the Canadian courts held a doctor to be a fiduciary so that a patient could claim equitable compensation for a failure to act in her best interests.

One reason for what might be called the timidity of the courts in defining who is a fiduciary was given by Mason (1985): 'realisation that breach of the fiduciary duty unleashes equitable remedies, particularly the constructive trust'. Thus if it is found that a particular category of person counts as a fiduciary this will mean that they will be liable in particular to proprietary remedies.[5]

The result is that where a relationship lies at the margins of fiduciary relationships the courts may be uncertain whether to brand it as

---

[1] This is the type of start to aim for: you have clearly identified that there is not one but two issues in this question.

[2] Although you will probably decide that there is no satisfactory all-embracing definition of a fiduciary, you still do need to look at the attempts which have been made.

[3] This is the first of a number of references to the views of academic authors in this essay. If you tackle an area such as this where there has been so much academic debate then you must show familiarity with it to gain a really good mark.

[4] You need to make this clear at the start. If the only example of a fiduciary was a trustee, we would know who a fiduciary was!

[5] The examiner will be looking for you to mention this as there is no point in identifying a person as a fiduciary for the sake of it – they are identified as fiduciaries to make them liable as fiduciaries.

[6] The reason for this example is not to describe the law on receipt of bribes by fiduciaries but to show how the courts veer from one view to another, possibly because of their reluctance to label a relationship as fiduciary and so unleash equitable remedies.

fiduciary which can then lead to conflicting case law. An example of this is the situation where persons receive bribes in breach of their fiduciary duty.[6] Do they become a constructive trustee of them? In **A-G for Hong-Kong v Reid** [1994] 1 AC 324 PC it was held, overruling previous authority (**Lister v Stubbs** (1890) 45 Ch D 1 CA) that they did but this was overruled by **Sinclair Investments (UK) Ltd v Versailles Trade Finance (In Administration)** [2011] EWCA Civ 347. In the latest case, **FHR European Ventures LLP v Mankarious** [2013] EWCA Civ 17 CA the court invited the Supreme Court to consider 'whether **Sinclair Investments** was right to decide that **Lister** is to be preferred to **Reid**' and so the law may be turning again to the position that a fiduciary who receives a bribe does become a constructive trustee of it.

[7] This is the second part of your answer and the transition needs to be clearly indicated.

Given the difficulty of finding an overarching principle based on the term 'fiduciary', we can look at the matter from the angle of the obligations which are imposed on a fiduciary.[7]

[8] Once you have mentioned this point do not spend too long on it as, although relevant, it is something of a side issue.

Resulting and constructive trusts can be left apart,[8] because, as Chambers (1997) points out (at p. 196), in most cases of resulting trusts all that is sought is the 'second measure of the surviving trust property'. In other cases it is accepted that the 'distinguishing obligation of a fiduciary is the obligation of loyalty' (Millett LJ in **Bristol and West Building Society v Mothew**). Precisely what that duty means can be seen by examining the two duties of fiduciaries which seem to be accepted as fundamental:

(a) Fiduciaries must not act in situations where there is a conflict between their duty as fiduciaries and their personal interest.

(b) Fiduciaries must not make an unauthorised profit out of their fiduciary position.

[9] You will earn extra marks for an awareness of this. It is a common error to assume that there can be only one principle here.

[10] You will need to decide at this point whether you have time to give all the facts of *Boardman* v *Phipps*, which cannot be easily stated, bearing in mind that you must bring out this principle.

Sometimes these are treated as one principle.[9] In **Boardman v Phipps** [1967] AC 46 HL, Lord Upjohn's statement that the 'no profit' rule is part of the 'wider rule that a trustee must not place himself in a position where his duty and his interest may conflict' is not universally accepted. The appellants were in a fiduciary relationship towards the trust, out of which they obtained the opportunity to make a profit. Thus we could say that they broke the 'no profit' rule.[10] However, the 'no profit' rule does not stand on its own: there is no law against a person making a profit. The 'no profit' rule applies where a person is, as a result of their fiduciary position, in a position where his duty and interest conflict. Was this so? Lord Upjohn, who dissented, said that there was not and observed that 'the appellants have bought for themselves and with their own money shares which the trustees never contemplated buying and they did so in circumstances fully known and approved of by the trustees'. Moreover, their actions benefited the trust as the trust's own shares increased in value. In ***Queensland Mines v Hudson*** (1978) 52 AJLR 399 PC they were treated as two distinct rules but, as Conaglen (2007) remarks (at p. 115), the facts of any one case can generally be explained on the basis that either the no-profit rule or the no-conflict of interest one was broken. It is suggested that it is preferable to treat them as one for the reason given by Lord Upjohn.[11]

[11] At the end of a discussion such as this show the examiner that you have thought about the issues yourself.

[12] This essay could have been quite different. Instead of ending with specific cases it could have consisted entirely of cases. However, our mark would have been reduced because a really good answer here demands a knowledge of principle.

Once a relationship has been identified as fiduciary then the 'no profit' and 'no conflict' rules can apply.[12] Thus, in ***Boston Deep Sea Fishing and Ice Co v Ansell*** (1888) 39 Ch D 339 HC a director bought ice for the company from another company in which he held shares and from which he received bonuses. The identification of the director as owing fiduciary duties to it enabled an action to be brought for an account of commissions and bonuses received by him. In ***Boardman v Phipps*** [1967] AC 46 HL the identification of Boardman, who was a solicitor to a trust, as owing fiduciary duties to it enabled the court to award an account of profits made by him when he had bought shares in a company using information available only to the trust.

So in the end it is impossible to arrive at a neat definition of a fiduciary. Thus, Denning MR, having mentioned that a trustee is a fiduciary, simply remarked that 'The cases show that the categories where the fiduciary relationship imposes the duty are open', without taking the matter any further. We could say that, using Mason's phraseology, the concept of a fiduciary has found principles and these are not the identification of fiduciaries themselves but the identification of fiduciary duties.

✓ Make your answer stand out

- Asking if, in fact, there is only one fiduciary duty: look at Conaglen (2005) at p. 466.
- Read Conaglen (2007) especially pp. 114–125 on the 'no profit' and 'no conflict' principles. ▶

- Look at the view of Smith (2003), who suggests that the distinguishing characteristic of a breach of fiduciary obligations is disloyalty by the fiduciary.
- Pointing out that other duties, for example that of good faith, are not fiduciary as they can arise in situations which are not fiduciary, for example in employment contracts.
- Referring to the thesis of Conaglen (2005) that the concept of fiduciary loyalty is not an end in itself but a means of ensuring that non-fiduciary duties are carried out.

Don't be tempted to . . .

- Think that the only fiduciaries are trustees.
- Just go through cases involving fiduciaries without attempting to address the issue of exactly who is a fiduciary.
- Neglect to deal with the idea of a 'concept' and a 'principle' at the start.
- Fail to ask if there are two rules: 'no profit' and 'no conflict of interest'.
- State various definitions of a fiduciary without attempting to consider whether they are satisfactory.

Question 4

'Equity will not allow a statute to be used as an instrument of fraud.'

Critically examine this maxim of equity and consider whether it has any continued usefulness today.

Answer plan

→ Explain what the maxim means.

→ Explain the maxim in operation, for example *Rochefoucauld* v *Boustead*.

→ Contrast this with cases where the maxim was not applied, for example *Midland Bank* v *Green*.

→ Critically consider the attitudes of different judges.

→ Provide other examples, for instance secret trusts.

→ Conclude by evaluating whether it is true that equity does generally apply this maxim.

Diagram plan

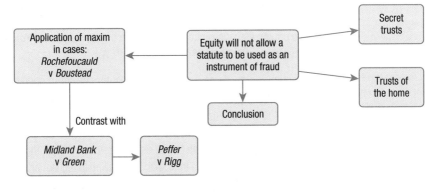

A printable version of this diagram plan is available from **www.pearsoned.co.uk/lawexpressqa**

Answer

This is a well-known maxim of equity which means that to shelter behind the requirements of a statute may be to allow a fraud to be committed and thus the statute becomes an instrument of fraud. Therefore, the question is asking whether equity will not allow a statute to be a means of achieving fraud.[1]

[1] This is a vital sentence, as it actually explains what the maxim means.

Is this true? In ***Rochefoucauld v Boustead*** [1897] 1 Ch 196 CA land was transferred to the defendant and it was alleged that he took it on trust for the claimant. She was having difficulty in repaying the mortgage and therefore she wanted him to take the land off her hands and repay the mortgage but the land would still be held on trust for her. The problem was that there was no written evidence of the trust as required by what was then section 4 of the Statute of Frauds 1677 (now section 53(1)(b) of the Law of Property Act 1925 (LPA 1925)).[2] If the lack of written evidence was fatal to her claim, then the defendant would commit the fraud of keeping the land absolutely and beneficially when he was not intended to. So equity imposed the trust despite the lack of written evidence. The effect was that oral evidence was admitted of the trust despite the statute providing that evidence of the trust must be in writing.

[2] Note how we have made it clear exactly what the problem in the case was and also how we have added the detail that the relevant statute has now been replaced by another statute – this last point will gain you marks for extra precision in your answer.

[3] This is where you can gain extra marks by pointing out that there is doubt as to exactly what type of trust was involved here.

[4] If you have time give the details of this case but at least mention this case or another fairly recent one as *Rochefoucauld*, although an excellent authority, is over 100 years old!

[5] Having mentioned one case (*Rochefoucauld*) now mention a case which seems to go the other way. You would be wasting your time by mentioning a *similar* case to *Rochefoucauld*, which just makes the same point.

[6] Boost your marks by bringing in the views of another judge in the same case.

[7] Where a case is of very doubtful authority, make sure that you say so!

The trust in this case appeared to be express but now section 53(2) of the LPA 1925 exempts resulting, implied and constructive trusts from the requirement of writing imposed by section 53(1)(b) and the tendency today is to categorise trusts imposed on the basis of this maxim as constructive.[3] An example of this is **Lyus v Prowsa Developments Ltd** [1982] 1 WLR 1044 CA.[4]

Although the above case is an example of the maxim in operation, equity operates on the basis of discretion and so we cannot expect to find that there is a rigid rule that equity will always act in the way it did in the above case.[5] In **Midland Bank Trust Co Ltd v Green (No 1)** [1981] AC 513 the House of Lords refused to hold that land was held on a constructive trust so that the failure to register an estate contract meant that a purchaser took free of the contract. This might have seemed a strong case for the intervention of equity because the contract was made between a father and son for the father to sell a farm to the son. The contract was not protected by registration as a land charge and, when the father and son fell out, the father took advantage of the lack of registration to make a sham sale of the farm to his wife with the sole object of defeating the son's contract. Yet the House of Lords was not persuaded and Lord Wilberforce said that 'it is not fraud to rely on the requirements of a statute'. In effect, the requirements of the Land Registration Acts were given precedence over the need to prevent a fraud, although Lord Denning in the Court of Appeal had held in favour of the son and would have imposed a trust.[6] Thus, we must often look at the policy behind decisions and not see the maxim as an all-embracing mantra which can be uttered to solve disputes.

Much also depends on the attitudes of different judges. For example, a constructive trust was imposed in the much-criticised case[7] of **Peffer v Rigg** [1977] 1 WLR 285 HC, where a party sought to rely on the lack of compliance with the Land Registration Act 1925. This point is also seen by contrasting **Binions v Evans** [1972] 2 All ER 70 CA with **Ashburn Anstalt v Arnold** [1989] 1 Ch 1 CA. In **Binions** Lord Denning in the Court of Appeal had imposed a constructive trust to prevent a licensee from being evicted by purchasers of a cottage despite a promise made when they bought it that she could remain. There was no written evidence of a trust (see s. 53(1)(b)) but the effect was that the licence was

[8] This is not an easy case to sum up briefly but the facts are useful, as they were the basis of a controversial decision and you need to show exactly *why* it was controversial.

held on trust for her and this gave her an equitable interest in the property which bound the purchasers as they had notice of it when they bought the cottage.[8] Yet in **Ashburn** Browne-Wilkinson V-C condemned as a heresy the notion that a constructive trust could give a licensee a right which was binding on purchasers.

A classic illustration of the maxim is found in the doctrine of secret trusts.[9] If I promise to leave X by will £1,000 on the strength of an oral promise by him that he will hold it on trust for Y then X can argue that the promise is not binding on him as it does not comply with the requirements of the Wills Act.[10] So equity holds that X is bound by a secret trust in favour of Y which it will enforce despite the failure to comply with the formalities. The alternative would be that X, despite his promise, keeps the money, which would be using the failure to comply with the statutory requirements as a means of committing fraud. This doctrine, unlike the cases mentioned above, does not depend on equitable discretion to any great extent and can be regarded as a rule. It has also applied to half-secret trusts, with less justification. Here I actually declare in my will that the property is left to X on trust but I do not say what the trusts are. Again, X will be bound if he has agreed with me that he will hold the £1,000 on trust for Y. The difference is that here there is no possibility of X committing fraud by keeping the property himself, as the will declares that there is a trust. Yet in **Blackwell v Blackwell** [1929] AC 318 HL it was held that half-secret trusts would be enforced.

[9] You will waste time – and so lose marks – if you just set out details of cases on secret trusts. Instead, concentrate on the principle behind them and show how it relates to the question. This is not a problem question on secret trusts!

[10] It helps to make this point clearer if you use an example of the general principle rather than a case, as we are not looking at the detailed application of the law.

Another example of the intervention of equity to prevent fraud is in the area of trusts of the family home, where an oral promise by one party to another that the home will be held on trust for both of them has been held binding despite the lack of writing and consequent failure to comply with section 53 of the LPA 1925.[11] A good, if old, example is **Eves v Eves** [1975] 3 All ER 768 CA.

[11] Again, you may not have time to go into detail here, so just bring out the principle and leave details of cases out.

One can sum up by saying that the picture is a confused one. One cannot state that there is an absolute rule that equity will always intervene to prevent a statute from being used as an instrument of fraud: much depends on the values which are felt to be competing against each other and the attitudes of the judges to resolving the tension which can exist between formal statutory requirements and the need to do justice in particular cases.

✓ Make your answer stand out

- Look in more detail at *Rochefoucauld* v *Boustead* – what type of trust was it? Why was it imposed?
- Look at the argument of Denning MR in *Midland Bank* v *Green* in the Court of Appeal and contrast it to that of Lord Wilberforce in the House of Lords.
- Do some research on the origin of this principle: how did it originate? You could then add a little more depth to the introduction or the conclusion.
- Contrast *Lyus* v *Prowsa Developments Ltd* with *Midland Bank* v *Green* to show that you understand that different courts and judges have different approaches.
- Think of other areas where this maxim could apply – over to you!

! Don't be tempted to . . .

- Go into great detail on the actual cases, for example on secret trusts – instead, bring out the principles.
- Set off on this question without explaining what lies behind the quotation.
- Come to very definite conclusions saying, for example, that the maxim is always applied or that it never is. The area of equitable maxims is not one for very final conclusions.
- Mention more than one case which makes the same point, as you are not adding anything to your answer and so not gaining any extra marks.

Question 5

'Estoppel must not be so governed by its own principles that it is unable to undertake its main function nor so wide and general that it is impossible to see what that function is.'

Critically evaluate this statement.

Answer plan

→ Begin by looking at what the question is about.

→ Consider the types of estoppel – make it clear that this answer will concentrate on proprietary estoppel.

→ Critically consider when proprietary estoppel can apply.

➜ Analyse the decision in *Yeoman's Row* v *Cobbe*.

➜ Similarly analyse the decision in *Thorner* v *Major* and contrast it with that in *Yeoman's Row* v *Cobbe*.

Diagram plan

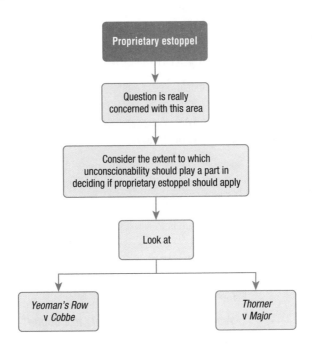

A printable version of this diagram plan is available from **www.pearsoned.co.uk/lawexpressqa**

Answer

[1] Promissory estoppel and proprietary estoppel are so different that a definition covering them both would be too wide to be of use, especially in an essay like this. Better to say at once that there are two types, which then leads you on to discuss proprietary estoppel in detail, which is what this question is about.

The idea behind this question is that estoppel needs to steer a middle ground. It must be governed by principles but at the same time the application of those principles must not be so rigid and inflexible that estoppel is unable to exercise its proper function.

There are two distinct types of estoppel.[1] As Hanbury (2012, p. 938) points out: 'Each has a separate origin and history.' Promissory estoppel applies in contractual relationships and essentially operates as a defence to prevent a party from going back on a promise. Its best-known application was in ***Central London Property Trust*** v ***High Trees Houses***

Ltd [1947] KB 130 HC. This doctrine does not create a new cause of action; instead it prevents a party going back on a representation as in *High Trees* itself. Proprietary estoppel, by contrast, is a sword: it enables rights, especially property rights, to be acquired when none existed before. It is founded on certain principles: there must be a representation by one person (X) to another (Y) which X intends Y to rely on and where Y's actual reliance is reasonable in the circumstances. An objective test applies: thus, the question is whether a promise by X can reasonably be understood as a commitment by X to Y. If so, then X will be estopped from going back on the representation and asserting his strict legal rights.

[2] Your discussion of the issue raised in the question will be much clearer if you have started by stating what the essential elements of estoppel are.

Provided that the above elements are present, the fundamental basis of the estoppel can be seen as unconscionability: would it be unconscionable for X, when Y has relied on X's promise to his detriment, to then depart from that promise?[2]

[3] However, as we will see later, the mention of promissory estoppel is not wasted even though the question is primarily about proprietary estoppel.

This question was prompted by recent cases involving proprietary estoppel and so this essay will concentrate on this[3] rather than on promissory estoppel.

The first issue is to ask if proprietary estoppel should be available where conduct has been unconscionable, even though the essential elements of it are not present. If this is so then there is of course the danger that estoppel will indeed be so wide and general that it is impossible to see what its function is.

In *Yeoman's Row Management Ltd* v *Cobbe* [2008] UKHL 55 HL an oral agreement between the company and Cobbe provided that a block of flats owned by the company would be demolished and Cobbe would apply for planning permission to erect houses in their place with any excess of the proceeds over £24 million shared equally with the company. After planning permission had been obtained, the company went back on the oral agreement and demanded more money, as it now realised that the land was worth much more. Cobbe claimed that the company was estopped from going back on the agreement.

Lord Scott asked: 'What is the fact that the company is estopped from asserting?' There was no question that the oral agreement was unenforceable and Cobbe did not claim a specific property right, merely a hope of entering a contract. He held that the Court of Appeal, which held in Cobbe's favour, had been influenced too much by the fact that it regarded the behaviour of the company as unconscionable without requiring the essential elements of proprietary estoppel to be present.

It is submitted that another case where estoppel acted too much as a general remedy is **Pascoe v Turner** [1979] 1 WLR 431 HC.[4] The claimant and defendant had lived in the claimant's house. When the relationship ended the claimant told the defendant that the house and everything in it was hers. In reliance on this the claimant, to the defendant's knowledge, spent money on the house. She was given notice to quit by the claimant but the court ordered the house to be conveyed to her although it was clear that her acts of reliance were only on the basis that she had a licence to live there for life.

[4] This case is outside the current debate but adds another angle to it. Mention of it ought to add to your marks.

However, although the courts should require that a proprietary estoppel claim satisfies the criteria set out above, there is also a danger of the courts going too far the other way and setting out criteria which would mean that proprietary estoppel would no longer apply to promises of future intentions such as promises to leave by will.[5]

[5] This is a crucial paragraph which links the first part of the answer to the second. You are showing that you are actually engaging with the question and writing a balanced answer which looks at two points of view. The type of paragraph which really adds to your marks!

In **Yeoman's Row Management Ltd v Cobbe** Lord Scott considered that proprietary estoppel should be restricted to representations of specific facts or mixed law and fact by X which stood in the way of a right claimed by Y.[6] This seemed to mean that proprietary estoppel was no different from promissory estoppel: it only applied as a defence to an action where those specific representations had been gone back on and not to enable an independent right to be asserted. In cases of promises to leave by will, Lord Scott would use the remedial constructive trust.

[6] This is an essential point: the view of Lord Scott needs to be carefully stated.

The problem is that proprietary estoppel has always applied to representations of what will happen and not just to specific present facts as where there is a representation to someone that she will acquire property on the death of the representor, as in **Gillett v Holt** [2001] Ch 210 CA, and in cases such as **Dillwyn v Llewelyn** (1862)[7] 4 De GF & J 517 HC, where a father's encouragement to his son to build a house on the father's land meant that on the father's death the land built on was ordered to be conveyed to the son.

[7] This is important: if Lord Scott's analysis was adopted then it would not only mean that promises to leave on death would be outside the scope of estoppel but others too. *Dillwyn* v *Llewellyn* is a good case to mention, as it has always been regarded as a classic estoppel case and it would seem startling if this type of case was no longer to be decided under estoppel.

However, in **Thorner v Major** [2009] UKHL 18[8] the majority did not accept that estoppel should be confined to representations of present fact. D had worked at P's farm for no payment from 1976 onwards, and by the 1980s, hoped that he might inherit the farm. No express representation had ever been made, but D relied on various hints and remarks made by P over the years. The House of Lords held that these amounted to an estoppel.

[8] *Thorner* v *Major* is the second recent case which is essential to mention.

[9] This rounds off the answer, as it mentions a slightly different point from that made by Lord Scott. It shows that you have really looked at what the judges actually said in these cases and will add to your marks.

Furthermore, the idea of Lord Walker in **Yeoman's Row** that the claimant must believe that they have been made an irrevocable promise was not accepted.[9] This would inevitably have meant that promises to leave by will would not be covered by promissory estoppel as a will can be revoked. However, in **Thorner v Major** it was held that the question is whether a party has reasonably relied on an assurance by the other as to that person's conduct.

In conclusion, estoppel should apply in as wide a variety of situations as possible but only if certain criteria are met. The decision in **Thorner v Major** is to be welcomed as keeping estoppel on the right track.

✓ Make your answer stand out

- By considering the extent to which detriment is an essential requirement of estoppel.
- By discussion of the remedial constructive trust.
- By examining the extent to which promissory estoppel has moved on from the *High Trees* decision.
- By including the further point made by Lord Scott – the need for certainty of subject matter as to the subject of the representation.
- By referring to cases following *Thorner v Major*, e.g. *Cook v Thomas* [2010] EWCA Civ 227.

! Don't be tempted to . . .

- Just describe estoppel.
- Go into the question without distinguishing between proprietary and promissory estoppel.
- Just reel off cases on estoppel without looking at the underlying issues.
- Miss the point that there are two distinct issues raised by the discussion of *Yeoman's Row v Cobbe* and *Thorner v Major*.

---

www.pearsoned.co.uk/lawexpressqa

Go online to access more revision support including additional essay and problem questions with diagram plans, You be the marker questions, and download all diagrams from the book.

Charitable trusts

How this topic may come up in exams

This is a favourite area for problem questions on whether particular objects of a trust are charitable. Watch for where a question asks you if a trust is valid rather than if it is just charitable. If this is so you may need to use material from our discussion of three certainties (Chapter 3) and non-charitable purpose trusts (Chapter 10). Essay questions may focus on public benefit, especially on the Charities Act 2011, and on political trusts. A final area is failure of charitable gifts together with failure of non-charitable gifts. These could be either problem or essay questions.

■ Before you begin

It's a good idea to consider the following key themes of charitable trusts before tackling a question on this topic.

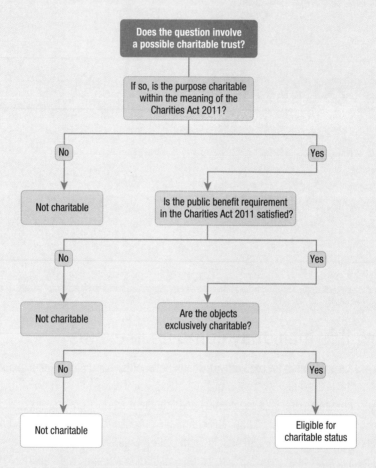

A printable version of this diagram is available from **www.pearsoned.co.uk/lawexpressqa**

Question 1

Albert's will contained the following dispositions:

(a) £10,000 to my needy brothers, Tim and Tom, to enable them and their families to have a better standard of living.

(b) £10,000 to the Malvern Brethren. This body meets on the Malvern Hills and worships various deities. Admission is by a rigorous process of scrutiny and the Brethren also publish an annual report on their work.

Advise Albert's executors on whether these dispositions are valid as charitable trusts.

Answer plan

→ Summarise the requirements for a valid charitable trust.

→ Discuss the law on public benefit in more detail and especially the relationship between statute and case law on the one hand and the Charity Commissioners' Guidance on the other.

→ Explain in part (a) the law on trusts for the relief of poverty and public benefit.

→ Note the distinction between the 'benefit aspect' of public benefit and the 'public aspect'.

→ Explain in part (b) the law on trusts for the advancement of religion and public benefit.

→ In both cases mention the requirement that the trusts must be exclusively charitable.

Diagram plan

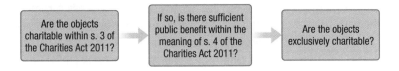

A printable version of this diagram plan is available from **www.pearsoned.co.uk/lawexpressqa**

Answer

[1] In problem questions it is often better to plunge straight in and start answering part (a) etc. However, here it will save time if you set these essential points out first – and it will also gain you marks at the start.

In these situations it is necessary to consider three points:[1]

(a) Are the objects charitable within the meaning of section 3 of the Charities Act 2011?

(b) If so, is there sufficient public benefit?

(c) If so, are the objects exclusively charitable?

[2] An examiner will look carefully to see if you have mastered these points. They are the foundation of the law on public benefit and must be set out clearly in any answer to a problem question on charitable trusts. As they appear in both parts of the question, it makes sense to set them out at the start. Make sure also that you insert this explanation of the relationship between the 2006 and 2011 Acts into every answer. It is vital to make this clear.

The law on public benefit is worth setting out at the start as it applies to both situations. Section 2(1)(b) of the Charities Act 2011 provides that any charitable purpose must be for the public benefit and section 4 of the Charities Act 2011 sets out the 'public benefit' test. Section 4(2) removes what is said to be the previous presumption that certain types of charities, including those for the relief of poverty, were presumed to be for the public benefit and so public benefit must be proved in all cases. Section 4(3) provides that 'any reference to the public benefit is a reference to the public benefit as that term is understood for the purposes of the law relating to charities in England and Wales'. The effect of this is to preserve the case law which existed before the 2006 Act. It was this Act which effected changes in charity law; the 2011 Act merely consolidates the statutory provisions relating to charity law.[2]

In addition, section 17 of the Charities Act 2011 obliges the Charity Commission to issue guidance on the meaning of public benefit and by section 17(5) charity trustees must have regard to this.

[3] You should make it a rule to first refer to the charitable purposes set out in section 3 of the Charities Act 2011 and see which of them could apply. It may be that more than one could apply, so do watch for this as an ability to recognise that more than one purpose could be relevant will obviously boost your marks.

(a) Albert wishes to leave '£10,000 to my needy brothers, Tim and Tom, to enable them and their families to have a better standard of living' and the word 'needy' could imply that this trust is for the prevention or relief of poverty, which is a charitable purpose by section 3(1)(a) of the Charities Act 2011. The question is whether 'needy' comes within the notion of poverty.[3] In *Re Coulthurst* [1951] Ch 661 CA, Evershed MR explained that 'poverty does not mean destitution, . . . it may not unfairly be paraphrased for present purposes as meaning persons who have to "go short" in the ordinary acceptation of that term . . . ' and in *Re Scarisbrick* [1951] Ch 622 a gift for 'needy persons' was held to be charitable. It could also be said that this trust is charitable under section 3(1)(j), 'the relief of those in need by reason of youth, age, ill-health, disability, financial hardship or other disadvantage', as Tim and Tom will be suffering financial hardship if they are needy.

[4] Remember that you need to separate any consideration of public benefit from the first question of whether the gift is charitable at all.

The next question is whether the trusts have sufficient public benefit.[4]

The problem here is that the benefits are restricted to Albert's brothers, Tim and Tom. The courts had established that trusts for 'poor relations' can be valid (see *Isaac v Defriez* (1754) Amb 595 HC) but a distinction was drawn between these and trusts for individuals (see Jenkins LJ in **Re Scarisbrick** [1951] Ch 622 CA). In **Dingle v Turner** [1972] AC 601 HL this distinction was expressly approved and the fact that trusts for the relief of poverty are subject to a more generous test of public benefit[5] was recognised in **Attorney General v Charity Commission for England and Wales** [2012] UKUT 420 (TCC): the continued existence of this was accepted. However, this case is a trust for individuals and so will not meet the public benefit test.

[5] Students sometimes say that trusts for the relief of poverty do not require public benefit at all. Do not make this mistake.

If the trust claims to be charitable under section 3(1)(j) of the Charities Act 2011, 'the relief of those in need by reason of youth, age, ill-health, disability, financial hardship or other disadvantage', it will fare no better as it will come up against the same problem of lack of public benefit.

[6] But you should mention this point.

Given that the trust is clearly not charitable, the question of whether it is exclusively charitable does not arise.[6]

(b) The gift of £10,000 to the Malvern Brethren may count as one for the advancement of religion as we are told that it worships various deities. Section 3(1)(c) of the Charities Act 2011 provides that a trust for advancement of religion is charitable and the fact that the brethren worship more than one deity does not affect this, as section 3(2)(a) of the Charities Act 2011 provides that, for the purposes of this Act, religion can involve a belief in more than one god. The next question is whether there is sufficient public benefit as required by section 4 of the Act. Membership is not closed even though it is by a 'rigorous process of scrutiny'. In **Gilmour v Coats** [1949] AC 426 HL a gift to a community of strictly cloistered and enclosed nuns was held not charitable because the benefit conferred on the public by their prayers was, per Lord Simonds, 'manifestly not susceptible of proof'. However, here an annual report is published which is presumably available to the public. Moreover, the report is on their work, which implies that the Brethren actually undertake some tasks beyond worship.

[7] Details of this case are on the website of the Charity Commission and this shows the importance of keeping a close watch on this.

A comparison can be drawn with the Preston Down Trust,[7] which runs meeting halls for the Exclusive Brethren. Most meetings, except Holy Communion services, were found to be open to non-members, although it was very rare for them to attend, but the Brethren did engage in street preaching and engaged to a certain extent in the wider community, including disaster relief work, encouragement of charitable giving and living out Christian beliefs in the community. This was sufficient public benefit although initially the Commission had felt that there was not. However, following some amendment to its trust deed registration as a charity was accepted. Here we could draw a comparison with **Neville Estates v Madden** [1962] Ch 832 HC where a trust for the advancement of religion among members of the Catford Synagogue was held charitable on this basis even though the services at the synagogue were only open to those on its list of members. There was a benefit in the actual holding of services and this was on the facts public benefit.

[8] You will not lose marks by failing to come to a definite conclusion provided that you have examined the arguments fully. Indeed, it is often weak students who come to extremely definite conclusions.

On the facts here it is impossible to tell whether there is sufficient public benefit and we would need more information on what the report contains and what activities the Brethren undertake and whether they are comparable with those of the Exclusive Brethren.[8] The admission of new members, albeit by rigorous scrutiny, may well tip the balance in favour of charitable status.

 Make your answer stand out

- Research the case of the Preston Down Trust – you can find it on the Charity Commission's website: www.gov.uk/government/publications/preston-down-trust
- Consider the argument of Hackney (2008) that in fact there never was any presumption of public benefit and that benefit was assumed. What had to be proved – and still does – is that this is public benefit.
- Consider the possibility that Article 9 of the European Convention on Human Rights might be relevant in considering whether a trust for the advancement of religion might have public benefit. See Harding (2008). Look also at Iwobi (2009).
- Look in detail at the Guidance issued by the Charity Commission and apply it to the question.

> **!** Don't be tempted to . . .
>
> - Go straight into the answer without setting out the statutory background in the Charities Act 2006, noting that it was this statute that changed the law and that the Charities Act 2011 was only a consolidating statute.
> - Fail to mention the Guidance on public benefit issued by the Charity Commission and how this relates to the Charities Act 2011.
> - Explain the law as it was before the Charities Act 2006.
> - Fail to distinguish between 'poor relations' trusts and trusts for individuals.

? Question 2

Isobel is drafting her will and wishes to leave some bequests and wants to know if they are charitable. If they are not, then she would like you to suggest revised wording to ensure that they are charitable.

(a) £50,000 to hold on trust to research into whether the works of Leo Tolstoy were in fact written by Charles Dickens.

(b) £100,000 to my trustees to hold on trust to provide scholarships for the relatives and dependants of workers in the pottery industry resident in Worcester. Preference to be given to those who are themselves employed in any trade in Worcester.

Advise her.

Answer plan

→ Explain the law on the requirements for charitable status and in particular public benefit in more detail and especially the relationship between statute and case law on the one hand and the Charity Commissioners' Guidance on the other.

→ Explain and analyse in part (a) the law on trusts for the advancement of education in the area of research and also the requirement of public benefit.

→ Explain in part (b) that no charitable purpose is stated and suggest what this might be.

→ Analyse the situation in part (b) in terms of public benefit.

Diagram plan

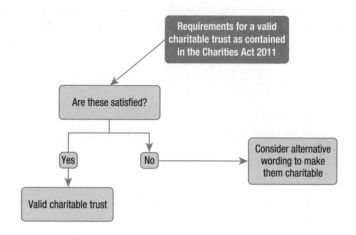

A printable version of this diagram plan is available from **www.pearsoned.co.uk/lawexpressqa**

Answer

[1] In problem questions it is often better to plunge straight in and start answering part (a) etc. However, here it will save time if you set these essential points out first – and it will also gain you marks at the start.

[2] It is vital at the start to relate your answer to the angle of the question. It is not: 'are these objects charitable?' but 'if they are not charitable, can they be amended so that they are charitable?' Keep coming back to this point.

[3] It is arguable that there never was a presumption at all – see Hackney (2008).

In these situations it is necessary to consider three points:[1]

(i) Are the objects charitable within the meaning of section 3 of the Charities Act 2011?

(ii) If so, is there sufficient public benefit?

(iii) If so, are the objects exclusively charitable?

If any of these requirements are not met then it is necessary to suggest appropriate wording so that, if possible, the trusts do have charitable status.[2]

The law on public benefit applies to each situation. Section 2(1)(b) of the Charities Act 2011 provides that any charitable purpose must be for the public benefit and section 4 of the Charities Act 2011 sets out the 'public benefit' test. Section 4(2) removes what was said to be the presumption[3] that certain types of charities, including those for the relief of poverty, were presumed to be for the public benefit and so public benefit must be proved in all cases. Section 4(3) provides that 'any reference to the public benefit is a reference to the public benefit as that term is understood for the purposes of the law relating to charities in England and Wales'. The effect of this is to preserve the case law which existed before the 2006 Act.

In addition, section 17 of the Charities Act 2011 obliges the Charity Commission to issue Guidance on the meaning of public benefit and by section 17(5) charity trustees must have regard to this. It is the Charity Commission which decides on applications for charitable status and so when advising Isobel, I will need to have the Guidance in mind.[4]

[4] This follows on from the previous comment: you are relating this point to the actual question. In fact the Guidance simply states the law but with examples.

[5] The price to be paid for a good mark in a question on charitable trusts is a wide knowledge of the case law, as this is where the detail of the law on charities is. Here our knowledge has paid off, as we have identified relevant cases on educational charities.

(a) The first proposed bequest is '£50,000 to hold on trust to research into whether the works of Leo Tolstoy were in fact written by Charles Dickens'. This could be for the advancement of education, which is charitable by section 3(1)(b) of the Charities Act 2011. Trusts for research can be charitable as in **Re Hopkins' Will Trust** [1964] 3 All ER 46 CA[5] where a gift to be applied towards finding the Bacon–Shakespeare manuscripts was held charitable. However, the court, aided by expert evidence, must make a judgment as to the educational value of the research. In this case Wilberforce J held that research must be of educational value to the researcher, or pass into the store of 'educational material' or 'improve the sum of communicable knowledge in a field which education may cover'. In this case, Wilberforce J held that discovering the Bacon–Shakespeare manuscripts would be 'of the highest value to history and to literature'. Researching the question of whether Dickens wrote the works of Tolstoy seems strange but we cannot judge this. Isobel must get expert advice as to whether this is a worthwhile endeavour.[6] If it is, then there must be public benefit. In **Re Besterman's Will Trust** (1980) The Times, 21 January HC it was emphasised that a trust for research will only be charitable if, in addition to the subject of that research being useful, there is the intention to disseminate it, and there is no mention of this in Isobel's proposed bequest. This will therefore need to be amended to include details of how and where the results of any research will be communicated to the public.[7]

[6] It is very important not to go off the point here and try to judge for yourself if this proposed bequest is charitable, as you could easily go into a long rambling discussion. Instead, deal with it as the courts would: expert evidence needs to be sought. You should do the same for any answer where you are uncertain of the actual merits of the proposed charitable gift.

[7] Do not forget that the question asks you for advice on suggested wording to make the gifts charitable if you feel that, at present, they are not.

There is also the possibility that the research could be charitable under section 3(1)(f), 'the advancement of arts, culture, heritage

[8] There is no need to go into detail on this point, as the same considerations apply as in the question of whether the bequest was educational. However, you will certainly gain credit for mentioning it.

[9] This shows the importance of taking time at the start of each question to read it very carefully!

or science', but the same considerations will apply here: is the research of value and the need to disseminate it.[8]

(b) The next proposed bequest is: '£100,000 to my trustees to hold on trust to provide scholarships for the relatives and dependants of workers in the pottery industry resident in Worcester. Preference to be given to those who are themselves employed in any trade in Worcester.' The initial problem is that the wording does not mention what the scholarships are for and so as such it cannot be charitable as no charitable purpose is stated.[9] It may be, for example, that they are for education and training perhaps in a particular skill, but this needs to be stated.

The next question is whether there is sufficient public benefit as required by the Charities Act 2011. Assuming that the purpose is educational then this will by itself be a purpose beneficial to the public but is there sufficient actual public benefit? The gift is for a specified class but the class is relatives and dependants of those employed in the pottery industry in Worcester which might count as a section of the public but then preference is to be given to those employed in any trade in Worcester. The result is that the class is very narrowly defined.

In *Oppenheim* v *Tobacco Securities Trust Co Ltd* [1951] AC 297 HL a trust was held not charitable where it was to provide for 'the education of children of employees or former employees of the British American Tobacco Co Ltd or any of its subsidiary or allied companies'. In this case we are not told how many firms there are in the pottery industry in Worcester. If there is only one then it seems that the objects are too narrow.

[10] Note the clear comparison between the facts of this case and the situation. A poor answer would just recite the facts of *Re Koettgen*.

In *Re Koettgen's Will Trust* [1954] Ch 252 HC a charitable educational trust with a preference to be given of up to 75 per cent of income to employees of a particular firm was held charitable because the gift to the primary class contained the necessary element of public benefit. However, here the preference in favour of those employed in any trade in Worcester could apply to 100 per cent of the income.[10]

[11] This is one of those answers where it is wise not to be too dogmatic, as this is not an area with black and white rules. The examiner will expect you to recognise this.

It may be that there is a reason for this restriction and, if so, Isobel should say what it is. As the wording stands, it would probably have a greater chance of success[11] as a charitable trust if the preference was removed.

Finally, if these suggestions are adopted there seems no reason why the trusts should not satisfy the final requirement that they must be exclusively charitable.

✓ **Make your answer stand out**

- Analyse the wording of each gift closely and never assume that because it may be for charitable purposes this automatically makes it charitable – apply all three requirements.
- Look closely at the facts of the problem and have a thorough knowledge of *Re Koettgen*.
- Mention the dissenting speech of Lord McDermott in *Oppenheim* v *Tobacco Securities*, who disagreed with the approach of Lord Simonds, who delivered the majority speech. Lord McDermott held that the question of whether a class was too small to have public benefit should be one of degree and a rigid approach was wrong.
- Compare the decisions in *Oppenheim* v *Tobacco Securities* with *Re Koettgen* and note the speech of Lord Radcliffe in *Cafoor* v *Income Tax Commissioner (Colombo)* [1961] AC 584 DC, who thought that *Re Koettgen* edged 'very near to being inconsistent with' *Oppenheim.* Why was this so?

! **Don't be tempted to . . .**

- Ignore the instruction in the question that you are asked if necessary to advise on revised wording to make the gift charitable.
- Spend too long on whether the gift can be charitable and not enough on whether it has sufficient public benefit.
- Fail to mention (even briefly) the requirement that all trusts must be exclusively charitable.
- Fail to analyse the exact wording of each gift.

❓ Question 3

You are asked to advise his executors and trustees on the validity of the following bequests contained in the will of Arthur, who has just died:

(a) £10,000 to the Barsetshire County Cricket Club.

(b) £100,000 to be held by my trustees to distribute it at their discretion among the employees and ex-employees of the National Health Service for their education and training, in gratitude for the excellent treatment by the NHS of me throughout my life.

Answer plan

→ Consider whether the gifts can be for a charitable purpose and if there is public benefit.

→ If not, can there be a valid non-charitable purpose trust or a gift to the members?

→ Can there be a valid private trust and, if so, will it satisfy the test for certainty of objects?

→ Consider the possible effects of the rules against perpetuities.

Diagram plan

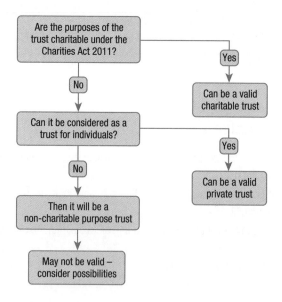

A printable version of this diagram plan is available from **www.pearsoned.co.uk/lawexpressqa**

Answer

We are asked whether these trusts are valid or not, and not whether they are, for example, charitable. Therefore, this answer will consider the whole range of possibilities.[1]

(a) The first gift is one of £10,000 to Barsetshire County Cricket club. This cannot be a private trust, as it is for purposes and not for individuals.[2] Is the purpose charitable? Trusts for amateur sport are charitable by section 3(1)(g) of the Charities Act 2011 and sport is defined by section 3(2)(d) of the Act as meaning 'sport or games which promote health by involving physical or mental skill or exertion'. This certainly includes cricket. We do not know, however, if Barsetshire County Cricket Club is an amateur club.[3] If it is, then the purposes will be charitable and it is suggested that the necessary element of public benefit is found by the gift enabling people to play cricket. If the club is professional then the gift cannot be charitable as, in *IRC v McMullen* [1981] AC 1 HL, Lord Hailsham stated that the playing of games was not in itself charitable and so charitable status depends on satisfying section 3(1)(g) above.

If the gift is not charitable then it falls within the category of non-charitable purpose trusts unless the cricket club is a company, as then there will be no trust at all and it will simply be a bequest to the company.[4] If it is not a company it will be an unincorporated association and, thus, as it cannot hold property itself, any property must be held on trust for its purposes, as in *Re Finger's Will Trust* [1972] Ch 286 HC. In this case the purposes were charitable and so there was a valid charitable trust but this is not so here. There is the possibility that the gift could be considered as either to be held on trust for the members of the club as in *Re Denley's Trust Deed* [1969] 1 Ch 373 HC or as a gift to the members who will hold it on a contractual basis as in *Re Recher's Will Trusts* [1972] Ch 526 HC.[5] The wording of the gift simply mentioned the club and not the members but this is not necessarily an obstacle to the court discovering either a trust for the members or a gift to them as in *Re Lipinski's Will Trusts* [1976] Ch 235 HC, where a gift to be used 'solely' for the construction or maintenance of the association's buildings was a gift to the members.

[1] This is an absolutely vital sentence, as it would be all too easy to take a quick look at this question, think that it concerned charitable trusts and devote all of your answer to this. In fact the question just asks if the trusts are *valid* and so we must consider all possibilities.

[2] This may seem an obvious point but it is a good idea to be aware of this possibility and in other questions of this kind there may be the possibility of a private trust. It also shows at the start that you are thinking of all possibilities.

[3] Do not assume that any sport club is amateur or professional unless you are given this information.

[4] Note that this part of the question refers to a 'bequest' and not a trust as in the second part. Thus it could be a direct gift.

[5] In any answer on this area you should consider both of these possibilities although how much time you spend on them will depend on the type of question.

If the court adopts either the solution in **Re Denley** or **Re Recher** then the gift will be valid, but if not, then unless the club is a company there will be an invalid non-charitable purpose trust and so the £10,000 will be held on a resulting trust for Arthur's estate.

If **Re Recher** applies there will be a gift to the members, but if there is a trust on the lines of **Re Denley**, the question is whether the gift infringes the rule against perpetuities. There are in fact two perpetuity rules and the applicable one here concerns inalienability of capital.[6] The period cannot exceed that fixed by section 15(4) of the Perpetuities and Accumulations Act 1964, as lives or lives in being plus 21 years. As no other period is specified here, this will apply. It is likely that the 'wait and see' provisions of the 1964 Act do not apply to non-charitable purpose trusts and so, as there is the possibility at the outset that the perpetuity period will be infringed, the gift will be void and the £10,000 will be held on a resulting trust for Arthur's estate.

(b) The gift of £100,000 to employees and ex-employees of the National Health Service for their education and training can first be considered as a charitable trust as the number of employees and ex-employees of the NHS give it the flavour of a trust for purposes rather than for individuals. If it is charitable then it can be for the advancement of education which is charitable under section 3(1)(b) of the Charities Act 2011, or possibly for the advancement of health or the saving of lives under section 3(1)(d). The next question is whether there is sufficient public benefit, as all the beneficiaries are linked by their employment in the NHS.

In **Oppenheim v Tobacco Securities Trust Co Ltd** [1951] AC 297 HL a trust was held not charitable where it was to provide for 'the education of children of employees or former employees of the British American Tobacco Co Ltd or any of its subsidiary or allied companies', even though the number of employees exceeded 110,000. Lord Simonds held that the fact that the group was large did not make the trust charitable if the connection between its members was based on some personal tie such as employment by a particular employee or employees, as here. This would seem to decide the matter, as the effect of section 4(3) of the Charities Act 2011[7] is that existing case law on charities is preserved.

[6] There is no need to discuss perpetuities at length but, as many students for some reason try to avoid the topic altogether, you will gain considerable credit for an accurate account of the law.

[7] Note that in the interests of accuracy we have not put 'section 4(3) of the Charities Act *says*' because the actual wording of section 4(3) does not expressly *say* that existing case law is preserved. However, this is what it means. If you are going for high marks – or simply do not want to drop marks – make sure that you get these small points right.

[8] If you mention *Oppenheim* then you should mention Lord McDermott's dissent too as it is often thought that his was the better view.

Lord MacDermott dissented, holding that there was the intention to benefit a class of substantial size and importance in such a way that the interests of the class as a whole were advanced.[8] If this view is accepted then it is arguable that there is sufficient public benefit.

If this trust is not charitable on the basis of **Oppenheim**, it might be valid as a private trust provided that it satisfies the requirement of certainty of objects laid down in **McPhail v Doulton** [1971] AC 424 HL, where Lord Wilberforce held that the test was: 'Can it be said with certainty that any given individual is or is not a member of the class?' Thus it is open to anyone to come forward and show that they are an employee or ex-employee of the NHS.

[9] This is clearly a point which the examiner is expecting you to mention and so you will lose marks if you end with *McPhail v Doulton*.

However, there must be very many employees or ex-employees of the NHS[9] and in **McPhail v Doulton** Lord Wilberforce said that even though a description of beneficiaries complied with the test he had laid down it might be 'so hopelessly wide as not to form anything like a class', and gave as an example 'all the residents of Greater London'. This principle was applied in **R v District Auditor, ex parte West Yorkshire Metropolitan County Council** [1986] RVR 24 HC, where a trust set up for the inhabitants of the County of West Yorkshire, of which there were about 2,500,000, was held void for administrative unworkability. If this is so the trust will be invalid.

✓ Make your answer stand out

- Look at McInnes (2008), who looks at recent Canadian case law – this could give any answer on sport and charity law a good comparative perspective.

- Mention that section 18 of the Perpetuities and Accumulations Act 2009 exempts non-charitable purpose trusts from the provisions of this Act.

- As the Perpetuities and Accumulations Act 1964 applies to private trusts, if the 'wait and see' principle in the Act does apply it will enable the trustees to exercise their powers within the perpetuity period, and any money not distributed at that time will go on a resulting trust for Arthur's estate.

- Mention that in *Dingle v Turner* [1972] AC 601 Lord Cross (with whom all the other Law Lords concurred) agreed with Lord MacDermott's view of public benefit in *Oppenheim v Tobacco Securities*, although this was *obiter*.

! Don't be tempted to . . .

■ Spend too long on any one area – recognise that this problem deals with many points, and marks will be allocated for each one.

■ Assume that the gifts are charitable and fail to consider other possibilities.

■ Deal with whether the gift is for a charitable purpose and then forget to consider if there is public benefit.

■ Start off without a clear plan in mind, as this is an area where the issues are closely linked.

🖉 Question 4

'It is indeed an essential feature of all charity in the legal sense that there must be in it some element of public benefit.' (Viscount Simonds in *IRC* v *Baddeley* (1955))

Critically consider, through an examination of the case law and other sources, how this requirement of public benefit has been interpreted.

Diagram plan

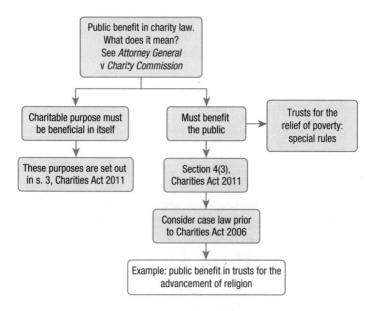

A printable version of this diagram plan is available from **www.pearsoned.co.uk/lawexpressqa**

Answer plan

➡ Explain why the requirement of public benefit is important in charity law.

➡ Assess the extent which, if at all, the Charities Act 2006 has changed the law in this area.

➡ Follow this by explaining the place of the statutory Guidance provided by the Charity Commission.

➡ Consider examples of how the courts have interpreted the requirement of public benefit.

Answer

[1] There are many detailed exemptions which charities receive from taxation but it is unlikely that you will need to remember them for a trusts exam. However, we do need one example of these exemptions to illustrate our point and the one chosen is easy to remember and unlikely to change.

[2] Most students do not make this point but it is very significant and you will gain marks if you do.

[3] You do need to be clear about the different effects of section 4(2) and section 4(3) for a good mark here.

The requirement that there must be an element of public benefit is a fundamental principle of charity law. This is because charities, in return for the benefits which they confer on the community, receive very considerable financial privileges such as exemption from income tax provided that the income is used for charitable purposes.[1]

In *Attorney General* v *Charity Commission* [2012] UKUT 420 (TCC) it was emphasised that there are two requirements: the charitable purpose must be beneficial (known as the 'benefit aspect') and it must benefit the public (known as the 'public aspect').[2] So the actual purpose must itself have benefit, such as the relief of poverty, and that benefit must be a public benefit. Thus, in *Re Compton* [1945] Ch 123 HC a trust for the education of the children undoubtedly had benefit but as it was for the children of three named families it was not charitable. However, in *Re Pinion* [1965] Ch 85 HC a studio and its contents were given to trustees to enable them to be used as a museum but no benefit from it could be shown as its contents were stigmatised by the court as 'a mass of junk'.

Prior to the Charities Act 2006 the law was said to be that charities for three purposes (poverty, education and religion) were charitable and in other cases public benefit had to be proved. Section 4(2) of the Charities Act 2011 appeared to remove this presumption and so it was argued that public benefit must be proved in all cases. However, this was confused by section 4(3)[3] which provides that 'any reference to the public benefit is a reference to the public benefit as that term is understood for the purposes of the law relating to charities in England and Wales.' The effect of this is to preserve the case law which existed before the 2006 Charities Act, a good deal of which was on the basis that there *was* a presumption of public benefit in certain cases.

In **Attorney General v Charity Commission**, which involved a number of charities concerned with the relief of poverty, the Upper Chamber took the opportunity to re-state the law on public benefit. It explained that public benefit is part of the nature of each charitable purpose. Thus education is by itself charitable and so is the relief of poverty. There could of course be cases where this was not so, one example often given being a school for pickpockets, but that does not affect the general principle. That being so, there is no question of any presumption of public benefit: that benefit is intrinsic to the charitable purpose.[4]

Section 17 of the Charities Act 2011 obliges the Charity Commission to issue guidance[5] on what is meant by public benefit but this cannot make the law nor change existing law but simply provide Guidance on the current legal understanding of public benefit.

A good illustration of the case law on public benefit is provided by trusts for the advancement of religion.[6] It appears that this requirement can be met in one of two ways.

The first is providing religious activities which are available to the public. It is on this basis that a trust for the provision of church buildings will be of public benefit, and also a trust for other religious activities such as the publication of literature or missionary work. In **Re Hetherington** [1989] 2 All ER 129 HC it was held that a trust for the celebration of masses was charitable because 'the public celebration of a religious rite edifies and improves those who attend it'. However, in **Gilmour v Coats** [1949] AC 426 HL a gift to a community of strictly cloistered and enclosed nuns was not held charitable because the benefit conferred on the public by their prayers was, per Lord Simonds, 'manifestly not susceptible of proof'. In addition, the possibility that the public might have been edified by the nuns' example of self-denial was too vague and intangible. This decision has been thought to be harsh and a different approach is seen in **Funnell v Stewart** [1996] 1 All ER 715 HC, where faith healing was simply accepted as a recognised public benefit provided that there was a sufficient religious element present. In 1990 the Charity Commissioners registered another contemplative community of nuns (the Society of the Most Precious Blood) who did, however, do counselling work by phone.[7]

[4] This is the first crucial point – the benefit aspect.

[5] The question mentioned 'case law and other sources'. This is clearly statute law and also this Guidance.

[6] Your essay will suffer if you try to cover too much. Instead, select a few areas and consider them in detail.

[7] Do not forget that the Annual Reports of the Charity Commission contain a great deal of material on what can be considered charitable and this case is an excellent instance of how you can boost your marks by including it.

The second way of demonstrating public benefit here is by the presence among the public of persons who have been edified by attendance at a place of worship. Here we see the clear division, which is not always apparent in the cases, between the benefit and public aspects.[8] In **Neville Estates v Madden** [1962] Ch 832 HC a trust for the advancement of religion among members of the Catford Synagogue was held charitable on this basis even though the services at the synagogue were only open to those on its list of members. There was a benefit in the actual holding of services and this was on the facts public benefit.

A problematic area is trusts for recreation. In **IRC v Baddeley** [1955] AC 572 HL it was held that a trust for the 'moral, social and physical well-being' of persons resident in East Ham and Leyton was not charitable because of the inclusion of social purposes. Even if they had not been included, it would have failed as possibly being limited to actual or potential Methodists in a certain area and so there was a lack of public benefit. It was a gift to a class within a class. Section 5 of the Charities Act 2011, which replaced the identical provisions in the Recreational Charities Act 1958, provides that recreational activities provided in the interests of social welfare can be beneficial[9] but the public benefit element of the decision in **Baddeley** remains.

However, trusts for the relief of poverty are subject to a unique test of public benefit.[10] In *Dingle* v *Turner* (1972) AC 601 HL a trust fund to pay pensions to poor employees of a certain company was held charitable. However, it is wrong to say that in trusts for the relief of poverty there is *no* requirement of public benefit: the point is that the line is drawn differently than on other cases. In **Dingle v Turner** the House approved the statement of Lord Cross in **Re Scarisbrick** [1951] Ch 622 CA that a distinction is drawn between 'whether the gift was for the relief of poverty amongst a particular description of poor people or was merely a gift to particular poor persons, the relief of poverty among them being the motive of the gift'. In the latter case it would not be charitable. It may be that, as in **Dingle v Turner**, that group is defined by reference to a personal connection (here, employment by a particular firm) but it is still a group.

Thus we can say that public benefit is still an essential feature of charity law, in the sense that both the actual purpose must have benefit and that benefit must be public benefit.

[8] This point will give you an added bonus as students do not often make it and it is now important in the light of *Attorney General* v *Charity Commission*.

[9] You do not need to give further details of section 5 as that would be getting away from the point as section 5 is primarily concerned with charitable purposes and not public benefit.

[10] Do mention this point in any answer especially as trusts for the relief of poverty were specifically mentioned as a separate class in *Attorney General* v *Charity Commission*.

✓ Make your answer stand out

- Read Fletcher (1996). This is very useful on *Funnell* v *Stewart* and *Re Hetherington*.
- Analyse other cases and assess if the courts have distinguished between the benefit and the public aspect.
- Look at the Charity Commission's website (gov.uk/government/organisations/charity-commission) for its views on what can be public benefit but remember that this is only Guidance and not the law.

! Don't be tempted to . . .

- Explain in a particular case why the objects were charitable or not. This is not the issue here – concentrate on the public benefit issue.
- Set out the facts of masses of cases so that you lose the focus of the essay.
- Compare the law as it was before the Charities Act 2006 with what it is now. This will take you away from the point. Instead, use your time to explain how the Charities Act 2006, which is now incorporated in the Charities Act 2011, has affected the law.

Question 5

'We have concluded that, while the (Charities Act 2006) has been broadly welcomed by the charitable sector, it is critically flawed on the issue of public benefit.'

(Post-legislative scrutiny of the Charities Act 2006 by the Public Administration Committee (2012))

Critically consider this view of the public benefit requirement in the Charities Act 2006.

Answer plan

→ What the question is about: the two problems of confusion in what is now the 2011 Act and misleading Guidance issued by the Charity Commission.

→ Explain carefully by analysing sections 4(2) and (3) of the Charity Act 2011 how this confusion arose.

→ Look at how the confusion seems to have been cleared up by *Attorney General* v *Charity Commission* [2012] but make the case that the legislation itself still needs amending.

→ Then look at the Guidance issued by the Commission showing the problems with its application in actual cases

→ Conclude by stating that legislation is needed to clarify the law on public benefit.

Diagram plan

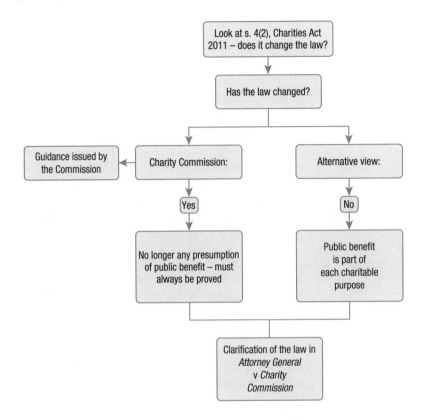

A printable version of this diagram plan is available from **www.pearsoned.co.uk/lawexpressqa**

Answer

[1] Here we are addressing the issue directly and in effect setting out a structure for our essay. Always aim for this type of start. Note carefully that the question only concerns the public benefit issue and so there are no marks for discussion of charitable purposes themselves.

The argument of the Public Administration Committee that the Charities Act 2006 is 'fatally flawed' on the issue of public benefit is based on two points[1]: first, the confusion on whether the presumption of public benefit was removed by the Act and secondly the requirement for the Charity Commission to produce public benefit Guidance when the law on which that Guidance was based was itself uncertain. This has led, as the Public Administration Committee says, to lengthy legal battles which could perhaps have been avoided if the law had been clear. Moreover, the Committee says that it has left the 'Commission, a branch of the executive, in an impossible position'. It should be made clear that the legislation is now in the Charities Act 2011 but the legislation is the same as the 2011 Act was a consolidating statute.[2]

The first issue is the debate on whether the presumption of public benefit in cases of trusts for the relief of poverty, the advancement of education and the advancement of religion was removed by the Act so that in all cases public benefit has to be proved. This was clearly the view of the Charity Commission as a spokesperson for the Charity Commission (quoted in Third Sector Online, 25 July 2012) said that: 'The Act stated that it is not to be presumed that a purpose of a particular description is for the public benefit.' The problem is that this referred to section 4(2) which indeed provides that in determining whether the requirement of public benefit is satisfied in relation to any such purpose, it is not to be presumed that a purpose of a particular description is for the public benefit.[3]

[3] This is a crucial provision which you must remember for the exam.

However, this does not go far enough as section 4(3) provides that any reference to the public benefit is a reference to the public benefit as that term is understood for the purposes of the law relating to charities in England and Wales.[4] The effect of this is to preserve the previous case law, but this means that cases such as **Oppenheim v Tobacco Securities Trust Co Ltd** [1951] AC 297 HL and **Gilmour v Coats** [1949] AC 426 HL, which laid down the law on public benefit in cases of education and religion respectively, are still good law.

[4] Your mention of section 4(2) above must be accompanied by contrasting it with section 4(3), clearly bringing out the differences between the two.

Hackney (2008) argued that the law has been misunderstood and that it has not indeed changed.[5] He says that the answer is that the 'law has always been that those seeking to establish a charity have had to prove that it was of a public character: this has not been presumed in any way nor was it a matter for dogmatic assumption'. He quoted the argument of counsel in **Oppenheim v Tobacco Securities Trust Co Ltd** [1951] AC 297 at 301: 'It is for the appellant to show that it is a charity. This cannot be a valid charitable trust unless it is of a public character, i.e., for a purpose directed to the benefit of the community or a section of the community.'

[5] This is an important argument to refer to and it connects with the next paragraph.

This argument seems to have been accepted in **Attorney General v Charity Commission** [2012] UKUT 420 (TCC) which involved a number of charities concerned with the relief of poverty but the Upper Chamber took the opportunity to re-state the law on public benefit.

It held that public benefit is part of the nature of each charitable purpose. Thus education is by itself charitable and so is the relief of poverty.[6] There could of course be cases where this was not so, one example often given being a school for pickpockets but that does not affect the general principle. That being so, there is no question of any presumption of public benefit: that benefit is intrinsic to the charitable purpose. Thus the actual purpose must itself have benefit, such as the relief of poverty, but in addition any actual benefit must be public benefit.

Nevertheless the Charities Act 2011 remains in force with the two sub-sections – 4(2) and (3) – and so there is a strong argument for a change in statute law to reflect the actual position.

The mistaken view of the law on public benefit was compounded by the fact that by section 17 of the Charities Act 2011 the Charity Commission is obliged to issue Guidance on the meaning of public benefit and this led to the lengthy legal battles to which the Public Administration Committee referred.[7]

One involved independent fee-paying schools. Guidance issued by the Commission said that any benefit must not be unreasonably restricted by ability to pay any fees charged but this section was successfully challenged in **Independent Schools Council v Charity Commission for England and Wales** [2011] UKUT 421 where the Upper Chamber held that the use of the word 'unreasonable' in the Guidance was wrong as charity law (see e.g. **Re Resch's Will Trusts** [1969] 1 AC 514 PC) had never imposed such a requirement. There was indeed a duty on educational charities to make provision for the poor and this must be more than minimal or tokenistic. Beyond that, the level of provision to be made for those unable to pay the full fees was to be decided by the trustees in the context of their charity's circumstances. There were no objective benchmarks about what was appropriate. As a result of this case and other problems the Commission revised its Guidance which now simply states what the law is with examples of how it might apply.

The other problem was that lack of clarity on public benefit led to allegations that the Commission was pursuing what was seen by some as a left wing, secularist anti-religion agenda[8] especially in the light of the rejection of the Commission's Guidance on fee paying by independent schools in the above case. This was seen also in the

[6] There is no time – and no need – in this essay to consider individual charitable purposes.

[7] You have now come to the other issue raised in the question.

[8] Not everyone agrees with this point and you should make this clear.

Commission's refusal to grant charitable status to the Preston Down Trust, which runs meeting halls for the Exclusive Brethren in Torquay, Paignton and Newton Abbot because the Commission was not satisfied that it had been established for the advancement of religion for public benefit. The Commission said that its decision took into account such matters as the nature of Christian religion embraced by the trust and the means through which this was promoted, including the public access to its services and the potential for its beneficial impact on the wider community. However, after this decision had been given considerable publicity the Commission changed its decision in the light of further evidence.

[9] You have rounded off your answer by referring back to the report quoted in the question. This is an excellent way to end but to do so you needed to have done your research on this report.

The Public Administration Committee[9] believes that it is essential for Parliament to revisit charity legislation and set the criteria for charitable status rather than delegating such decisions to the Charity Commission and the courts. This must be the right course of action.

Make your answer stand out

- Look at the Preston Down Trust case in more detail. It was raised in Parliament. See http://www.lawandreligionuk.com/2012/11/07/charitable-status-public-benefit-and-closed-congregations-update/.
- Read Hackney's (2008) article, quoted in the answer, in full.
- Go to the Charity Commission's website (www.charity-commission.gov.uk) and look at the Public Benefit Guidance. If you can use this to add in some actual examples of how the Commission works this will add greatly to your answer.
- Annual Reports of the Charity Commissioners – available on the above website.

! Don't be tempted to . . .

- Concentrate too much on the public benefit issue to the exclusion of the others.
- Go through all of the heads of charity set out in section 3 of the Charities Act 2011 and in each case decide if the law has changed. This will take you too long and you will not have time to discuss the issues.
- Discuss whether the Charities Act 2006 (now Charities Act 2011) has changed the law without explaining exactly what its provisions are.

 **Question 6**

'There is a sharp theoretical dividing line in the modern law of charities between charitable and political purposes: the former exclude the latter.' (Moffat, 2009, p. 1023)

Critically consider this statement.

Diagram plan

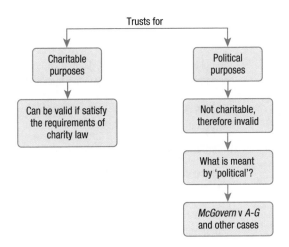

A printable version of this diagram plan is available from **www.pearsoned.co.uk/lawexpressqa**

Answer plan

→ Explain what the question is saying – stress the word 'theoretical'.

→ Give an explanation of what 'political' means in the context of charity law and follow this with examples from the cases.

→ Consider the problem which 'campaigning' can bring for charities and the Guidance given by the Charity Commission.

→ Consider whether the list of charitable objects set out in section 3(1) of the Charities Act 2011 has made any difference to the concept of political activity.

→ Conclude by mentioning the changing role of charities in the context of this question.

Answer

1 This is an excellent clear
start which will impress
the examiner at once. You
have picked up on the word
'theoretical' and contrasted it
with the position in practice.
The challenge is now to follow
this through in this essay.

There is undoubtedly a theoretical dividing line between charitable and political purposes but it will be argued that it is not always a clear one in practice.[1] In a letter to the *Daily Telegraph* (8 August 2013) Sir Stephen Bubb, the CEO of the Association of Chief Executives of Voluntary Organisations pointed out the long history of political campaigning by charities from the presentation of a petition to Parliament in 1787 advocating the abolition of the slave trade to the establishment of societies for the prevention of cruelty to animals in the Victorian era.

The initial question is what 'political' means in this context and if the courts have given it a wider meaning than just party political.

[2] It is essential that you start with an explanation (not a definition, which is not possible) of exactly what political is. The advantage of using the explanation given by Slade J in this case is that you can then use it to illustrate how it was applied to the facts of the case.

In *McGovern* v *A-G* [1982] Ch 321 HC Slade J said that the term 'political trusts' included trusts to:[2]

1 further the interests of a particular political party;

2 procure changes in the laws of either the United Kingdom or a foreign country;

3 procure a reversal of government policy or of particular decisions of governmental authorities whether in the United Kingdom or in a foreign country.

In this case a trust was established by Amnesty International with four main objects:

(i) the relief of prisoners of conscience and their relatives;

(ii) seeking the release of such prisoners;

(iii) the abolition of torture or inhuman treatment or punishment;

(iv) research into human rights and the dissemination of the results of that research.

[3] This case is especially good as an illustration of the law, as it gives examples of where some activities were charitable and some were not.

Although objects (i) and (iv) were held by themselves to be charitable, objects (ii) and (iii) involved attempting to procure changes in the law and the reversal of government decisions, whether in the United Kingdom or abroad.[3] The trust was therefore held not to be charitable, on the basis that it was not exclusively charitable.

Slade J gave the following reasons why political activities are not charitable:

(i) The courts cannot judge if a change in the law is for the public benefit, because it will not normally have evidence before it to enable it to do this.

(ii) Even if the court does have such evidence, to hold that a change in the law is desirable would usurp the function of the legislature.

(iii) In the case of trusts campaigning to secure the alteration of foreign laws, not only would there be the evidential problem referred to at (i) above, but the enforcement of such a trust might prejudice the relations of this country with that of the foreign country concerned.

However, the boundary between political and charitable activities is not in fact always clear, especially where the trust has an educational flavour. If the objects are connected with propaganda then they will not be charitable, as in **Re Bushnell** [1975] 1 All ER 721 HC where the object was to use a fund 'for the advancement and propagation of the teaching of socialised medicine'. The court held that the dominant or essential object of the primary trust was to promote or bring about the establishment of a state health service in accordance with the testator's own theory. Therefore, as it was not a trust to educate the public so that they could decide for themselves upon the advantages or otherwise of such a service it was not charitable. On the other hand,[4] in **Re Koeppler's Will Trusts** [1985] 2 All ER 869 HC a gift was construed as being for a project involving conferences on issues of current political debate but which did not involve the propagation of political opinions or any activities of a party political nature. Instead, the object of the project was a genuine attempt to find and disseminate the truth, and accordingly the gift was held to be for the advancement of education and thus charitable. In **Southwood v A-G** [2000] WTLR 119 HC the actual trust deed was ambiguous and so the court held that it could look at the actual activities of the trust. Here they were not charitable.[5]

Problems have also arisen with the activities of university or college students' unions. These are charitable bodies, as they are connected with the advancement of education, and so their funds must not be

[4] It would have been easy to follow *Re Bushnell* with another case where the trust was held not to be charitable but this would have made the same point and would not have boosted your marks by very much. Instead, the next case makes a contrasting point.

[5] There is no need to set out the facts of this case, as it makes a similar point to those above. Instead, it is this particular point which is significant.

used for political purposes, as in **Baldry v Feintuck** [1972] 2 All ER 81 HC, where the use of union funds to campaign for free school milk to be restored was held to be political. In **Webb v O'Doherty** (1991) *The Times,* 11 February HC an injunction was granted to restrain a students' union from spending money in support of a campaign against the Gulf War. The court distinguished between campaigning by seeking to influence public opinion, which is not charitable, and mere discussion of political issues, which can be charitable.

It is this distinction between charitable and non-charitable activities, especially in the area of campaigning, which the Charity Commission seeks to draw in its Guidance *Speaking Out: Guidance on Campaigning and Political Activity by Charities* (March 2008).[6] The problem is that a charity may have identified a particular problem as part of its activities in, for example, the area of famine relief, and as a result may feel impelled to take action to remove this. The key points, set out at B1, are that: 'Campaigning and political activity can be legitimate and valuable activities for charities to undertake.' However, it emphasises that: 'political campaigning, or political activity, as defined in this guidance, must be undertaken by a charity only in the context of supporting the delivery of its charitable purposes. Unlike other forms of campaigning, it must not be the continuing and sole activity of the charity.' Thus, campaigning may be a legitimate activity only if it arises out of the work of the charity.

Another issue is whether the new list of charitable objects set out in section 3 of the Charities Act 2011 could enable a charity to engage in political activity. One obvious possibility is section 3(1)(h): 'the advancement of human rights, conflict resolution or reconciliation or the promotion of religious or racial harmony or equality and diversity'. This could on its face allow campaigning against the policies of a country where it is believed that human rights are being infringed, for example. However, we must remember that by section 4(3) of the 2011 Act the existing case law is preserved[7] and so any activities in the promotion of human rights must be charitable according to previous decisions of the courts. In this instance actual research into human rights and the dissemination of its results was held charitable in **McGovern v A-G** and this will be what is made charitable by section 4(3).

[6] This is one area where you will lose marks if you do not refer to what the Charity Commission is saying. This is especially important as, with the establishment of the Charity Appeal Tribunal by the Charities Act 2006, fewer charity cases will come before the courts and so important decisions will come from the Charity Commission.

[7] Section 4(3) is one of the lynch-pins of the Act and its importance should be stressed in any essay on charities.

A final point is that the debate on what is a political purpose needs to be looked at in the context of the enhanced role which governments see for charities or the 'Third Sector', as they are called.[8] The boundary between charities and political activity may be theoretically clear but it is still likely to give rise to problems in the future.

[8] This is a really excellent point to end on – it means that your answer ends on a suitably challenging note.

 Make your answer stand out

- Read Dunn (2008). This article looks at the role of charities in promoting social reform and the increasing role of the state in promoting social welfare. It then looks at the rules which restrict the political activities of charities.
- Mention the different approach taken in the United States. There is a very useful summary of the US cases in the judgment of Carnwath J in *Southwood* v *A-G*.
- Look at investigations undertaken by the Charity Commission into particular charities, e.g. the investigation into OXFAM (in 1991).
- Look at the activities and objects of any charity and see if, in your opinion, the boundary between charitable and political activity is crossed.
- Could the restriction on the 'political activities' of charities be an infringement of their rights under Article 10 of the European Convention on Human Rights, which provides for freedom of expression?
- In *Aid/Watch Incorporated v Commissioner of Taxation* (2010) 241 CLR 539 the High Court of Australia held that there is no longer any prohibition in Australia on charities having political purposes. The court specifically recognised the public benefit in charities campaigning for both changes in the law and in government policy.

! Don't be tempted to . . .

- Restrict yourself to the case law only.
- Say that political means *only* party political.
- Give your own view on this area without backing it up with evidence.

❓ **Question 7**

John, who died in April 2014, left the following charitable bequests in his will made in 2006:

(a) £10,000 to Hanbury College, where John took his LLB. Hanbury College provided law courses but it no longer exists. When it was dissolved in 2009 its assets were transferred to Chamberlain College, which provides a range of business courses including legal courses.

(b) £50,000 to the Association for Distressed Retired Lawyers, a registered charity. In July 2014 this was wound up. There is in existence an Association for the Relief of Retired Lawyers which is also a registered charity.

(c) £20,000 to the Swinton League for the Rescue of Sick Cats. There has never been such a body.

(d) £15,000 to the Earlsdon College for Young Ladies, an international finishing school for girls aged 16–18. There is a condition attached to the gift that it can only be used for the education of girls who are of German nationality, as John was keen to promote Anglo-German understanding. The school has, however, refused to accept the gift with this condition.

You are asked to advise his executors, Teresa and Richard, on what action they should take with regard to the above bequests.

Diagram plan

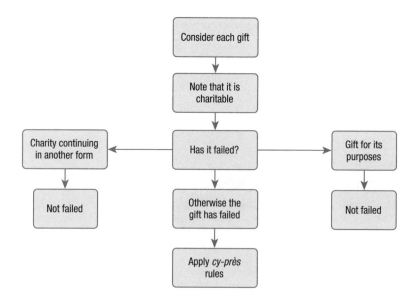

A printable version of this diagram plan is available from **www.pearsoned.co.uk/lawexpressqa**

Answer plan

→ Identify that the bequests are all charitable.

→ Consider whether the gifts have failed at all.

→ If the gifts have failed, is *cy-près* application possible?

→ Is a general charitable intention required and, if so, is it present?

→ If the gift has failed and if *cy-près* application is not possible, then the property will have to be held on a resulting trust for the estate.

Answer

The first point is that we are told that all the bequests are charitable and so there is no need to discuss if they have charitable status.[1]

(a) The charity to which the gift was left, Hanbury College, no longer exists as a separate entity. The first question is whether the gift can be said to be for the purposes of this charity rather than necessarily to the actual charity, so that, if it is continuing under another form, the gift can still be applied to those purposes. This looks on its wording like a gift to Hanbury College rather than to its purposes. However, if it is for the purposes of the college we must then ask if these are continued under the work of Chamberlain College, which has taken over its assets. This college provides a range of courses which includes the legal courses which were run by Hanbury College and so it may be possible to say that Hanbury College is continuing in another form. In **Re Faraker** [1912] 2 Ch 488 HC a testatrix bequeathed a legacy to 'Mrs Bailey's Charity, Rotherhithe', the object of which was to benefit poor widows. However, the charity had been amalgamated with others with the object of benefiting the poor in general of Rotherhithe. The court held that the amalgamated charities were entitled to the gift. If this principle applies here, Chamberlain College will be entitled to the gift. However, the extent to which the legal courses form part of the work of Chamberlain College is not clear. If, for example, the business courses are very large in comparison to the legal courses then it may be that the purposes of Chamberlain College are different to Hanbury College and so it could not claim the gift on this basis. In **Re Roberts** [1963] 1 All ER 674 AC it was held that the **Re Faraker**

[1] If you did not spot this point then you would have wasted time and marks by discussing in detail if each gift has charitable status. It is quite common for questions dealing with the failure of charitable gifts to actually tell you that the gift is charitable. This is because the examiner considers that there is enough in the question on the issue of failure of the gift to occupy you. You must not assume this, however, and so you need to check in each case if you are told that the gift is charitable.

principle could not apply as the original trust in this case had been terminated under a power which allowed the fund to be used for purposes which might have no relation whatever to the old charity. Although our case seems nearer to **Re Faraker** if the court takes the same view as in **Re Roberts** then the solution in that case, that of a *cy-près* scheme, could also apply here.[2]

Under the *cy-près* rules where a gift has failed then it may be applied for other charitable purposes *cy-près* (so near) to the original intention of the testator. Section 62 of the Charities Act 2011 lays down when a gift has failed and one of these, that the original purposes cannot be carried out (s. 62(1)(a)(ii)), applies here, as the Hanbury College no longer exists. There is a further condition required before *cy-près* application is possible, which is that the testator must have shown a general charitable intention.

Where the gift is for the purposes of a particular institution then it may be that there will be no general charitable intention, as in **Re Rymer** [1895] 1 Ch 19 HC where there was a gift to a seminary which had ceased to exist. In **Re Roberts** Wilberforce J observed that the 'gift there was of a particularly local character by reason not only of the gift itself but by reason of the other context in the will'. Thus, whether there was a general charitable intention will depend on an examination of the rest of the will and here there are three other gifts to charity. This may indicate such an intention (**Re Jenkins' Will Trusts** [1966] 2 WLR 615 HC). If not, and if *cy-près* application is not possible, then the gift of £10,000 will be held by Teresa and Richard on a resulting trust for John's estate.[3]

(b) The crucial point is that the Association for Distressed Retired Lawyers was wound up in July 2014 and John died in April 2014.[4] Thus the principle in **Re Slevin** [1891] 2 Ch 236 HC provides that the requirement of a general charitable intention need not be satisfied where the charity ceases to exist *after* the testator's death, because the property would already have vested in the recipient and so it can be applied *cy-près*. In this case money was left to an orphanage which existed at the testator's death but ceased to exist before the money was paid over. *Cy-près* application was ordered. The only requirement necessary for *cy-près* application is then that the gift has failed and, as in (a) above,

[2] This is where you can start to earn those extra marks. The examiner has deliberately left open the question of whether the principle in *Re Faraker* applies. You should then examine the situation if it does not and go on to explore the possibility of a *cy-près* application.

[3] It is essential to round off an answer in this way. Remember that you must always find a home for the property and often it may be uncertain if in fact *cy-près* application is possible. Therefore, you should have the possible solution of a resulting trust in mind.

[4] If you do not recognise this point your marks for this part of the answer will be very poor. If you receive a question on failure of charitable gifts check for one where you are told the date of the testator's death and the date when the gift failed. If the gift failed *after* the death of the testator then you should answer as shown here.

section 62(1)(a)(ii) applies as the original purposes cannot be carried out as the Association no longer exists. It would seem appropriate for a *cy-près* scheme to be ordered under which the Association of Retired Lawyers can receive the gift.

(c) The gift of £20,000 to the Swinton League for the Rescue of Sick Cats has obviously failed under section 62(1)(a)(ii) of the Charities Act 2011, as the league does not exist, and so the question is whether it can be applied *cy-près.* In **Re Harwood** [1936] Ch 285 HC a gift to the Belfast Peace Society, which had never existed, was applied *cy-près* because the testator showed a general intention to benefit societies whose object was the promotion of peace. However, the mere fact that an institution has never existed is not always evidence of a general charitable intention. Although **Re Koeppler's WT** [1986] Ch 423 HC doubted **Re Harwood** on the ground that promotion of peace was political and not charitable, this does not affect its application here. However, it would be wrong to simply assume that **Re Harwood** applies as in every case it has to be shown that there is a general charitable intention.[5] If this is not the case here, the £20,000 will be held on a resulting trust for John's estate.

(d) Where a gift has a condition attached to it and the charity will not accept the gift with the condition, as here, then it may be possible to apply the gift *cy-près* with the condition removed. In **Re Lysaght** [1966] Ch 191 HC a gift to the Royal College of Surgeons (RCS) to hold on trust to found medical studentships contained a condition stating, *inter alia,* that the students should not be of the Jewish or Roman Catholic faith. The RCS refused to act as trustee unless this condition was removed, which it was. A general charitable intention must, of course, also be found in these cases.[6] In **Re Lysaght** it was held that the general charitable intention was the foundation of medical studentships and so in this case it would presumably be the intention to further the education of girls aged 16–18. If not, then the gift will be held on a resulting trust for John's estate.

[5] Too often students quote *Re Harwood* and assume that this automatically means that the gift can go on a *cy-près* application. Boost your marks by showing that this is not necessarily so.

[6] This is really the same point as before but in another context. Always remember that *cy-près* application of property is never possible without a general charitable intention except where the principle in *Re Slevin* applies.

Make your answer stand out

■ Take a clear and logical approach especially in part (a) where you must not assume that the gift has actually failed.

■ Read Garton (2007). This is a really interesting account of the history of the *cy-près* doctrine and its present-day role.

■ Do some research into the latest case on this area: *Kings* v *Bultitude* [2010] EWHC 1795 (Ch) and see Picton (2011).

■ Consider if the decision in *Re Harwood* was justified. If a charity to which a gift is left does not exist then how can it be said that there is any charitable intention at all?

❗ Don't be tempted to . . .

■ Forget that where the purposes of the charity seem to be carried on in another form then the gift may not have failed at all. Only mention *cy-près* if you think that the purposes may not be being carried on in another form.

■ Forget that for a *cy-près* application to succeed two requirements must be satisfied: the gift must have failed and, except in the *Re Slevin* type of case, there must be a general charitable intention.

■ Just apply cases to this area without asking whether there is a general charitable intention.

www.pearsoned.co.uk/lawexpressqa

 Go online to access more revision support including additional essay and problem questions with diagram plans, You be the marker questions, and download all diagrams from the book.

10

The beneficiary principle and purpose trusts

How this topic may come up in exams

This topic can arise in problem questions dealing with the validity of gifts made to, for example, unincorporated associations, and also bequests in wills for the care of animals and the maintenance of monuments. A frequent essay question is to ask you if the law of trusts has, in effect, got it right here in the first place. Why, for example, should a gift to an unincorporated association cause problems at all? Look out as well for questions which link material in this chapter with the three certainties (Chapter 3) and charitable trusts (Chapter 9).

Before you begin

It's a good idea to consider the following key themes of the beneficiary principle and purpose trusts before tackling a question on this topic.

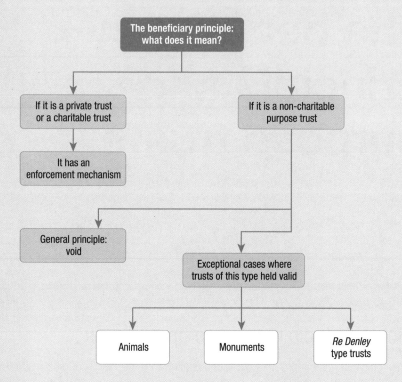

A printable version of this diagram is available from **www.pearsoned.co.uk/lawexpressqa**

Question 1

'Although non-charitable purpose trusts have long been regarded as generally void, it is difficult to identify any clear rationale as to why this should be the case.' (Virgo, 2012, p. 218)

Critically examine this statement.

Diagram plan

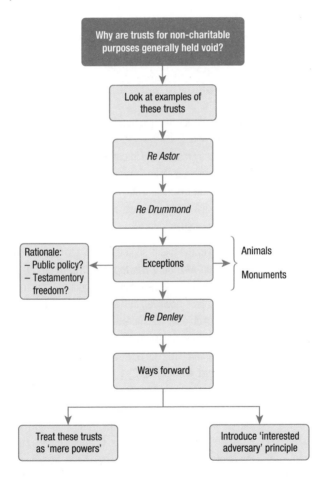

A printable version of this diagram plan is available from **www.pearsoned.co.uk/lawexpressqa**

Answer plan

➡ Consider the beneficiary principle as a rationale of this rule and how it has been applied in the cases.

➡ Mention that this rule is of fairly recent development.

➡ Consider the exceptional cases where trusts for animals and monuments have been held valid, and ask what rationale there is for these, if any, stressing that in some cases the rationale seems to rest on general public policy grounds.

➡ Then look at the cases where the courts have tried ways to hold these trusts valid and again look for a rationale.

➡ Critically consider the various ways in which it has been suggested that these trusts could be held valid.

Answer

[1] The point of this question is not to invite you to write all that you know on this area but, in effect, to look at the rationale behind it. This paragraph both shows that you have understood this and also sets out a structure for your essay. A perfect start.

The rationale for the rule that trusts for non-charitable purposes are generally void is, as the question says, difficult to see. The result is that perfectly reasonable intentions are prevented from being carried out and moreover the rule is subject to exceptions which themselves have no clear rationale. Finally, attempts to hold that these trusts can be valid have led to unnecessarily complex case law. We shall look at these three issues in turn.[1]

The origin of the rule is sometimes said to be the dictum of Grant MR who said in **Morice v Bishop of Durham** (1804) 10 Ves 522 that 'there must be somebody in whose favour the court can decree performance'. In fact, however, this was a trust which failed through lack of certainty of objects. It is more accurate to say that the basis of the rule is found in the beneficiary principle: a trust must have a beneficiary who can enforce it.[2] The point was made by Roxburgh J in **Re Astor's Settlement Trusts** [1952] 1 All ER 1067 HC: 'it is not possible to contemplate with equanimity the creation of large funds devoted to non-charitable purposes which no court and no department of state can control or, in case of maladministration, reform'. Private trusts can be enforced by the beneficiaries. Charitable trusts can be enforced by the Attorney General rather than by a beneficiary and so are subject to control. A trust for non-charitable purposes, rather than persons, has no beneficiary who can enforce it and the settlor will not be allowed to do so.[3] The lack of a beneficiary who can enforce the trust is why these trusts are sometimes known as trusts of imperfect obligation.

[2] This will impress the examiner at once as you are looking very precisely at exactly what the rationale for these trusts is.

[3] In this context it is important to demonstrate how non-charitable purpose trusts are the odd ones out as the other two types have an enforcement mechanism.

[4] There were in fact a number of purposes mentioned in the trust in this case but it is only necessary to select some to make the point that they were not charitable. You could mention other cases at this point such as *Leahy* v *A-G for NSW* but they simply illustrate the same point.

The effect of the rule that trusts for non-charitable purposes are void is seen in **Re Astor's ST** where a fund was left to be held for various non-charitable purposes including the maintenance of good relations between nations and the independence of newspapers.[4]

Although the beneficiary principle is stated to be the rationale for holding non-charitable trusts void, in fact trusts of this type were held valid in cases before **Re Astor**. For instance, in **Re Drummond** [1914] 2 Ch 90 HC a trust was upheld where the objects were the Old Boys of Bradford Grammar School and to acquire premises for a clubhouse. Suppose that in this case the trustees did not perform the trust then presumably the Old Boys could take action if they wished to. Conversely, if the trustees do perform the trust then there is no problem at all.

[5] We are now developing our answer by looking at the next issue: the anomalous cases where non-charitable purpose trusts have been enforced but tying this in to the main theme: what is the rationale here, if any?

The idea that the rationale is the beneficiary principle breaks down altogether in two cases where trusts for non-charitable purposes have long been held valid.[5]

One is trusts for the care of specific animals as in **Re Dean** (1889) 41 Ch D 552 HC and the other is a trust for the building or maintenance of a tomb or monument as in **Re Hooper** [1932] 1 Ch 38 HC where a testator made a gift for the care of some family graves and monuments and a tablet in a church window. In neither of these cases has the lack of an enforcement mechanism to enforce the trust caused difficulty, although these are of course very limited situations.

[6] At this point some research detail really helps to boost your marks and keeps the focus on the essential issue: the rationale for these trusts.

What is the rationale here?[6] Brown and Pawlowski (2012) argue that the rationale in **Re Dean** was simply that the court felt it was socially acceptable for testators to leave gifts in their will to look after their favourite pets as otherwise the cost would fall on the testator's family or the public. This is really a public policy ground and can be said to derive from the much broader principle of testamentary freedom: that a testator should be free to dispose of her estate as she pleases, a principle upheld by the HL in **Blathwayt v Baron Cawley** [1976] AC 397 HL.

The only exception is where the courts consider that the purposes of the trust are useless or capricious as in the Scottish case of **M'Caig v University of Glasgow** 1907 SC 231 where the object of the trust was to construct stone statues and towers in the likeness of the testator and his relatives at prominent points in Oban. The object was held by Lord Kyllachy as having 'no utility, private or public' and 'perpetuating at great cost, and in an absurd manner, the idiosyncrasies of an eccentric testator'.

Concern by the courts that the rule against the validity of non-charitable purpose trusts can cause perfectly worthwhile trusts to fail has led to complex attempts to hold them valid which themselves lack any clear rationale.[7] In **Re Denley's Trust Deed** [1969] 1 Ch 373 HC what appeared to be a trust for purposes was held to be one for individuals, and although this was an important development it cannot apply where the trust is one for purposes as such. Another possible case, that of trusts for masses, seems to have been taken out of this category by the decision in **Re Hetherington** [1989] 2 All ER 129 that these trusts are likely to be charitable.

[8] This should be where you really earn your extra marks. This area has been controversial for a long time and there have been various proposals for reform. It is essential that you are aware of these.

The question is whether there is any way forward so that these trusts can be, at least in some circumstances, enforced. There are in fact two possible ways.[8]

One is to hold that these trusts could take effect as mere powers. This would have the advantage that the enforceability point did not matter: a power is discretionary anyway and does not have to be carried out.

[9] It does help in making your argument clearer, and so adding to your marks, if you have separate paragraphs for each point as here.

[10] Here you are thinking laterally and using your knowledge from another area. Do this whenever possible: it is a perfectly valid approach as the law of trusts is a unity and it will undoubtedly impress an examiner.

The other and more radical solution is the introduction of an 'interested adversary principle'[9] where persons or institutions might be identified as being watchdogs to act in enforcing the trust. A bold decision of the courts might bring this about and the developing law on trusteeship may help.[10] In **Schmidt v Rosewood Trust Ltd** [2003] AC 709, an action concerning disclosure of trust documents, Lord Walker held that 'the more principled and correct approach is to regard the right to seek disclosure of trust documents as one aspect of the court's inherent jurisdiction to supervise, and if necessary to intervene in, the administration of trusts. The right to seek the court's intervention does not depend on entitlement to a fixed and transmissible beneficial interest.' Thus it might be possible to develop this line of argument to give the courts power to supervise a non-charitable purpose trust and it is interesting that Lord Walker mentions that the right to seek the courts' intervention does not depend on the existence of a beneficial interest. Thus an enforcer, who would not have a beneficial interest in the trust as of course there are no beneficial interests, might be allowed to intervene to enforce it.

For now, it is suggested that the question is correct: that the law does not have a clear rationale and so the adoption of the above ideas may help to achieve this.

Make your answer stand out

- Read and refer to Hayton (2001) who considers how this area can be developed in a more satisfactory way.
- Read and refer to Matthews (1996), another attempt at charting a way forward. This essay also gives a stimulating and clear account of the present law.
- Look at Brown (2007). This has some very interesting research detail on the extent to which trusts for animals, monuments and masses are used today and a suggestion that a promise given by a nominated person and contained in a 'deed of commitment and enforcement' could be a way of enforcing them.
- Mention, if only with a brief example, how the perpetuity principle has affected the operation of non-charitable purpose trusts.

! Don't be tempted to . . .

- Leave out the theoretical issues and plunge into the cases at once.
- Just give examples of cases where these types of trusts have been held to be invalid. You must discuss the background to the law first.
- Give very detailed accounts of the facts of cases. This is not a problem question where you need to set the facts alongside those of the problem. Instead use the cases to illustrate your points.

? Question 2

Jim, by will, directed his trustees, Frank and Brendan, to hold the following bequests on trust:

(a) £10,000 to hold on trust to look after my dog, Felix.

(b) £20,000 to care for and maintain the monument to myself which will be erected in the park of my home town Barset.

(c) £5,000 to the priest of St Peter's Church, Worcester to say masses for the repose of my soul.

(d) £50,000 to promote the admirable sport of fox hunting.

Consider whether these bequests are valid.

Answer plan

→ Consider in each case whether the gift could be charitable.

→ If it is not, then explain the general attitude of the law to non-charitable purpose trusts and mention the rationale for this.

→ Analyse each situation to establish if it comes within any of the exceptional cases where a trust for non-charitable purposes can be valid.

→ Consider whether the trust is affected by the rules against perpetuities.

→ Finally, look at any other reasons why the trust might fail, e.g. illegality.

Diagram plan

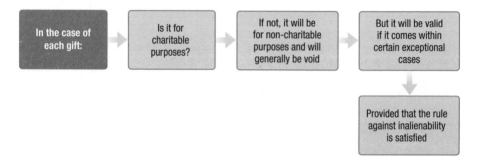

A printable version of this diagram plan is available from **www.pearsoned.co.uk/lawexpressqa**

Answer

[1] Although the conclusion turns out to be that the gift is not charitable, in a question like this you will be expected to first ask if it *could* be charitable.

[2] There is also the point that there is no public benefit but, as the purpose is not charitable anyway, there is no need to consider this.

[3] In addition to stating the law on why these trusts are generally invalid, you will gain credit if you explain briefly why this is so. This is a controversial area and the examiner will expect you to be aware of the rationale for the principle stated in *Re Astor*.

(a) The gift of £10,000 to look after the testator's dog Felix is not for charitable purposes,[1] as it does not come within any of the purposes set out by section 3 of the Charities Act 2011. Trusts for animal welfare are charitable by section 3(1)(k) of the Act but this is a trust for a particular animal.[2] It is therefore a trust for non-charitable purposes. These are generally void (**Re Astor** [1952] Ch 534 HC), as they are trusts of imperfect obligation in that there is no one to compel performance of them.[3] However, trusts for the care of specific animals form an exception to this principle and are valid as in **Re Dean** (1889) 41 Ch D 552 HC, where money was left for the maintenance of the testator's horses and hounds. However, such gifts must be limited to the perpetuity period. There are in fact

[4] Many students for some reason try to avoid the topic of perpetuities altogether and you will gain considerable credit for an accurate account of the law.

[5] You will see that we actually give the facts of three cases for this point. This is because the law is not settled and so we are looking for possible principles on which to base our answer.

two perpetuity rules and the applicable one here concerns inalienability of capital which prevents capital being tied up for too long a period.[4] The period cannot exceed that fixed by section 15(4) of the Perpetuities and Accumulations Act 1964, as lives or lives in being plus 21 years. As no other period is specified here, this will apply. In **Re Dean** itself the court seemed to ignore the perpetuity point as the gift was valid even though it was for 50 years provided that any of the horses and hounds should live that long.[5] However, in the Irish case of **Re Kelly** [1932] IR 255 HC the court stated that the life span of animals could not be taken as the measuring point for the perpetuity period and that lives meant human lives. In **Re Haines** (1952) *The Times,* 7 November judicial notice was taken of the proposition that a cat cannot live for more than 21 years and this validated the trust, but this is a trust for a dog and so it is suggested that expert evidence will be needed on how long a dog can live for. It is likely that the 'wait and see' provisions of the 1964 Act do not apply to non-charitable purpose trusts and so if there is the possibility at the outset that the perpetuity period will be infringed, as a dog is capable of living for more than 21 years, then the perpetuity period will apply and the gift will be void. Thus, the £10,000 will be held on a resulting trust for Jim's estate.

(b) The gift of '£20,000 to care for and maintain the monument to myself which will be erected in the park of my home town Barset' will not be charitable unless the monument is of such artistic value that it comes under section 3(1)(f) of the Charities Act 2011 as being for the advancement of arts, culture or heritage.[6] If not, it will be a non-charitable purpose trust and in principle void under the principle in **Re Astor**. However, a trust for the building or maintenance of a tomb or monument has been held valid as in **Re Hooper** [1932] 1 Ch 38 HC, where a testator made a gift for the care of some family graves and monuments and a tablet in a church window. On this basis the gift can be valid, although it must comply with the perpetuity period and no period is mentioned. As we have mentioned above, it is not possible to wait and see if, for example, the monument does not last for more than the perpetuity period and so this gift will be void.

[6] This is a good point which will earn you extra marks as once again you are showing your awareness of the *possibility* of charitable status.

(c) The gift of '£5,000 to the priest of St Peter's Church, Worcester to say masses for the repose of my soul' may be valid as a charitable trust under section 3(1)(b) of the Charities Act 2011 as being for the advancement of religion. In **Bourne v Keane** [1919] AC 815 the House of Lords established that gifts and trusts for the saying of masses were not void as being for superstitious uses as had at one time been the case but it did not decide that such trusts were charitable.[7] Thus there was a view that they came within the same category as trusts for animals and monuments as valid non-charitable purpose trusts, but in **Re Hetherington** [1989] 2 All ER 129 HC it was held that a trust for the celebration of masses was charitable because 'the public celebration of a religious rite edifies and improves those who attend it'.[8] The fact that the masses could be said in private was not a bar to charitable status as there was, in effect, one purpose, the saying of masses, capable of implementation in two different ways. One, public masses, is charitable, the other, private masses, is not. The court applied the principle that where a gift has a single purpose which could be performed by either charitable or non-charitable means, it should be construed as a gift to be performed by charitable means. A further ground for holding that the gift was charitable was that it was for the advancement of the priesthood as the gifts made provision for priests. The perpetuity point does not arise, as the rule against inalienability of gifts does not apply to charities on the basis that as charities are for the public benefit their continuance is to be encouraged.[9]

(d) The gift of £50,000 'to promote the admirable sport of fox hunting' will not count as a charitable trust as it does not come within any of the charitable purposes set out in section 3 of the Charities Act 2011. It is sometimes said that in **Re Thompson** [1934] Ch 342 HC the court held that a trust for the promotion of fox hunting was valid presumably as a non-charitable purpose trust.[10] In fact, the case concerned a gift to be applied to the promotion of fox hunting with a gift of residue to Trinity Hall, Cambridge. The issue was whether the trust was void, as there was no beneficiary, but the court held that it was not as the purpose was sufficiently certain. A trust for the promotion of fox hunting would now be void anyway, as it promotes an illegal purpose contrary to the Hunting Act 2004. Thus, this gift will fail and there will be a resulting trust of the £50,000 for Jim's estate.

[7] This is an area of law which has developed over the years and your answer will gain more marks if you set this out.

[8] Notice how you are building up your argument: the first case, *Bourne* v *Keane,* held that gifts for the saying of masses could be valid but in *Re Hetherington* it went further and held that in principle they were charitable. This is the type of approach which will impress an examiner.

[9] This point is not always understood, even by the courts, and so you will boost your marks by stating it correctly.

[10] The examiner will be checking to see if you fall into the common error of saying that this case held that trusts for the promotion of fox hunting are valid. As you can see, it did not.

Make your answer stand out

■ Read Parry (1989) who analyses the decision in *Re Hetherington* and looks at the history of the law on trusts for the saying of masses.

■ Mention some criticisms of the rule in *Re Astor* that trusts for non-charitable purposes are void, and possible ways in which the law could be changed so that they were valid. See, for example, Brown (2007) for one idea. This article is also useful in providing a very helpful and clear account of the law.

■ Explain that the cases where trusts for non-charitable purposes have been held valid are regarded as an anomaly and that the categories will not be extended.

! Don't be tempted to . . .

■ Fail to consider at the start of each answer if the gift could be charitable.

■ Omit to state that a gift will be valid without considering the perpetuity period.

■ Fail to find a home for the property if the trust fails.

Question 3

'It would astonish a layman to be told that there was a difficulty in his giving a legacy to an unincorporated non-charitable society which he had, or could have had, supported without trouble during his lifetime.' (Brightman J in *Re Recher's Will Trusts* [1972] Ch 526 at 536)

Examine what these difficulties are and critically consider whether the solutions to them adopted by the courts are satisfactory or whether a new approach to the problem of gifts to unincorporated associations is needed.

Answer plan

➔ Outline the fundamental problem – trusts for non-charitable purposes are void.

➔ Identify and analyse problems which flow from these: e.g. the fact that the society is not incorporated and the rule against inalienability.

➔ Explain how the decision in *Re Denley* might provide a solution.

➔ Explain how the decision in *Re Recher* might provide a solution.

➔ Conclusion – evaluate possible reforms of the law to make it easier to make gifts to unincorporated non-charitable bodies.

Diagram plan

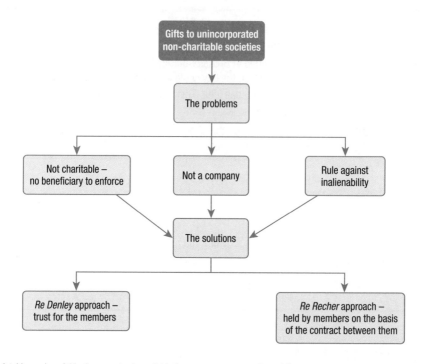

A printable version of this diagram plan is available from **www.pearsoned.co.uk/lawexpressqa**

Answer

[1] You need to get this essential point over very clearly at the start of the answer.

[2] You need to say something about why this rule exists but not too much as most of your answer will be devoted to explaining how the courts have attempted to avoid the consequences of this rule.

[3] This is another stage in your answer at which you could go off the point and you need to resist the temptation. Keep the idea of gifts to societies in mind.

The reason why there is a problem with gifts to unincorporated non-chari- table societies is that these gifts can infringe a number of rules. The crucial point is that as they are not charitable and as they are not private trusts for the benefit of identifiable beneficiaries they take effect as non-charitable purpose trusts which are generally void.[1] The basis of the rule is found in the beneficiary principle: a trust must have a beneficiary who can enforce it.[2] As Harman J said in **Re Wood** [1949] Ch 498 HC, 'a gift on trust must have a *cestui que* trust'. Thus, as there are no identified beneficiaries to enforce it as in the case of a private trust nor the Charity Commission in the case of a charitable trust, the trust is void. There are certain exceptions to this principle, for example trusts for the care of specific animals, but these do not affect gifts to societies.[3]

The next problem, which follows from the first, is that the society is not incorporated. If it was incorporated as a company then the gift would vest in that company immediately and there would be no question of a trust. As the society is not incorporated there cannot be a gift to it as it cannot hold property, and so any gift can only be for its purposes which are not charitable. The result is that we come back to the problem that there cannot be a trust for non-charitable purposes. In ***Re Finger's Will Trust*** [1972] Ch 286 HC a testatrix left shares of her residuary estate to various charities. One of these was an unincorporated association but as the gift was for charitable purposes it was valid. Had they not been charitable, it would have failed.[4]

The final problem is that trusts in these cases must comply with the rules against inalienability.[5] The inalienability rules are concerned with the tying up of money for an excessive time. As such they are applicable to non-charitable purpose trusts which could tie up a fund. The effect is that such a trust will be void unless from the beginning it is certain that persons will have become absolutely entitled by the end of a period fixed at lives or lives in being plus 21 years, and it should be noted that the 'wait and see' provisions of the Perpetuities and Accumulations Act 1964[6] do not apply to purpose trusts (see s. 15(4)). It is possible to fix a shorter time. If the gift had been charitable then the rule against inalienability would not have applied and if the gift had been to a company then it would have been irrelevant as the gift would have vested in the company at once.

Given these problems the courts have devised various solutions in an attempt to have some at least of gifts made to unincorporated non-charitable societies held valid.[7]

The first is that of Goff J in ***Re Denley's Trust Deed*** [1969] 1 Ch 373 HC, where he was able to construe what appeared to be a trust for purposes as one for individuals. A plot of land was conveyed to trustees 'for the purpose of a recreation or sports ground primarily for the benefit of the employees of the company' and also for the benefit of such other persons as the trustees might allow. This was held valid as a trust for the employees because they were entitled to the use of the land.

This decision has, however, been difficult to classify. Was the trust one for individuals, in which case there is no problem, or is it a kind of hybrid trust, being partly private and partly for purposes?[8]

---

[4] This is good examination technique as you are showing that although the facts of this case are not strictly relevant you have appreciated the principle behind the decision.

[5] This is a difficult area and you will boost your marks by a clear statement of the problem. Students often put the two rules in this area together under one heading of 'perpetuity' when in fact what we are concerned with is the inalienability of the gift. Remember that in this question you do not have to do the difficult job of actually applying the rule to a problem.

[6] Note that the Perpetuities and Accumulations Act 2009 does not apply here, as it only applies to cases where an interest may vest at too remote a time. Indeed, section 18 expressly states that it does not apply to any rule of law which limits the duration of non-charitable purpose trusts. The 1964 Act applies where the gift may be inalienable.

[7] This is the kind of linking sentence which you must always aim for in an answer. You have set out the problems and, as you are approaching halfway through the essay, it is time to turn to the possible solutions.

[8] This extra thinking will gain extra marks.

Another approach, and one which applies particularly to gifts to societies, is to hold that the gift is to the members of the society who will hold it, not on trust, but on the basis of the contract between them. In **Re Recher's Will Trust** [1972] Ch 526 HC a gift made to the London and Provincial Anti-Vivisection Society was held to be a beneficial gift to the members, not so as to entitle each of them to an immediate share but as an addition to the funds of the association subject to the contract between the members as set out in the rules. This approach was followed in **Re Lipinski's Will Trusts** [1976] Ch 235 HC, where a testator bequeathed half of his residuary estate in trust to an association to be used solely in constructing or maintaining the association's buildings. This was held valid as a gift to the members subject to the contract between them as members even though the word 'solely' might have indicated that a trust was intended for the purpose specified.

[9] An answer will always gain marks if it shows that you are aware of recent developments. This is an especially useful case to mention, as it illustrates the application of both the trust and the contract approaches explained earlier.

The most recent decision,[9] **Re Horley Town Football Club; Hunt v McLaren** [2006] EWHC 2386 (Ch), shows a development of this approach. This concerned a surplus arising on a sale of land held in trust as an endowment for an unincorporated association. It was held that the beneficial interest vested in the current full members and was held on a bare trust for them. This entitled them to call in a general meeting for the assets to be transferred to them as individuals. This decision follows the line of authority in **Re Recher** in basing the solution on contract, but the device of a trust is used to solve the problem of exactly where the legal ownership of the property lies pending any distribution between the members.

One problem with the approach in **Re Recher** is that a gift to the members may offend the rule against inalienability if there is something in the gift or its circumstances or the rules of the association which prevents the members from dividing the gift between them on the basis that they are solely entitled in equity. This is what caused the gift to fail in **Re Grant's Will Trusts** [1979] 3 All ER 359 HC, where a gift was made to the Chertsey Labour Party but the members could not change the rules and divide the gift between themselves because the rules were subject to control by the National Executive Committee of the Labour Party.

[10] A conclusion will always impress the examiner if it contains some new idea to lift the answer at the end. This is much better than a lame summary of what you have already said.

Therefore, there is no doubt that, as Brightman J said in **Re Recher**, a layman would indeed be astonished by the difficulties in making gifts to an unincorporated non-charitable society. One possible solution[10] is to allow a trust for non-charitable purposes to have an enforcer, who could in the case of a will be the residuary legatee, who would be able to take action if the terms of the gift were felt to be infringed. This would be a sensible reform, given that there is no objection on the grounds of public policy to these gifts and every reason for enforcing them.

 Make your answer stand out

- Refer to Brown (2007). This article gives a very helpful summary of the law and of its practical effects and then goes on to consider proposals for change.
- Look into what the basis of the decision in *Re Denley* was: see Matthews (1995).
- The decision in *Re Horley Town Football Club* is analysed by Luxton (2007).
- Consider the possibility that gifts to unincorporated non-charitable associations could be valid under the *Quistclose* principle (see Chapter 7).

! Don't be tempted to . . .

- Fail to make the distinction between charitable and non-charitable purposes clear.
- Miss the point that gifts to companies will vest at once.
- Fail to explain the inalienability rule.
- Quote too many cases on one area.

? Question 4

You are asked to advise on what should be done with surplus funds in the following cases:

(a) The Hanbury Park Association of Retired Lecturers in Land Law and Equity was founded to provide benefits for the spouses of these persons after they had died. It was a large and popular organisation with a lively membership which held a number of social events that were attended by members of the public and where funds were raised by an entry fee and the sale of raffle tickets. In addition, an anonymous donation of £5,000 was received which was believed to be from a grateful ex-student. However, the Association has only one member left, who is the Chairman. The surplus funds amount to £20,000.

(b) A collection was held for victims of a flood disaster in 1947 with the object of 'cheering them up' by providing them with holidays. However, all the victims of the flood have now died and a surplus of £5,000 remains. The trustees seek advice on what to do with this money.

Answer plan

→ Are the organisations charitable? If so, consider application of the funds *cy-près*.

→ Note that neither organisation is a company and so we must deal with the law on unincorporated associations.

→ In the case of the Hanbury Park Association, consider where the money came from in each case: the entry fee, the proceeds from the sale of raffle tickets and the donation, and apply the relevant law.

→ In the case of the fund for flood disaster victims, consider the possibility of the money going to the Crown as *bona vacantia* or being held as a private trust.

Diagram plan

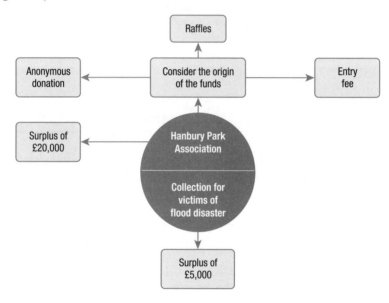

A printable version of this diagram plan is available from **www.pearsoned.co.uk/lawexpressqa**

[1] Check in a question of this kind whether you are told that the funds were *not* held for charitable purposes. If so, you should leave this first paragraph out. In this case, although it is fairly obvious that the organisation is not charitable, you should spend a paragraph, but no more, on this point.

Answer

(a) The first question is whether the association is charitable.[1] If it is then it will be possible for the surplus funds to be applied *cy-près* for other charitable objects provided that there was a general charitable intention and that the gift has failed within the meaning of section 62 of the Charities Act 2011. However, there

[2] Never in any answer just
refer to 'charitable purposes'
but always to 'charitable
purposes as defined by
section 3(1) of the Charities
Act 2011', as you are
making it clear that you are
concerned with the legal
definition of charity.

[3] This again is a point to
include if you are not told the
status of the organisation.
Almost certainly the
organisation will not be a
company, as this is a trusts
exam and not a company law
exam, but still watch for it.

[4] The opening paragraph
was, as it were, clearing the
ground and now you can
come to the main issue.

[5] It is worth showing the
examiner that you know
this, as it makes a clear
starting point for your answer.
However, you should then
move on quickly to consider
the question posed here.

[6] It is likely that you will not
be told what the rules are so
that you have to continue and
consider the various solutions
adopted by the courts. Even
so, you must always mention
that the association's rules
are the starting point.

[7] Although this is not likely
to be the answer you should
mention the resulting trust
solution, as it was adopted in
many cases.

is no evidence that the association was established for charitable purposes as defined by section 3(1) of the Charities Act 2011,[2] as there is no evidence that it was for the relief of poverty or the advancement of education. In addition, the class of beneficiaries is too small to have any public benefit. Thus, we must assume that it was not charitable. The other point is that the association is obviously not a company[3] and so it is an unincorporated association. Thus the distribution of its funds will be governed by trust law and not by company law.

Thus we need to examine the case law on the distribution of the surplus funds of unincorporated non-charitable associations.[4] The usual rule is that the actual funds of an association are held by the members (**Neville Estates Ltd v Madden** [1962] Ch 832 HC). The alternative, that they are held on trust, is only possible if the trust is charitable. [5] However, in this case we are dealing with a claim to the surplus assets of the association when it is dissolved.

The first step must be to see what the rules of the association say, as these form a contract between the members and so will govern the matter.[6] It would seem strange that an association of lawyers specialising in equity and land law should have an association which did not provide for what was to happen if it was dissolved, but we are not told of any and so must assume that there were none.

The anonymous donation could be held to go on a resulting trust[7] for those who contributed it, as in **Re Gillingham Bus Disaster Fund** [1958] 2 All ER 749 HC, where a surplus remained from a fund raised mainly from street collections and other non-identifiable sources. The court held that the money was to be held on a resulting trust for the donors because, as Harman J said, 'the donor did not part with his money out and out absolutely' but only to the extent that his wishes as declared by the trust could be carried into effect. Thus, when 'this has been done any surplus still belongs to him'. This is a most unfortunate solution, as the money may simply remain in court as the donor may never come forward. A preferable solution is that adopted in **Re West Sussex Constabulary's Benevolent Fund Trust** [1970] 1 All ER 544 HC, where it was held that the donors, as they were anonymous, must have intended to have parted with their money out and out. The relationship was one of contract, not trust, and so the sum would go to the Crown as *bona vacantia.*

[8] This gives you an opportunity to deal with these separately. The examiner obviously intended you to do this, otherwise they would not have been mentioned.

This solution could apply to the money paid to attend fund-raising events and raffle tickets, [8] where it was held in the **West Sussex** case on similar facts that the relationship was one of contract not trust: those who paid for the entertainment had had their entertainment and so no longer had any claim to the money. Thus, again, the money will go to the Crown as *bona vacantia.* However, the *bona vacantia* solution is also unsatisfactory, as the contributors can never have intended their money to end up in the hands of the Crown.

The other solution would be to follow **Re Bucks Constabu-lary Widows' and Orphans' Fund Friendly Society (No 2)** [1979] 1 WLR 936 HC and hold that as all the funds are assets of the association they should be held for the members alive at the date of the dissolution. The problem here is that Walton J held that, where there is only one member of an association left, as here, then the association must cease to exist and the surviving member cannot claim the funds. In that case the only destination of the assets would be as *bona vacantia* to the Crown.

[9] This is now the leading case to refer to in this area.

However, in the recent case of **Hanchett-Stamford v Attorney General** [2008] EWHC 30 (Ch),[9] the last surviving member was allowed to claim the funds. The claimant was, on her husband's death, the last surviving member of the Performing and Captive Animals Defence League, which was an unincorporated non-charitable association. She wished the assets, amounting to nearly £1.5 million, to be held on trust to select a charity with similar objects to whom the funds could be given. Lewison J could not see the logic in saying that 'if there are two members of an association which has assets of, say, £2m, they can by agreement divide those assets between them and pocket £1m each, but if one of them dies before they have divided the assets, the whole pot goes to the Crown as *bona vacantia*'. In addition, he took account of Article 1 of the First Protocol of the European Convention on Human Rights. This provides that no one is to be deprived of their possessions except in the public interest and subject to the conditions provided by law.[10]

[10] This is the kind of extra detail which will gain you marks.

(b) The problem with the fund raised for victims of flood disasters is that it does not seem to have been charitable, as the provision of holidays may not be considered a charitable purpose as defined by section 1(1) of the Charities Act 2011. There is no evidence that the fund was for the relief of poverty, and funds raised for victims of disasters cannot give benefits to victims which exceed their needs. This problem arose with funds contributed to the Penlee Lifeboat Disaster Fund in 1981 (see **Re Picarda** (1982) 132 NLJ 223). If the fund is not charitable then it could go to the Crown as *bona vacantia,* as it will now be impossible to trace the subscribers. If they could be traced, it would be held on a resulting trust for them. The solution in the Penlee Lifeboat case was to simply treat the fund as a private trust which, as it is for the benefit of individuals, makes sense both legally and in practice as it allowed the money to be distributed among the families. In this case it could be distributed among the descendants of the victims.

[11] Do not forget this last point. We cannot be certain that it is *not* charitable.

Finally, if the fund is charitable[11] then it will be possible for the surplus funds to be applied *cy-près* for other charitable objects provided that there was a general charitable intention and that the gift has failed within the meaning of section 62 of the Charities Act 2011.

 Make your answer stand out

■ Read and refer to Baughen (2010), which analyses the decision in *Hanchett-Stamford* v *Attorney General*. This is an important decision and you can expect questions on it in an exam.

■ Mention, by way of comparison, the position on the distribution of the surplus funds of pension schemes – see *Davis* v *Richards and Wallington Ltd* [1990] 1 WLR 1511 and *Air Jamaica Ltd* v *Charlton* [1999] 1 WLR 1399.

■ See if you can find any details on what actually happened to the money contributed in *Re Gillingham*.

! Don't be tempted to . . .

- Forget to deal first with the possibility that the organisations are established for charitable purposes.
- Fail to identify that they are not companies and so are unincorporated.
- Deal with only one possible solution to the question of where the surplus goes.
- Come to very definite conclusions. We cannot be certain, for example, that the trust for flood victims is *not* charitable.

www.pearsoned.co.uk/lawexpressqa

 Go online to access more revision support including additional essay and problem questions with diagram plans, You be the marker questions, and download all diagrams from the book.

Trusteeship and variation of trusts

How this topic may come up in exams

This is a fertile area for essay questions with obvious ones on the nature of trusteeship, the idea of a fiduciary, the relationship between the Trustee Acts and the trust instrument and, if it is in your syllabus, variation of trusts. Problems can be on particular duties and powers of trustees, with likely candidates being investment, inspection of trust documents, maintenance and advancement.

Obvious links are with constructive trusts (Chapter 8) as a constructive trust can be imposed where a trustee is in breach of fiduciary duty, and remedies for breach of trust (Chapter 12) as these will be relevant once you have decided that the trustee has broken a term of the trust.

Before you begin

It's a good idea to consider the following key themes of trusteeship and variation of trusts before tackling a question on this topic.

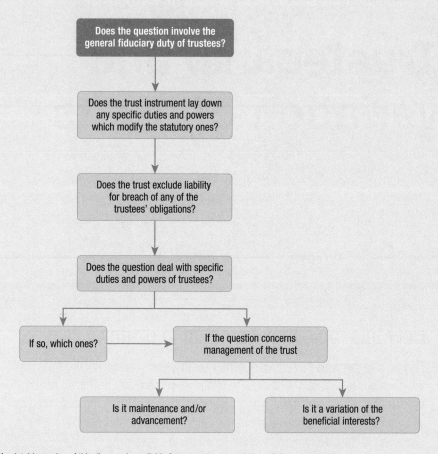

A printable version of this diagram is available from **www.pearsoned.co.uk/lawexpressqa**

❓ Question 1

Tim and Ted are trustees of a fund of £500,000 established by the will of Edgar to be held for each of Edgar's children in equal shares on their reaching the age of 25. There are three children, Ben, aged 17, Sue, aged 19 and Jack, aged 22. Tim is a solicitor and Ted is a family friend.

Jack is a trainee investment manager and tells Tim and Ted that shares in a property company in South America represent a 'fantastic investment opportunity' and that they should act quickly and give him a cheque for 'as much as they can' out of the trust funds. Tim and Ted write to Ben and Sue saying 'What do you think of this?' and asking for an 'urgent reply'. They both reply at once. Ben says 'Why not?' and Sue says 'This is a wonderful idea!'

Tim and Ted hand over a cheque for £300,000 drawn on the trust made out to Jack personally. Jack did not invest the money as promised but instead spent all the money on a racehorse which collapsed and died in its next race.

Advise Sue and Ben on any action which they can take and against whom.

Answer plan

→ Explain the significance of the general duty of care in section 1 of the Trustee Act 2000.

→ Explain the rules in the Trustee Act 2000 on investment.

→ Critically consider how the rules on delegation apply, especially in the context of investment powers.

→ Explain possible remedies of the beneficiaries.

→ Consider any possible defences available to the trustees.

Diagram plan

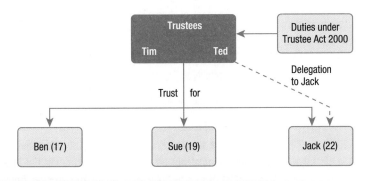

A printable version of this diagram plan is available from **www.pearsoned.co.uk/lawexpressqa**

Answer

[1] This shows the examiner at once that you are aware that there are two areas to this question and so makes an excellent start. There is no point in looking at possible remedies until you have identified if there have been any breaches of trust. Then go on and make a habit of asking if there are any express powers contained in the trust instrument. This not only shows a logical approach but is also exactly what you would do in practice. Finally, make a note to mention the possibility of an exclusion clause as well at the start. There is no need for any more detail on this in this answer.

[2] Although this question deals with a particular area, that of liability for breach of trust in the exercise of the power of investment, it is important to begin with this general principle and then go on to deal with particular specific areas.

[3] This is important: make the contrast between section 3, which deals with what the trustees can legally do, and section 4 which deals with the actual criteria when investing.

This question first asks us to consider if there have been any breaches of trust and then, if so, to look at what remedies are available and against whom. The question does not say that there are any express powers in the trust instrument and so this answer is on the basis that the trustees' powers are statutory. Nor are we told that there is any clause purporting to exclude the liability of trustees.[1]

Section 1 of the Trustee Act 2000[2] provides that a trustee must exercise such care and skill as is reasonable in the circumstances having regard in particular to:

(a) Any special knowledge or experience which he has or holds himself out as having.

(b) If he acts in the course of a business or profession, to any special knowledge or experience that it is reasonable to expect of a person acting in the course of that business or profession.

In this case Tim is a solicitor whereas Ted is a family friend. Solicitors are not investment experts but they should know the law and it is suggested that this may place a higher standard on him. On the other hand Ted as a family friend may have extra knowledge of the circumstances and needs of the beneficiaries.

Section 3 of the Trustee Act provides that a trustee may make any investment that he could make if he was absolutely entitled under the trust. Thus the trustees did have power to make the investment[3] suggested by Jack of shares in a property company in South America. However, when trustees are investing they must have regard to the standard investment criteria in section 4, which are:

(a) the suitability to the trust of particular investments;

(b) the need for diversification of investments, so far as this is appropriate.

These criteria reflect the portfolio theory of investments whereby investments must not be considered in isolation but looked at in the context of the portfolio as a whole and an overall investment strategy.

In this case the trustees proposed to invest £300,000 out of a total trust fund of £500,000 in an overseas company. This is clearly a speculative investment which might be appropriate in some trusts but here there is a family trust which will end at the latest date in eight years when Ben, the youngest beneficiary, reaches 25. A speculative investment, which may take years to realise its potential, does not seem to satisfy the criteria in section 4.[4]

[4] Note this practical point relating the very general rules in sections 3 and 4 to the facts. It shows how you can analyse a situation and will gain you extra marks.

Finally, section 5 provides that trustees must obtain and consider 'proper advice' about the way in which the power on investment should be exercised having regard to the standard investment criteria. Proper advice is defined as the advice of a person reasonably believed by the trustees to be qualified to give it by reason of their ability in and practical experience of financial matters relating to the proposed investment. Clearly Jack, who was an investment trainee aged only 22, does not come into this category. Although trustees need not obtain advice if they reasonably conclude that in the circumstances it is unnecessary or inappropriate to do so, this obviously does not apply here.

[5] Although the investment was never made the trustees still intended to make it and so this issue needed to be explored.

Thus even if the investment proposed by Jack had been made it would have been in breach of trust.[5]

However, the trustees simply delegated the investment decision to Jack by handing him a cheque made out to him personally. Section 11 of the Trustee Act 2000 provides that trustees may delegate all decisions except those contained in a list set out in the section. Investment is not in this list and so may be delegated. However, by handing over the cheque to a person who cannot reasonably be considered a suitable agent the trustees are clearly in breach of their statutory duty of care laid down in section 1. In addition they have in effect employed Jack as an agent and they can be liable for his acts. Section 23 of the Trustee Act 2000[6] provides that a trustee is not liable for the acts or defaults of the agent unless he has failed to observe the standard of care when appointing the agent or keeping the arrangement under review. Clearly both trustees are liable for Jack's acts. Having established that there has been a breach of trust we now turn to consider the remedies.

[6] We have mentioned two sections of the Trustee Act 2000 whereas many students would only have mentioned one. They are both relevant and so your marks will be increased.

One which is not open to the beneficiaries is a tracing remedy under which they can follow the trust property as the proceeds of the trust fund were all invested in a racehorse which is now dead.[7] Thus any remedy will be a personal remedy against the trustees for their breach of trust.

However, Jack, one of the beneficiaries, actually instigated the breach of trust and so he cannot claim any compensation, and under section 62 of the Trustee Act 1925 his interest in the trust may be impounded to satisfy the claims of the other beneficiaries.

It may be argued that any action by Ben and Sue is barred as they consented to the breach of trust. However, Ben is 17 and so as he was not of full age when he wrote his letter of apparent consent, he can still claim. Sue is 19 and of course over full age but she could argue, first, that the letter from Tim and Ted did not give all the relevant facts as it just said 'What do you think of this?' and, second, that she was put under pressure as they asked for an 'urgent reply'. Thus it is suggested that they can both claim.

Tim and Ted may try to use the defence in section 61 of the Trustee Act 1925 under which the court may relieve a trustee from liability if he has acted honestly and reasonably and ought fairly to be excused both for the breach and for omitting to obtain the directions of the court. In **Nationwide Building Society v Davisons Solicitors** [2012] EWCA Civ 1626 it was emphasised that the standard of trustees under section 61 was reasonableness not perfection but it is suggested that in view of Tim and Ted's conduct outlined above they would not be held to have acted reasonably and so could not rely on section 61.

[8] It is essential that you mention the actual remedy in the question such as this as this is what the question has been leading up to.

Assuming that Ben and Sue claim against Tim and Ted, the measure of liability will be to restore to the trust all the property (the £300,000) which was wrongly taken from it, with interest.[8]

[9] Problem questions in this area often involve two or more trustees and if this is so then you must state and apply this rule.

Tim is a solicitor whereas Ted is a family friend. Although all trustees are individually liable for their own actual breaches, they are jointly and severally liable to compensate the beneficiaries and the fundamental equitable rule is that no regard is taken of fault.[9] Accordingly, a beneficiary can sue one or some or all of them and recover the entire loss from those trustees against whom he brings the action (**Bahin v Hughes** (1886) LR 31 Ch D 390). Thus Ben and Sue may claim against either or both trustees.

Make your answer stand out

- Explore the implications of Tim being a solicitor.
- Research the Law Commission in its Report *Trustees' Powers and Duties* No 260 (1999) especially Part III (Duty of Care) and Part IV (Trustees' Powers of Delegation). These will add value to your answer by giving extra detail on why the Trustee Act 2000 was passed and what the law was before.
- Read Clements (2004). This is a very valuable survey of the background to the Trustee Act 2000.
- Consider *Re Evans* [1999] 2 All ER 777 which dealt with section 61 of the Trustee Act 1925.
- End your answer by referring to *Re Partington* (1887) 57 LT 654 where the breach was committed solely on the advice of one trustee who had to indemnify his co-trustee and explain that this is not so here.

! Don't be tempted to . . .

- Fail to check the ages of the beneficiaries at the start.
- Ignore the remedies for breach of trust issue.
- Jump straight to the remedies for breach of trust issue and fail to start by asking if there has been a breach of trust at all.
- Miss the point that one trustee is a solicitor. You would not have been told this for nothing.

❓ Question 2

Fred died on 1 September 2014 and has left £400,000 to Anne and Sue to hold on trust for his two children, Jack and Charles, in equal shares for them on reaching the age of 21. You are asked to advise Anne and Sue on whether they should agree to any of the following requests made to them by the beneficiaries:

(a) Jack is 19 and a promising opera singer. He has asked for £120,000 to be paid to him now so that he can go to Milan for specialist opera tuition for a year and to meet his accommodation and living expenses whilst there. He intends to ask his girlfriend Maria to accompany him.

(b)   Charles is 14 and is a promising cricketer. He has asked the trustees to pay the fees of £5,000 a year at a specialist cricket academy in Australia for five years so that he can improve his skills as a cricketer and at the same time continue with his academic studies there.

How, if at all, would your answer differ if Fred had died on 1 November 2014?

Answer plan

➜ Explain that Anne and Sue as trustees have statutory powers and do not appear to have any additional ones conferred by the trust instrument.

➜ Distinguish between powers and duties and explain what each means.

➜ Note the ages of the beneficiaries as Jack is over 18 and so is automatically entitled to income.

➜ Analyse powers of maintenance in relation to Charles.

➜ Analyse powers of advancement in relation to Jack.

➜ End by applying the relevant provisions of the Inheritance and Trustees' Powers Act 2014.

Diagram plan

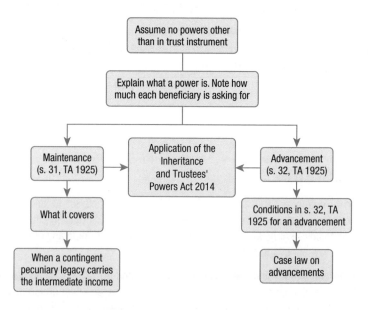

A printable version of this diagram plan is available from **www.pearsoned.co.uk/lawexpressqa**

Answer

¹ Make it a habit to begin any answer to a problem question on this area by explaining the relationship between statutory powers and those in the trust instrument. You should then as here check whether there are in fact any relevant powers in the trust instrument. Finally you should mention as we have done that trustees have powers and what this means. Put all of these three points in at the start of your answer and you have laid a solid foundation for a really good mark.

² Always note ages of beneficiaries: this is one reason why you should do so.

³ Begin the details of your answer by stating the law clearly and concisely.

⁴ State exactly what section 32 says and then go on to the cases.

This question is concerned with the statutory powers of trustees, in sections 31 and 32 of the Trustee Act 1925, of maintenance and advancement. These are additional to any powers contained in the trust instrument and are also subject to the general provision in section 69(2) of the Trustee Act 1925 that the statutory powers conferred on trustees only apply in the absence of a contrary intention. As we are not told of any specific powers in the trust instrument we will assume that there are none and assume that the trustees' powers are in sections 31 and 32. The other general point is that the trustees have a power¹ and not a duty and as powers are discretionary they do not have to agree to any request for maintenance and advancement.

(a) Jack is 19 and the statutory power to pay maintenance ceases at the age of 18² and he is entitled to the income unless there is a contrary intention, of which there is no evidence here. Thus Jack is entitled to the income. However, Jack is not entitled to the capital until he is 21 and so he must ask the trustees to exercise the power of advancement. Section 32 allows trustees to make advancements out of capital provided that:³

(i) The total sum which is paid does not exceed half of the beneficiary's share. Jack is entitled to half of a fund presently standing at £400,000 which means that he is entitled to £200,000 at 21. Half of this is £100,000 and so Jack cannot be advanced more than this.

(ii) If a beneficiary has a prior interest he must be of full age and consent in writing to the advancement. However, this does not apply here.

It is also worth noting that if an advancement is made to Jack then he must bring the amount of the advancement into account when the fund is distributed (s. 32(1)(b)), otherwise he would be paid twice.

The question is then whether the trustees should exercise their power of advancement. Section 32 refers to 'advancement or benefit'.⁴ Advancement has been held to refer to establishing the beneficiary in life through, for example, buying or furnishing a house, and the word 'benefit' seems to give a wider meaning to the term (**Re Kershaw's Trusts** (1868) LR 6 Eq 322 HC). It is suggested that if there is evidence that this course will indeed enable Jack to pursue a career as an opera singer then an advancement could be made but the amount, even reduced to £100,000, does seem high.[5] In **Re Pauling's Settlement Trusts (No 1)** [1964] Ch 303 HC the court held that where trustees prescribe a particular purpose for which the money is to be used they cannot leave the beneficiary entirely free to spend it for that purpose or in any other way that he chooses and so the trustees should make sure that the sum of £100,000 will be used for this purpose.

The other point is that the advancement should not be used to benefit others, as in this case Maria, but Jack might use **Re Kershaw's Trusts** where an advancement to the beneficiary's husband to enable him to set up a business in England and so prevent the family from separating was held valid. He might argue that if £100,000 is paid to him for Maria's benefit also then it will prevent them from separating.

(b) Charles has asked for £5,000 a year for five years, which will take him to the age of 19. As he is entitled to £200,000 at 21 this sum might come out of income, in which case the trustees could exercise their power of maintenance.[6] This is a power to pay such income as the trustees consider reasonable for the maintenance, education or benefit of an infant beneficiary. Moreover, trustees must consider the age of the infant, his requirements and all other circumstances. Trustees may pay the income to the infant (minor's) parent or guardian, if any, or otherwise apply the money (s. 31(1)(i) of the Trustee Act 1925). Thus the money could be paid direct to the academy. However, section 31(3) provides that maintenance can only be paid when a person is entitled to the income. Here there is a contingent pecuniary legacy as the sum is contingent on the beneficiaries attaining the age of 21.[7] A contingent pecuniary legacy does not carry the intermediate income unless any of the following apply:

(i) The legacy was given by the father of the minor or some person *in loco parentis* to the beneficiary, provided that no other fund is set aside for the maintenance of the legatee (**Re West** [1913] 2 Ch 345 HC) and the contingency is the attainment of the legatee's majority (*Re Jones* [1932] 1 Ch 642 HC).

(ii) The testator shows an intention to maintain the legatee (*Re Churchill* [1909] 2 Ch 431 HC).

(iii) The testator sets the legacy aside so as to be available for the legatee as soon as the contingency arises (*Re Medlock* (1886) 55 LJ Ch 738 HC).

It appears that (i) above will apply unless there is another fund set aside for Charles' maintenance and there is no evidence that this is so. Thus the trustees will have power to pay the sum requested out of income or, if there is insufficient income, out of capital. The only point is that the trustees may be reluctant to enter into a commitment for some years ahead but as the power of maintenance ceases at 18, Charles will have the income paid direct to him during his last year at the academy and so the commitment will only be for four years. It is suggested that the trustees could agree to this request.

If Fred had died on 1 November 2014 then my answer would differ as the trust would be governed by the Inheritance and Trustees' Powers Act 2014 which, by section 10(4) applies to trusts created or arising after the Act came into force on 1 October 2014.[8] In relation to the exercise of the power of advancement in relation to Jack in (a), section 9 of this Act allows the trustees to advance the whole of the capital but subject to the same considerations as before. So the trustees can, if they wish, advance Jack the £120,000 that he asks for but as was pointed out the sum of £100,000 is high and so £120,000 will be even more so.

Section 8 of the Act widens the powers of maintenance by amending section 31[9] so that trustees may pay such maintenance as they think fit rather than such as they consider reasonable and the requirement to consider the age of the infant, his requirements and all other circumstances has gone. The effect is to widen the discretion of the trustees and make it less likely that its exercise can be challenged. However, trustees still have a discretion but it is suggested that in relation to Charles in (b) it may still be reasonable to enter into this commitment, the only caveat being the length of time that the commitment is for.

[8] This is clearly going to be a feature of questions on this area so do note this date carefully.

[9] Note that the rules on when a contingent pecuniary interest carries the intermediate income are still in force.

Make your answer stand out

- Read and refer to the recent decision in *Southgate* v *Sutton* [2011] EWCA Civ 637 which is considered in the answer to Question 4 below. The effect was to confer on the trustees a wider power to make advancements. Read and refer to Ker (1953) on intermediate income. This may help you to understand what can be a difficult area.

- Read the Report of the Law Reform Committee (1982) Cmnd 8733 Paragraphs 4.43 and 4.44 on the effect of inflation on advancements. You may be able to include a brief mention of this in your answer.

- Read and refer to *X* v *A* [2006] 1 WLR 741: an interesting case providing an illustration of when an advancement can be refused.

! Don't be tempted to . . .

- Forget to make a note at the start of the ages of the beneficiaries and when they will be entitled to maintenance and advancement.

- Forget when beneficiaries are entitled to income anyway.

- Leave out the first paragraph setting out three basic points.

- Leave out any mention of contingent pecuniary interests as if you do your answer will be incomplete and you will lose marks.

Question 3

'Relaxing the traditional means of controlling trustees by relying on intervention from those holding beneficial interests has led to possibilities of abuse.' (Davies, 2004, p. 1)

Critically consider this statement in the context of disclosure of trust documents to beneficiaries.

Answer plan

→ State the present law in Lord Walker's judgment in *Pitt* v *Holt*.

→ Explain how a robust law on disclosure of trust documents is an essential weapon in controlling trustee decisions.

→ Critically consider the case law before *Schmidt* v *Rosewood Trust Ltd* on access of beneficiaries to trust documents.

→ Evaluate the effect of the decision in *Schmidt* v *Rosewood Trust Ltd* on this area.

→ Consider the decision in *Breakspear* v *Ackland* and see if it can be distinguished from *Schmidt* v *Rosewood*.

→ Conclude by mentioning the twin ideas of confidentiality and accountability.

Diagram plan

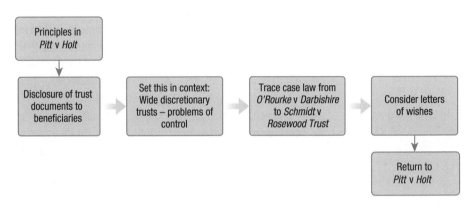

A printable version of this diagram plan is available from **www.pearsoned.co.uk/lawexpressqa**

Answer

The principles on when the courts can control the discretionary actions of trustees were set out by Lord Walker in **Pitt v Holt** [2013] UKSC 26: 'Trustees must act in good faith, responsibly and reasonably. They must inform themselves, before making a decision, of matters which are relevant to the decision. These matters may not be limited to simple matters of fact but will, on occasion (indeed, quite often) include taking advice from appropriate experts, whether the experts are lawyers, accountants, actuaries, surveyors, scientists or whomsoever.'

Lord Walker's judgment was delivered in the context of litigation involving undoing of mistakes by trustees and the so-called rule in **Re Hastings-Bass** [1975] Ch 25 HC but it was intended to have wider application.

[1] This is vital: the law on disclosure of trust documents must be seen against the general law on control of discretionary decisions by trustees of which it forms part.

The problem is that even though **Pitt v Holt** represents a tightening up of the extent to which the courts can control decisions of trustees, if beneficiaries are denied access to trust documents then their means of control are blunted.[1]

The starting point is **McPhail v Doulton** [1971] AC 424 which upheld the validity of wide discretionary trusts.[2] However, as Davies (2004) points out 'as with **Donoghue v Stevenson** some 40 years earlier, control mechanisms are scarcely able to limit them' as the only persons allowed to seek the intervention of the courts were those with defined beneficial interests and in the case of very wide discretionary trusts there might be few if any of these.

[2] The link to wide discretionary trusts is an absolutely crucial point in the success of this essay.

The first modern case on disclosure of documents is **O'Rourke v Darbishire** [1920] AC 581 CA where Lord Wrenbury said that: 'The beneficiary is entitled to see all trust documents because they are trust documents and because he is a beneficiary. They are in this sense his own . . . ' The effect was to limit the right to challenge decisions to those with specific beneficial interests.[3] In **Re Londonderry's Settlement** [1965] Ch 918 CA the Court of Appeal refused the beneficiary access to documents that would show why the trustees chose to distribute the fund in the way that they did. Disclosure had been sought of minutes and agendas of trust meetings and correspondence between the trustees and their agents. The court held that trustees of a discretionary family settlement such as this could not discharge their duties if: '[A]t any moment there is likely to be an investigation for the purpose of seeing whether they have exercised their discretion in the best possible manner.'

[3] This is where you link with the theme which you set out at the start.

However, it is arguable that the court failed to clarify the basis on which beneficiaries could assert a right to see documents. Nor did it clearly address the fundamental question of exactly what are trust documents. Salmon LJ simply said that they are 'documents in possession of the trustees containing information about the trust which the beneficiaries are entitled to know', but this lacks any precision. At the heart of the court's reasoning in **Re Londonderry's Settlement** is the perceived need for confidentiality in trustees' decision making, especially in family type trusts, supported by the decision in **Re Beloved Wilkes' Charity** (1851) 3 Mac & G 440 HC that as a general rule a trustee is not required to disclose his or her reasons for exercising a discretionary power. Here we return to **Pitt v Holt**[4] as it is arguable that a principle allowing the courts to exercise greater control over the decisions of trustees is stymied by a rule that denies access to the trustees' reasons for their decisions.

[4] Do emphasise the change in the law made by *Pitt v Holt*.

[5] This is a crucial link in this answer. It was necessary to deal with the earlier cases as they contained the law on disclosure of trust documents, but you must now make the point that the question is concerned with trusts which give trustees a wide discretionary power and discuss how to apply the law on disclosure of trust documents to this type of trust.

With the decision in **Schmidt v Rosewood Trust Ltd** we move from family trusts to a quite different type of trust[5] with which this question is concerned: the very wide discretionary trust of the kind approved in **Re Hay's Settlement Trusts** [1982] 1 WLR 202 HC.

There were three issues: first, who is entitled to seek disclosure; second, what evidence do they need to show in order to make out a case for disclosure; and, third, on what principles should it be ordered?

The facts of **Schmidt v Rosewood Trust Ltd** concerned an application by the administrator of the estate of Schmidt who was a possible object of the very wide power conferred by the trust to add any number of beneficiaries but under **O'Rourke v Darbishire** he was not at this point an actual beneficiary and so did not 'own' the documents.

[6] Here we get to the heart of the matter: the fact that in this case the court recognised the need for a different approach.

However, the Judicial Committee rejected the proposition that the right to seek the court's intervention depended on entitlement to a fixed and transmissible beneficial interest and that the beneficiaries had to have a proprietary interest in the documents.[6] Instead it held that Schmidt had a strong claim as the right to seek disclosure of trust documents was one aspect of the court's inherent jurisdiction to supervise, and if necessary to intervene in, the administration of trusts. The Judicial Committee recognised that the courts are now dealing with a completely different type of trust from that, for example, in **Re Londonderry's Settlement** where there was a family trust and where one could rely on, in Davies' phrase, 'the integrity of trustees'. With wide discretionary trusts there is more scope for abuse and so a restrictive approach to who is entitled to seek disclosure of trust documents would simply mean that there would be less chance that any possible abuse would go undetected.[7]

[7] This is a vital paragraph for gaining high marks as you are linking the different approaches in the cases to the policy reasons for requiring greater control of trustees' decisions by the courts, and so you are going right back to the central issue in the question.

[8] This is where you will gain marks provided that you can demonstrate how this case is relevant to the question. Do not treat it as just another case on disclosure of documents.

Another area where there has been recent discussion of disclosure of documents has been letters of wishes.[8] These have gained in popularity as a means of the settlor setting out how he/she wishes the trustees to exercise their discretion, although they have no binding force.

In **Breakspear v Ackland** [2008] EWHC 220 (Ch) the settlor signed a letter of wishes stating that his third wife, who was a beneficiary under a trust set up by him along with children by his first marriage, should be adequately provided for. The issue was whether this letter should be disclosed by the trustees to the children. Briggs J emphasised that letters of wishes should generally be kept confidential from the beneficiaries. Trustees are accountable for the financial management of the trust assets and so trust financial statements must be disclosed to the beneficiaries but letters of wishes are clearly not in this category and thus disclosure would not be ordered.

[9] This leads on from the previous footnote as now we are showing how the case ties in with the rest of our answer.

This decision can be reconciled with **Schmidt v Rosewood Trust Ltd** as **Breakspear v Ackland** concerned a family trust as in **Re Londonderry's Settlement**.[9] However, the consequence may be that we are moving to two sets of laws in this area, one for family-type trusts of the kind as in this case and the other for large discretionary trusts, with confidentiality the watchword in the first case and accountability in the second. However, if there is too much emphasis on confidentiality, how will it be possible for courts to make trustees accountable and exercise more detailed control over discretionary decisions of trustees as indicated by **Pitt v Holt**? If access to trust documents is still denied will there still be 'possibilities of abuse' as mentioned in the question?[10]

[10] Note how in our last sentence we have come back to the words of the question.

✓ Make your answer stand out

- Read and refer to Davies (2004) 'The integrity of trusteeship' in full. It is a most valuable summary of the law and contains a clear account of *Schmidt* v *Rosewood Trust Ltd*. Note in particular his criticism of the decision because: 'It is not however obvious what an applicant for a disclosure order will have to demonstrate before the order is issued.'

- Consider the type of trust set up in *Re Hay's Settlement Trusts* as this will give you more background to the question.

- Read and refer to Griffiths (2008) 'An inevitable tension? The disclosure of letters of wishes'. The author looks at the shift from confidentiality to accountability.

- Look at cases post-*Schmidt* v *Rosewood Trust Ltd*, such as the New Zealand decision in *Foreman* v *Kingstone* [2004] 1 NZLR 841.

- Forget to deal with the general issue of control by the courts of trustees: this question focuses on one issue, disclosure of documents, and you must concentrate on this.
- Just look at the details of the law on disclosure of documents but *link this* to the general theme of control of trustees.
- Ignore the letter of wishes issue.
- Ignore any underlying reasons for the decisions of the courts – a good example is *Re Londonderry's Settlement.*

Question 4

'The court has discretion to approve an arrangement under the Act, even though the settlement may make it crystal clear that the settlor or testator does not want any departure from any of the strict terms of the trust.' (Mummery LJ in *Goulding* v *James* [1997] 4 All ER 239 CA)

Critically consider the jurisdiction of the courts to vary beneficial interests under a trust especially in the light of this observation by Mummery LJ on the operation of the Variation of Trusts Act 1958.

Answer plan

→ Set the scene by explaining when trusts can be varied and when the consent of the beneficiaries is needed.

→ Set out the provisions of the Variation of Trusts Act dealing with when the court can approve a variation in the beneficial interests under a trust.

→ Emphasise the fundamental point that the court cannot approve a variation unless it is for the benefit of those on whose behalf it is sought.

→ Critically consider cases where the intentions of the settlor seem to have been overridden by the courts in consenting to a variation.

→ End by looking at the parallel jurisdiction of the courts under section 57 of the Trustee Act 1925 and how it has been exercised in *Southgate* v *Sutton.*

Diagram plan

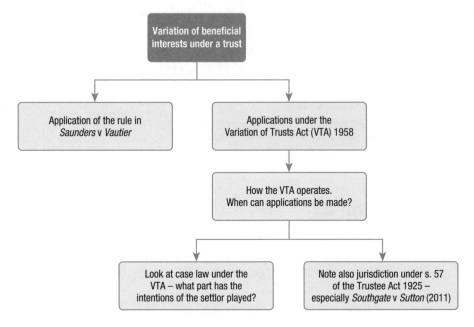

A printable version of this diagram plan is available from **www.pearsoned.co.uk/lawexpressqa**

[1] Read the question carefully and you will see that it asks you to 'Consider the jurisdiction of the courts to vary beneficial interests under a trust *especially* in the light of this observation . . . ' Thus it is not asking you only to consider the observation of Mummery LJ, although you must certainly do this, but also to consider the jurisdiction of the courts to vary trusts *in general*. If you had concentrated only on the point made by Mummery LJ then you would have lost marks.

[2] This fundamental point needs to be stressed at the outset.

Answer

It is first important to clarify exactly when the interests of beneficiaries under a trust can be varied.[1] If the beneficiaries are of full age then they will need to give their consent personally[2] to any variation of their beneficial interests where, for example, the shares to be taken by each beneficiary are to be altered. This is clearly fair. In fact, if all the beneficiaries are of full age and capacity and absolutely entitled then they can all agree under the rule in **Saunders v Vautier** (1841) 41 ER 482 to terminate the trust and claim the fund absolutely. However, not all the beneficiaries may agree to the proposed variation, as in **Southgate v Sutton** [2011] EWCA Civ 637 (below), or there may be discretionary beneficiaries in which case **Saunders v Vautier** will not apply.

[3] It is vital to make it clear that the VTA only applies in a limited number of cases.

However, the Variation of Trusts Act (VTA) 1958 does give the court power to give consent to a variation on behalf of a number of classes of persons.[3] These are:

(a) infants and persons who by means of (mental) incapacity are incapable of assenting;

(b) persons who have only an expectation of succeeding, such as a potential future spouse;

(c) persons unborn;

(d) persons with a discretionary interest under a protective trust.

How should the court exercise its powers? The only guidance given to the courts is contained is section 1 of the VTA which provides that (apart from category (d)) the court shall not approve any variation on behalf of any person unless this would be for 'the benefit of that person'[4] and in deciding this the courts have taken a wide view of what constitutes 'benefit'.

[4] This is the crucial phrase: omit it and you will lose marks.

[5] Now that you have set the scene, you can focus on the observation of Mummery LJ mentioned in the question.

The classic objection to any legislation on variation of trusts is, as Mummery LJ pointed out in *Goulding* v *James* [1997] 2 All ER 239, that the settlement 'may make it crystal clear that the settlor or testator does not want any departure from any of the strict terms of the trust'.[5] Thus by varying the trust the court may be going against the wishes of the settlor in creating the trust. Has this in fact been the case?

[6] It is impossible to give an answer which discusses the issues in the required depth and demonstrates some critical analysis if at the same time you mention a great many cases. Note the approach adopted here: only two cases are discussed but these are discussed in detail and they are analysed.

[7] It is essential to mention this to explain that not in all cases are the settlor's wishes ignored.

[8] Here we begin to look at the two cases in detail.

The cases show some variation in approach.[6] In *Re Steed's Will Trust* [1960] Ch 407, Evershed MR emphasised that the intentions of the settlor must be considered.[7] Here a testator had left his property to his housekeeper on protective trusts to prevent her from 'being sponged upon by one of her brothers'. The court refused to sanction the removal of the protective element, which would mean that she would be absolutely entitled to the trust property, because this would undermine the testator's intention that she should not be exposed to risk. However, in *Re Remnant's Settlement Trusts* [1970] Ch 560[8] a will contained a forfeiture clause, under which children who practised Roman Catholicism or married a Roman Catholic would forfeit their interests. The testator had two children, one of whom stood to forfeit her interest as she had married a Roman Catholic and had become a Roman Catholic herself. The other sister was a Protestant. The court approved the deletion of the forfeiture clause and

Pennycuick J observed that: 'a forfeiture provision of this kind might well cause very serious dissension between the families'. In fact both sets of families agreed to the deletion of the clause.

[9] If you are aiming for high marks then this is the kind of paragraph to include. You have, as the previous paragraph shows, researched this case and now you are using this research to critically analyse the decision.

If we are to treat fidelity to the intentions of the settlor as an important consideration then this decision is hard to understand.[9] It was not unlawful to include this forfeiture clause and the will was made just after the daughter had married a Roman Catholic. Thus it seemed clear that the settlor intended that her daughter's marriage to a Roman Catholic should result in the forfeiture of her interest.

In **Goulding v James** itself Mrs Froud, the testatrix, had set up a trust under which her daughter, J, took a life interest in her residuary estate followed by an absolute gift of the estate to her grandson, M, on his attaining the age of 40. If M predeceased J, or if M failed to reach 40, the estate would pass to such of the testatrix's great-grandchildren as should be living at the date of M's death. The variation proposed by J and M, would give each of them an absolute, 45 per cent share in the estate and the remaining 10 per cent would be held on trust for any great-grandchildren.

[10] This is excellent research detail: we have contrasted the approach of the High Court with that of the Court of Appeal. Try to do this in other answers.

The result would be to give much more generous provision for the unborn great-grandchildren than the value of their current interest in residue. However, the High Court refused the application,[10] on the ground that the proposed variation would be contrary to the testatrix's strongly held wishes. Her intention was that J should not be able to touch the capital of the estate at any time as she disliked J's husband, and M's interest should be postponed until he reached the age of 40 as she regarded him as immature. However, Mummery LJ approved the application on appeal. He pointed out that the question of benefit had to be considered in relation to the interests of the beneficiaries on whose behalf approval was sought, in this case the unborn great-grandchildren, and the approximately five-fold increase in the value of their share was clearly for their benefit.

In fact, most variations will merely remove some technical obstacle in the trust document rather than thwarting the settlor's intentions, but it now seems clear that where the proposed variation is for the benefit of those on whose behalf approval is sought then the fact that it conflicts with the settlor's intentions is a less important factor.

In order to give a complete picture of the law in this area it should be mentioned that section 57 of the Trustee Act 1925 gives power to the court to approve proposals by trustees concerning the management or administration of trust property where this 'is in the opinion of the court expedient'. This is traditionally used to approve, for instance, changes to investment powers of trustees. However, it does not give jurisdiction to vary the beneficial interests (***Chapman v Chapman*** [1954] AC 429 HL). However, in ***Southgate v Sutton*** [2011] the Court of Appeal approved what really amounted to a variation in the beneficial interests in an application under section 57[11] where it agreed to the creation of a sub-trust of separated funds for the benefit of the US beneficiaries as distinct from the UK beneficiaries. The object was to avoid a double tax burden on the US beneficiaries. It could be argued that a partition of the fund would vary the beneficial interests as the beneficiaries would enjoy the income of part of the fund instead of enjoying a share of the income of the whole fund as previously, but the court sanctioned the arrangement. To sum up, it seems from the cases that the courts are increasing their jurisdiction to vary beneficial interests under trusts and that fidelity to the wishes of the settlor is a less significant factor.[12]

[11] The inclusion of this case will add value to your answer and increase your marks in two ways: it shows an ability to 'think outside the box' and demonstrate that you are aware of the significance of another statutory provision, and it also shows knowledge of recent case law.

[12] You do need to round off this answer but at the same time you must avoid just summarising what you have said. A one sentence conclusion as here can be fine.

✓ Make your answer stand out

- Have a clear structure – do not just mention the issue of the intentions of the settlor where a variation is sought but, as the question asks, set this in the context of this area of law as a whole.
- Select some cases and research these in depth.
- Research how and why the VTA was passed: look at the HL decision in *Chapman* v *Chapman* [1954] AC 429 HL and the debates in Parliament when the Variation of Trusts Bill was being considered.
- Read and refer to Luxton (1997): this looks at *Goulding* v *James* [1997] 2 All ER 239 CA, and at the extent to which the court in that case may have laid down rules restricting the exercise of the discretion of the courts in consideration of applications under the VTA.

! Don't be tempted to . . .

- State all of the cases where the court can give its consent on behalf of certain persons to a variation in the beneficial interests. Some of them are complex and would not add to this answer.
- Fail to emphasise the fundamental criterion: that any variation must be for the benefit of those on whose behalf it is sought.
- Spend too long on the details of the VTA at the expense of analysis of the cases.
- Mention too many cases at the expense of a critical analysis of the issue.

www.pearsoned.co.uk/lawexpressqa

Go online to access more revision support including additional essay and problem questions with diagram plans, You be the marker questions, and download all diagrams from the book.

Remedies for breach of trust

How this topic may come up in exams

This topic can arise in two types of problem questions. One involves the situation where property may have been received in breach of trust, often linked to possible assistance in a breach of trust. The other is where a person in a fiduciary position misapplies trust property and you have to apply the techniques of tracing. You will find examples of both here. Another remedy is that of money payments where there has been a breach of trust, which is considered in a question in Chapter 11. A final possibility is an essay question which could ask you about the relationship between the different remedies.

■ Before you begin

It's a good idea to consider the following key themes of remedies for breach of trust before tackling a question on this topic.

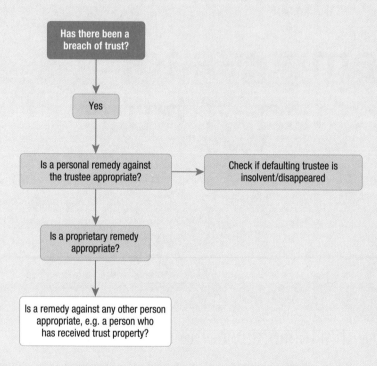

A printable version of this diagram is available from **www.pearsoned.co.uk/lawexpressqa**

❓ Question 1

John, Ted and Mal run 'Trig's Gigs', which provides equipment for gigs and other entertainments. The van which carries the equipment was purchased for £9,000, John, Ted and Mal contributing £3,000 each. However, the van was registered in John's name. The van had the words 'Trig's Gigs' painted on the side.

John sold the van to Ed for £8,000. Ed also provides equipment for gigs and he had seen John, Ted and Mal using the van at gigs. John asks Ned, a friend who has helped at gigs where Trig's Gigs provided the equipment, to drive the van to Ed's house, as John has lost his driving licence, and Ned does so. John is never seen again.

Ted and Mal ask your advice on any remedies which they may have explaining the relevant law fully.

Answer plan

→ Identify that Ted and Mal have a beneficial interest in the van, as it was bought with money provided by them.

→ Identify that Ed may be liable as a constructive trustee on the basis of knowing receipt of trust property.

→ State and explain the law on the test for liability in knowing receipt cases.

→ Outline common law remedies.

→ Then move on to consider Ned's liability, setting out the relevant tests and explaining first that there is some debate on exactly what this liability should be called.

Diagram plan

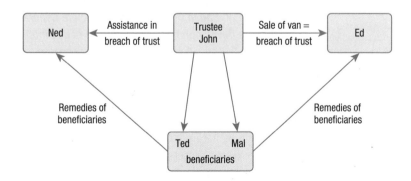

A printable version of this diagram plan is available from **www.pearsoned.co.uk/lawexpressqa**

Answer

John bought the van for £9,000 but, of this, Ted and Mal each provided £3,000. Thus, as they provided part of the purchase price, equity will presume that a resulting trust arises under which John holds the van on trust for all of them in proportion to their contributions. This presumption can be displaced by evidence that only a loan was intended[1] (***Dyer* v *Dyer*** (1788) 2 Cox Eq Cas 92 HC) but there is no evidence of that here.

Although there seems to have been no trust deed, it is clear that the van was held for the purposes of the trust and so is trust property. When John sold the van to Ed he committed a breach of trust as it is clear that Ted and Mal did not consent to the sale.[2] Ted and Mal would be able to pursue personal remedies against John for an account of profits but as John cannot be traced this would be pointless.[3]

Ed has bought the van and so he has received trust property. The question is whether an action *in rem* may be brought to recover the trust property as a result of which Ed can be made to hold it on a constructive trust for Ted and Mal. However, a beneficiary cannot recover trust property where it is in the hands of a *bona fide* purchaser of the legal estate for value without notice of the beneficiary's equitable right. The question is then whether Ed did have notice of Ted and Mal's rights.[4]

The courts have found difficulty in establishing an all-embracing principle for determining when a stranger who has received trust property can be liable.[5] In ***Baden Delvaux Lecuit* v *Société Générale pour Favoriser le Développement du Commerce et de l'Industrie en France*** [1983] BCLC 325 HC, Peter Gibson J proposed five categories which stretched to 'knowledge of circumstances which would put an honest and reasonable man on enquiry'. There has, in more recent years, been a move away from this. Megarry V-C in ***Re Montagu's Settlement Trust*** [1987] Ch 264 HC emphasised that the question was whether the recipient had knowledge and not notice and that liability should not be imposed unless the conscience of the recipient was affected. His choice of words as a test for liability was whether the recipient was guilty of a 'want of probity'. The present law is probably best summed up by the decision in ***BCCI (Overseas) Ltd* v *Akindele*** [2001] Ch 437 CA,[6] where Nourse LJ held the categories

Margin notes

[1] This is a good point for extra marks; equity only presumes a resulting trust in these cases and so you should look for any evidence that in fact none was intended.

[2] Although they did not consent to the sale in this case, it might not be so straightforward in other cases and so you should watch for this point.

[3] Students often waste time at this point. Do not be one of them!

[4] Do notice how this argument has been developed: we have not just said that Ed will be liable if he has notice of the beneficiary's rights but explained exactly *why* notice is important. It is this logical approach, mentioning all relevant points, which will enable you to pick up those extra marks.

[5] This is an important point and means that rather than just use one test for liability in your answer, you can pick up marks by a more general survey of the law before you come to the most recent authority.

[6] It is at this point that you come to the most recent authority and this is the one which you should apply to the facts.

in **Baden** were more appropriate to cases of assistance in a breach of trust but he approved of the approach in **Re Montagu**, with its emphasis on knowledge. He held that there should be a single test of knowledge: did 'the recipient's state of knowledge . . . make it unconscionable for him to retain the benefit of the receipt?' This, he felt, would enable there to be common-sense decisions in the context of commercial transactions.

If we apply this to the facts here we see that Ed also provides equipment for gigs and he had seen John, Ted and Mal using the van at gigs. Moreover, the van had 'Trig's Gigs' painted on the side. On these facts it seems that, although we have no direct evidence that Ed actually knew that the van was the property of Trig's Gigs, there is equally no evidence that Ed thought that the van was the sole property of John. On this basis, it is suggested that Ed's state of knowledge would make it unconscionable for him to retain the van[7] solely and beneficially and so he will hold it on trust for Ted and Mal. Ed's primary duty will be to restore the van to Ted and Mal. If Ed unreasonably delays in doing this then, under the rule in **Saunders v Vautier** (1841) 41 ER 482 HC, Ted and Mal could terminate the trust, as they are absolutely entitled provided that they are both of full age, and recover the van.

[7] It is vital to apply the exact words on any test for liability to the conduct which is in issue – this shows a clear analytical approach and will certainly add to your marks.

There could be possibilities of common law actions open to Ted and Mal but they do not seem to be applicable here.[8] The common law action for money had and received, as in **Lipkin Gorman v Karpnale Ltd** [1991] 2 AC 548 HL, obviously cannot apply as the claim does not involve money, and a possible action based on unjust enrichment is really applicable where the recipient is an innocent volunteer and here Ed is a purchaser.

[8] Make it a habit in questions on receipt of trust property to mention the possibility of actions at common law. Even if, as here, they will not apply, you have shown the examiner that you are aware of them and can use them if appropriate.

The other question is whether Ned can be made liable in an action by Ted and Mal for knowing assistance in the breach of trust by John in selling the van to Ed. Here, Ned is a friend of John's who has helped at gigs where Trig's Gigs provided the equipment, and Ned agrees to drive the van to Ed's house as John has lost his driving licence.

Here there is no acquisition of trust property and the general view is that it is incorrect to speak of a person who assists in a breach of trust as a constructive trustee. The remedy is a personal one against the wrongdoer and is called liability for 'dishonest assistance' in a breach of trust.[9] If this is so, the better term would be 'accountable in equity'

[9] This is an important point which an examiner will expect you to mention.

as suggested by Lord Millett in *Dubai Aluminium Co Ltd v Salaam* [2003] 2 AC 366 HL.

In *Royal Brunei Airlines Sdn Bhd v Tan Kok Ming* [1995] 2 AC 378 DC, Lord Nicholls held that the accessory's liability should depend on whether he had been dishonest. He disposed of the debate on whether it mattered if the trustee had been dishonest[10] and held that the liability of the person who assisted in the breach of trust did not depend on the trustee's own state of mind. In fact in this case it seems clear that John was fraudulent.

[10] Note that the question asks you to 'explain the relevant law fully' and this is an indication that you are expected to explain points in some detail even where the answer is actually clear. However, you should not use this as an excuse to bring in irrelevant issues.

In *Twinsectra Ltd v Yardley* [2002] AC 164 HL, Lord Hutton held that a person will not be dishonest unless it is established that his conduct had been dishonest by the ordinary standards of reasonable and honest people and that he realised that by those standards his conduct was dishonest. *Abou-Rahmah v Abacha* [2006] EWCA Civ 1492 clarified this by explaining that the test for dishonesty is predominantly objective in that although the defendant must have known that he was acting contrary to normal standards of honesty he need not have been actually conscious that he was doing wrong.

[11] Note two points: you need to make use of all the information given. Note how the point about the driving licence can be integrated into the answer. The other one is that you only need to come to a conclusion on the issue of Ned's possible liability as you have already dealt with that of Ed.

On this basis, Ned may not have known that he was acting in a way that was 'contrary to normal standards of honesty', as John did not tell him why he was to drive the van to Ed's house and it could have been that Ed simply wished to borrow the van. John's explanation that he could not drive it as he had lost his licence seems plausible on the facts and it is suggested that Ned will not be liable.[11]

 Make your answer stand out

- Do read the judgment of Nourse LJ in *BCCI* v *Akindele*: this contains an excellent review of the law and a discussion of the extent to which constructive notice and dishonesty has been required. You could then use some of this in your answer.
- Consider whether the test of unconscionability is really very helpful – is this term sufficiently clear?
- There is a general survey of the whole law on knowing receipt in Mitchell and Watterson (2010, pp. 115–58). They look, for example, at exactly what duties a constructive trustee, such as Ed in this question, might owe to the beneficiaries. You could usefully mention this point.

Don't be tempted to . . .

- There is a very useful survey of the law on liability for dishonest assistance which you could read and refer to: Ridge (2008).
- Is the language of a constructive trustee inappropriate in cases of knowing receipt as well as knowing assistance? In what real sense is Ed, for example, a trustee?
- Have a look at *Barlow Clowes International Ltd (in liquidation)* v *Eurotrust International Ltd* [2005] UKPC 37. Does this decision on liability for dishonest assistance differ from that in *Twinsectra* v *Yardley* and, if so, how?
- Start by discussing possible remedies which Ted and Mal have without first identifying that there is actually a trust. If there is no trust there can be no remedies for breach of trust.
- Do not confuse liability on the part of Ed for possible knowing receipt and on the part of Ned for possible knowing assistance. Deal with these issues separately.
- Do not refer to Ned as constructive trustee without at least explaining the controversy about whether he should be described in that way.

? Question 2

Nick is a trustee and also treasurer of 'Green Fingers', a small charity established to encourage gardening among young people. He is also sole trustee of a family trust set up under the will of his late wife, Edith, for the benefit of their three children, Ben, Ned and Sue.

Nick pays in £2,000 of the funds of Green Fingers into his own bank account, which previously had £5,000 in it, and then pays in £3,000 from the family trust. The total funds in his bank account are now £10,000. Nick then withdraws £8,000 to purchase a racing yacht which wins first prize of £10,000 in the 'Round the Isle of Thanet' yacht race. Nick pays this sum into his account which now stands at £12,000. He writes himself a note: 'This is to make good what I took out. All settled now.' He then withdraws £5,000 and gives it to his son, Fred, who buys premium bonds with it and wins £100. Nick then withdraws £5,000 and gives it to his local hospital to go towards its heart scanner appeal. The balance remaining is £2,000, which Nick spends on a horse which he intends to race. Unfortunately, the horse dies at the start of its first race. Nick has now retired to a monastery in Tibet to 'try to make amends for my past misdeeds'. His total assets are £100 in a bank account.

The beneficiaries under both of the trusts have now discovered the losses and ask for your advice on whether and how they can recover the lost funds.

Answer plan

→ Identify that breaches of trust have occurred.

→ Explain the possibility of a personal action for an account against Nick but point out that it will be of little use in view of the amount involved.

➜ Then move on to explain what the tracing process is.

➜ Explain the fundamental requirements for tracing.

➜ Now analyse the situation in detail, applying the tracing rules at each stage.

Diagram plan

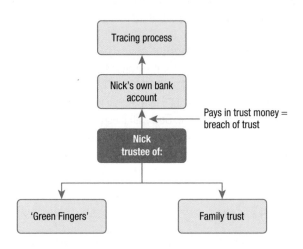

A printable version of this diagram plan is available from **www.pearsoned.co.uk/lawexpressqa**

[1] It is of course obvious that Nick has acted in breach of trust but you still need to say this.

[2] You should always consider the possibility of a personal action first but do look for where the question says that the trustee in breach is insolvent. Here you simply need to say that a personal action would be pointless. Note that we have mentioned that this action is restitutionary. This shows that we are aware of the nature of equitable remedies as distinct from the corresponding common law remedy of damages, which is compensatory.

Answer

The first point is that Nick has acted in breach of trust in parting with the funds of two trusts[1] and so we need to consider the possible remedies for breach of trust available to the beneficiaries. The starting point is to consider any possible remedies against Nick personally. He has £100 in his account and this is available to the beneficiaries under a personal action for an account. This is a restitutionary remedy and so the £100 must be restored to the trust funds.[2]

We then need to look at the possibility of proprietary actions to recover trust property which has been wrongly parted with, or to recover other

³ Tracing is technically not a remedy itself but the process by which a remedy is obtained. For instance, it may be that as a result of the use of tracing a constructive trust is imposed.

⁴ Although these requirements will be satisfied in most cases, you will still gain marks for setting them out.

⁵ It will help in the discussion which follows if we use this shorthand.

property representing it. The process by which this takes place is known as tracing.³

There are certain requirements to be satisfied in order to be able to trace.⁴ First, there must be a fiduciary relationship which there is here as there are two trusts. Secondly, those seeking to trace must have an equitable proprietary interest which they have as beneficiaries.

The first breaches of trust are where Nick pays in £2,000 of the funds of Green Fingers (we shall refer to this as Trust A)⁵ into his own bank account which previously had £5,000 in it. He then pays in £3,000 from the family trust, which we shall refer to as Trust B. The total funds in his bank account are now £10,000.

Nick then withdraws £8,000 to purchase a racing yacht, which still appears to exist. Can Trust A or B trace into this?

In **Re Hallett's Estate** (1880) 13 Ch D 696 CA the rule was established that when making withdrawals from an account a trustee is presumed to spend his own money first. However, once the amount in the account falls below the amount of trust funds then it is assumed that part of the trust funds must have been spent. Here there was £5,000 in his bank account before he had paid in any money from trust funds and so, of the £8,000 used to buy the yacht, £5,000 is his own money. The reason for this rule is to protect beneficiaries where sums are left in a trustee's account as it makes it more likely that money left will belong to the beneficiaries and can be claimed by them.⁶

⁶ You could answer this question without mentioning the reasons behind this rule but it shows that you have really understood it if you do and so will add to your marks.

However, this leaves £3,000, which must have come from the funds of one or both of the trusts. To decide which of the funds it came from, we apply the Rule in **Clayton's Case** (1816) 35 ER 781 HC, which provides that, in the case of an active continuing bank account, the trustee is regarded as having taken out of the fund whatever had been first put in. 'First in, first out.' Thus, as this is certainly an active bank account, if for the wrong reasons, this rule will apply and as the money from Trust A was first in, this will be the account that the money to buy the yacht will come from first. However, as there is only £2,000 in this account, the other £1,000 must have come from Trust B.⁷

⁷ There will usually be something left over, as here, so that you can apply the rules starting with *Clayton's Case.*

⁸ If you mention *Clayton's Case* then you must also mention this authority.

The authority of the rule in **Clayton's Case** was weakened in **Barlow Clowes International Ltd (in liquidation) v Vaughan** [1992] 4 All

ER 22 CA[8] when it was not applied to claims by investors to share in the assets of a company which had managed investment plans for them. The investments were in a collective scheme by which investors' money was mixed together and invested in a common fund and it was held to be wrong that those who invested first could expect least. The court held that the rule in **Clayton's Case** is only one of convenience and would therefore be displaced here, and instead investors would share rateably in the company's assets in proportion to the amounts due to them. If this principle applied here, it could be argued that the loss to the trust fund should be borne rateably by the two trusts, and so the loss of £3,000 will be borne in the proportion of 40:60 between Trust A and Trust B.

The yacht wins first prize of £10,000 in the 'Round the Isle of Thanet' yacht race. Nick pays this sum into his account, which now stands at £12,000. Of this, £2,000 is money belonging to Trust B, which is still in the account. It can be argued that the prize of £10,000 belongs to the trusts, as it is the traceable proceeds of the yacht which was bought with their money (see **Re Tilley's Will Trusts** [1967] Ch 1179 HC). On the other hand, it was held in **Roscoe v Winder** [1915] 1 Ch 62 HC that where a trustee makes any later payments into his bank account these are not treated as repayments of the trust money unless the trustee has shown an intention to do this. In this case Nick writes himself a note: 'This is to make good what I took out. All settled now.' Thus on the basis of both rules it seems clear that the £10,000 will belong to the trusts. So on the basis of 40:60, it can be argued that Trust A receives £4,000 and now stands at this figure and Trust B receives £6,000 and now stands at £8,000 adding the £2,000 already in the account.[9]

[9] A tip: if by now you are getting bemused by the arithmetic, then give it up, as it is more important to be able to apply the principles and if you get the sums wrong it may mean that you get the law wrong too.

Nick then withdraws £5,000 and gives it to his son Fred who buys premium bonds with it and wins £100. If the rule in **Clayton's Case** applies this will come from Trust A which will now be exhausted, and £1,000 will come from Trust B. As Fred was given the money he will be a volunteer, albeit innocent, and tracing will be possible against him. Thus he will be liable to restore the £5,000 plus the win of £100 (**Re Tilley's Will Trusts**). When the money is restored it is suggested that Trust A and B will be put back to where they were before.

Nick then withdraws £5,000 and gives it to his local hospital to go towards its heart scanner appeal. In **Re Diplock** [1948] Ch 465 CA it was held that tracing was not possible where money has been paid by innocent volunteers who were charities on improving their own land and it may be that this will apply here. This rule used to be explained on the basis that tracing would be inequitable but it is now considered to rest under the principle that there has been a change of position[10] (see **Lipkin Gorman v Karpnale Ltd** [1991] 2 AC 548 HL). If **Clayton's Case** applies, then this will come from Trust A, which will now be exhausted, and £1,000 from Trust B.

Finally, the balance remaining is £2,000, which Nick spends on a horse which he intends to race. Unfortunately, the horse dies at the start of its first race. As the property is no longer identifiable, the right to trace is lost. This £2,000 will come from Trust B as Trust A is exhausted.

In the end, all that is left is the £5,100 which on the facts will probably go to Trust B.[11]

[10] The idea that tracing will not be possible where money has been innocently received and spent by a charity often appears in exam questions but you will gain marks by pointing out that the law has moved on from regarding the loss of the right to trace as based on the fact that it would be inequitable to do so.

[11] You do not need a long conclusion as you have been summing up as you went along.

✓ Make your answer stand out

- Explain that there can be no tracing at common law as mixing money in an account makes it unidentifiable at common law (*Agip (Africa) Ltd* v *Jackson* [1990] Ch 265).

- Mention *Russell-Cooke Trust Co* v *Prentis (No 1)* [2002] EWHC 2227 (Ch) as another means of deciding how to allocate loss between more than one fund which has been wrongly applied.

- Consider the application of the rule in *Re Oatway* [1903] 2 Ch 356 – would the different principle which it establishes to that in *Roscoe* v *Winder* produce a different result in the case of trust money spent on the yacht? Note that this is a case of mixed funds.

- Look at *Foskett* v *McKeown* [2001] 1 AC 102 and especially at the speech of Lord Millett. He held that where trust money is mixed with the trustee's own money then the beneficiary is 'entitled to locate his contribution in any part of the mixture' and to subordinate the claims of the defaulting trustee and their successors to those of the beneficiary.

> **! Don't be tempted to . . .**
>
> - Set out all the rules on tracing first and only then apply the law. You will lose marks and get into a real muddle!
> - Confuse common law and equitable tracing – make it clear that you are dealing with equitable tracing.
> - Say that tracing is a remedy in itself.

Question 3

The term 'equitable compensation' in relation to breach of trust gives the impression that this area is primarily concerned with compensation in the same way as the common law is. In fact equity approaches the question of remedies for breach of trust from a quite different standpoint.

Critically consider this statement.

Answer plan

→ Distinguish between different types of breaches of trust and contrast actions for breach of trust with common law actions in contract and tort.

→ Explain the right of the beneficiary to require the taking of an account.

→ Then move on to look at the two possibilities: falsifying the account and surcharging the account.

→ Look at the reasoning of Lord Browne-Wilkinson in *Target Holdings* v *Redferns* and note that there seem to be different rules for bare commercial type trusts and others.

→ Conclusion: ask if the principles here are clear.

Diagram plan

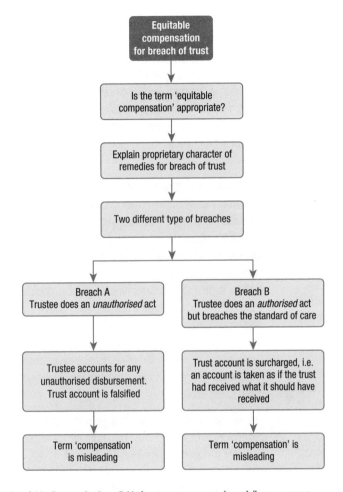

A printable version of this diagram plan is available from **www.pearsoned.co.uk/lawexpressqa**

Answer

[1] Aim for this type of start: it is clear and confident and shows the examiner that you know exactly where you are going.

It is indeed arguable that the use of the term 'equitable compensation' is misleading. Moreover many lawyers would not refer to equitable compensation at all precisely because compensation is a term used in common law actions in contract and tort.[1] It is true that in equity the term 'damages' is not used, unlike at common law, but the use of 'compensation' in equity can still mislead.

It is vital to distinguish between different types of breaches of trust and, at a more basic level, to note the distinctive character of remedies for breach of trust. This rests on the proprietary interest in the trust property held by the beneficiaries and is entirely different from an action at common law for compensation for, for instance, personal injury where there is no pre-existing legal relationship between the parties. Here there is: that of trustee and beneficiary, and the remedy sought is proprietary.[2] In common law actions for damages the remedy sought is personal.

[2] This is an absolutely vital point. Keep hold of it throughout your answer.

The two types of breaches of trust are first where a trustee misapplies trust money by, for instance, distributing it to the wrong person. The essence is that the trustee has done something which she must not do. The second is where the trustee, for instance, makes unauthorised investments and, in doing so, fails to show the necessary standard of care. Here the trustee has done something that she is entitled to do, make the investments, but has done it negligently. As Millett LJ said in *Armitage v Nurse* [1998] Ch 241: 'a breach of trust may be deliberate or inadvertent'.[3] We will call the first breach A and the second breach B. There is an obvious parallel between breach B cases and those for the tort of negligence at common law and here it is tempting to use the term 'equitable compensation' but even here it can cause confusion.

[3] Up to this point in this paragraph we had not mentioned any authority but, although we are dealing with fundamental issues, a mention of a relevant authority, even if only briefly as here, can only increase your marks.

The fundamental duty of the trustee is to produce accounts for the beneficiary to examine.[4] This flows from the beneficiaries' proprietary interests in the trust property. As the trust assets are the beneficiary's in equity then she has the right to know in what state they are. In *Ultraframe (UK) Ltd v Fielding* [2007] WTLR 835, Lewison J said, 'The taking of an account is the process by which a beneficiary requires a trustee to justify his stewardship of trust property.' Where a breach of trust has occurred then the beneficiaries can require the taking of an account which will show that a sum has been misapplied. As Lewison J explained, there are then two possibilities.

[4] Any discussion of equitable compensation and indeed other remedies must consider the right of the beneficiary to accounts. This is really the starting point here.

One is that the account is falsified.[5] This means that the sum misapplied is disallowed. Lewison J instanced where trustees have made an unauthorised investment that falls in value (type A breach). The account is taken as if the expenditure had not been made and thus as

[5] Note the argument: first, the taking of an account and then, for a type A breach, falsifying the account. Do not let the term 'falsifying' put you off! It is a technical Chancery procedural one.

if the unauthorised expenditure has not formed part of the trust assets. In this sense the account is falsified. The trustee is then required to account to the trust for the unauthorised disbursement, that is, the full amount of what he had taken out of the trust account wrongly, and so the trustee is restoring the trust property and the claim is for performance of the trustee's obligation to deliver the assets of the trust (substitutive performance). Thus the term 'compensation' is misleading as the beneficiaries are not compensated for harm suffered, and so questions of causation have no place. Thus Blackburne J in **Re Lehman Brothers International (Europe) (in administration) (No 2)** [2009] EWHC 2141 (Ch) said that a beneficiary's remedy for breach of trust 'is principally directed to securing performance of the trust, rather than to the recovery of compensation or damages'.[6]

[6] Although we have been setting out the basic principles here it is, as always, vital to anchor your discussion in an authority and this quote is easily recalled.

The other possibility is that the account is surcharged where there is a type B breach[7] where, for example, the beneficiary alleges that the trustee has not exercised due care and diligence in making an investment. The account is taken as if the trust had received what it would have received if the trustee had exercised due diligence. This is sometimes known as a reparation claim.

[7] This is the next logical step in the answer: you have dealt with the remedy for a type A breach, this is the remedy for type B.

In principle equity does not ask if the loss was foreseeable but in questions of loss arising due to negligence questions of causation may arise and can this look like common law damages for negligence. **Target Holdings Ltd v Redferns** [1996] AC 421 HL[8] illustrates this. Money was lent by a finance company (X) to developers (Y) on the security of two properties which were fraudulently overvalued. Redferns acted for both parties and received the mortgage advance on a bare trust for the claimant to release it to Y when the transfers of the properties were executed. However, in breach of trust they released it early. This was in fact a type A breach as the trustees had misapplied trust money.[9] Y subsequently went into liquidation, and X sold the properties for much less than their value. X claimed against Redferns for their loss on the transaction but failed.

[8] Although this decision may have generated more heat than light it is essential to mention it in a discussion on equitable compensation.

[9] You do need to identify this point as the discussion hangs on it.

The House of Lords held that the rule in assessing compensation for breach of trust in commercial dealings such as this, especially as the solicitor was only a bare trustee,[10] is that a trustee is only liable for losses caused by the breach and not for losses which would have occurred anyway. Thus, although the solicitors, the trustees, acted in breach of trust by releasing the funds early, the claimants obtained the mortgage

[10] Make sure that you point this out and that you know what a bare trustee is.

securities later anyway. The early release of the funds did not decide if the mortgage would go through, and it was this which caused the loss.

[11] This is an absolutely vital sentence in the context of the question. If you are not careful you could get stuck into a long account of *Target Holdings* when in fact, as we are about to demonstrate, it is not the actual decision which the question is asking you about but the implications of Lord Browne-Wilkinson's remarks.

The decision seems correct but the remarks of Lord Browne-Wilkinson have caused debate.[11] He felt that X should have to prove a causal link between its loss and the breach of duty by the solicitors, which looks like the common law position. He distinguished between bare commercial type trusts such as that in **Redferns**, where the issue of reconstituting the trust fund did not arise as the transaction had been completed and so the purpose of the trust had ended, with other trusts such as a family type one which was still running and where the trust fund would need to be reconstituted. The result is that in a **Redferns** type situation one needs to look at questions of causation in a common law context but if the trust is still subsisting causation of loss is obvious as it is the value of the misapplied property.

It is clear that in principle equitable remedies work quite differently from those of the common law and so it is suggested that the use of the term 'equitable compensation' can mislead. The problem lies not with where the obligation is simply to restore what has been wrongly taken out but with where the loss is not precisely measurable and the trust is still subsisting. One suspects that the principles here are still in a stage of development.

 Make your answer stand out

- Demonstrate that you are absolutely clear on the fundamental issues in this area. They take some time to unravel so make sure that you do this well.
- Note this quote from Ipp J in *Permanent Building Society (in liquidation)* v *Wheeler* (1994) 14 ACSR 109 at 157: 'the existence of a fiduciary duty does not mean that every duty owed by a fiduciary to the beneficiary is a fiduciary duty'. One example given is the duty to exercise reasonable care. Could a re-labelling of which duties are fiduciary (equitable remedies) and which are not (common law remedies) bring clarity to this area?
- Read Millett (1998). This is a stimulating survey of the debate and contains an extremely clear exposition of the law on claims by beneficiaries against trustees. Note his disagreement with the views of Lord Browne-Wilkinson mentioned in the question.
- Research the decision of the High Court of Australia in *Youyang Pty Ltd* v *Minter Ellison Morris Fletcher* (2003) 212 CLR 484 which applied *Target Holdings* v *Redferns* and also the UK decision in *Swindle* v *Harrison* [1997] 4 All ER 705.

! Don't be tempted to . . .

- Miss the basic distinction between common law and equitable remedies.

- Just describe the law but instead look critically at it. This applies especially to the decision in *Target Holdings* v *Redfern*.

- Spend too long on the facts of *Target Holdings* v *Redferns* without relating them to the issue in the question.

- Write about equitable compensation in areas other than breaches of trust under section 2 of Lord Cairns Act (Chancery Amendment Act) 1858. The question only asks you about remedies for breach of trust.

- Mention too many areas superficially.

www.pearsoned.co.uk/lawexpressqa

Go online to access more revision support including additional essay and problem questions with diagram plans, You be the marker questions, and download all diagrams from the book.

A mixture of questions

How this topic may come up in exams

In many exams in equity and trusts questions are set which incorporate a variety of topics and this chapter contains a selection of these. You will almost certainly get questions which range across the whole area of equity and it is easier to look at these after you have familiarised yourself with particular subject areas.

Some cases appear in more than one question as they are really excellent illustrations of equitable principles and these can be used in more than one context. Learn these cases really well rather than learning many cases superficially. You can then use them to gain a really good mark and, at the same time, reduce the number of cases you have to learn. A bonus all round!

Before you begin

It's a good idea to consider the following key themes before tackling a question that ranges across a variety of topics in equity and trusts.

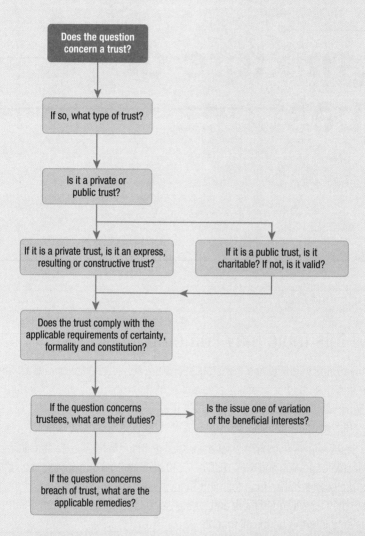

A printable version of this diagram is available from **www.pearsoned.co.uk/lawexpressqa**

❓ Question 1

John owned a house 'The Laurels' and 500 shares in Hanbury Park Ltd. He told his daughter, Mary: 'Now that you are 18 it is time to think of your future. One day you will have this house so I will take care of it for you until you are 25 and then transfer it to you.' The next day John contacted a firm of builders about a possible extension to the house to enable him to house his model railway.

Later that day he met Mike, an old friend, and said to him: 'You know, I have more wealth than I need. I would like to do something to help others and so I am going to transfer my shares into your name for you to hold on trust at your discretion for my old workmates. You know who they are.' John then told his accountant, Peter, to deal with the formalities for a transfer of his shares to Mike. Peter sent a form to John to sign but did not explain what it was about and John put it away until he had a chance to ask Peter for more advice.

John is also a beneficiary under a trust of £500,000 set up by his Uncle Jack. He telephoned Uncle Jack and said: 'I do not need the money in the trust fund. Please hold on trust for my sister Amy.'

A week later John made his will in which he left all his property to the League of Friends of Sick Cats and appointed his Aunt Molly and Mary as executors.

John has now died. Advise his executors on who is entitled to:

(a) 'The Laurels'

(b) the 500 shares in Hanbury Park Ltd

(c) John's interest in the trust fund.

Answer plan

→ Separate the different intended gifts and note who the executors are.

→ Consider the intended trust of the house: identify and apply three certainties and formal requirements. Possible application of the rule in *Strong* v *Bird*.

→ Now consider the intended trust of the shares: identify and apply any formal requirements, consider the question of certainty of objects and whether the trust is constituted.

→ Finally, consider the intended transfer of the beneficial interest in the trust fund: identify and apply formal requirements.

Diagram plan

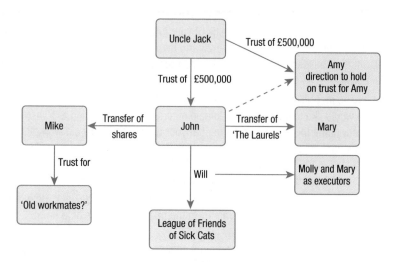

A printable version of this diagram plan is available from **www.pearsoned.co.uk/lawexpressqa**

[1] Many students, realising that this question concerns a possible trust, would rush to consider the formalities point. But wait! There are marks to be gained by spending time first on whether there is a trust at all and so looking at the three certainties.

[2] This is not a question just about certainties but also about a number of other issues. So resist the temptation to go into detail on this point, and wrap up this part of your answer fairly quickly.

[3] Formalities should *always* be mentioned *after* you have checked if the three certainties are present. There is no point in discussing if the trust satisfies the formal requirements if there is no trust!

Answer

(a) The first question is whether John has declared a trust of 'The Laurels' in favour of Mary.[1] There is certainty of subject matter (The Laurels) and objects (Mary), so the only question is whether John actually intended to declare himself a trustee. He says that he will take care of the house for Mary until she is 25 and then transfer it to her. The question is whether the words 'take care' of the house coupled with a clear statement that he will transfer it to her at 25 are enough. This is borderline and all we can say[2] is that if the courts decide that there is no trust then of course Mary's claim fails and the house will devolve on John's death to the charity. If there is a trust then as it is a trust of land it must comply with section 53(1)(b) of the LPA 1925. This provides that 'a declaration of trust concerning land or any interest therein must be manifested and proved by some writing signed by some person who is able to declare the same or by his will'. If not, the trust will not be enforceable.[3] The actual declaration of trust need not be in writing. The words 'manifested and proved' require only written evidence.

The problem here is that John has declared the trusts orally, which will not satisfy section 53(1)(b), and so as Mary cannot enforce it the house will remain part of John's estate and will pass to the charity.

However, Mary is also an executor of John's estate[4] and so we must investigate if the rule in **Strong v Bird** (1874) LR 18 Eq 315 HC will assist her. This provides that if an incomplete gift is made during the donor's lifetime and the donor has appointed the donee his executor, then the vesting of the property in the donee completes the gift. **Strong v Bird** dealt with a debt owed to the executor but in **Re Stewart** [1908] 2 Ch 251 HC[5] the rule in **Strong v Bird** was extended from cases of forgiveness of debts to those where there has been an incomplete transfer of property to a person who is also appointed executor under the will of the transferee. The effect is that the transfer may now be valid.

However, in addition, the rule in **Strong v Bird** requires that there must be a *continuing* intention to make the gift.[6] In **Re Gonin** [1979] Ch 16 HC a mother wished to leave her house to her daughter but instead she wrote a cheque for £33,000 in the daughter's favour, which was found after her death. The court held that there was no continuing intention on the mother's part that the daughter should have the house, as the giving of the cheque indicated that she had changed her mind. So in this case the fact that the next day John contacted a firm of builders about a possible extension to the house to enable him to house his model railway may indicate that John has changed his mind about the trust for Mary. The evidence is inconclusive but, if **Strong v Bird** applies, Mary can claim the house. If it does not, she cannot.[7]

(b) John then says to Mike that he is 'going to transfer my shares into your name for you to hold on trust for my old workmates. You know who they are.' There is certainty of intention,[8] as John says that Mike is to hold on trust[9] and the subject matter will be clear provided that the only shares in his estate are the 500 shares in Hanbury Park Ltd.[10] If not, evidence may be brought to identify them. If there is no certainty of subject matter then all the shares will form part of John's estate on his death and will

[4] Always check before beginning an answer on constitution if the intended donee is also the executor under a will of the donor. If so, this is a sure sign that you will be expected to apply *Strong* v *Bird*.

[5] Mentioning this case immediately marks your answer out as a good one. Most students would only mention *Strong* v *Bird* but as the problem concerns a trust you need to link the rule in *Strong* v *Bird* to trusts and this is what this case does.

[6] Where the question involves the possible application of *Strong* v *Bird* you should watch also for any indication of a lack of a continuing intention by the transferor.

[7] Aim for pithy conclusions like this which encapsulate your answer in one sentence.

[8] Remember the drill: certainties first!

[9] A small point but one you must never forget! Many students, seeing that the answer is obvious here as John actually says that he is creating a trust will just say that there is certainty of intention. But if you do you will lose marks. Always give evidence for your conclusions.

[10] The question said that John simply referred to 'my shares', instead of being more specific.

pass to the charity. The problem is then certainty of objects as John refers to 'my old workmates'. This is a discretionary trust, as indicated by the word 'discretion' in the gift, and so the test for certainty of objects is that laid down in **McPhail v Doulton** [1971] AC 424 HL: can it be said with certainty if a person is or is not a beneficiary? It is submitted that evidence could be brought to show who John's 'old workmates' are. If, however, the test of certainty is not satisfied, then Mike will hold the shares on a resulting trust for John and, as they will then form part of John's estate, they will pass to the charity on his death.

Assuming that there is a valid trust then although the declaration of trust is not in writing, this does not affect the enforceability of the trust, as section 53(1)(b) of the LPA 1925 only applies to trusts of land.

However, there is a problem with constitution of the trust as the subject matter, the shares, is not transferred to Mike. If John had done all in his power to effect the transfer then, under the principle in **Re Rose** [1952] Ch 499 CA, it would bind him, but here Peter, John's accountant, sent a form to John to sign and John put it away until he had a chance to ask Peter for more advice. However, in **Pennington v Waine** [2002] EWCA Civ 227 it was held on the facts of that case that, although the transferor had *not* done all in her power to effect a transfer of shares it did still bind her. In this case the transferor had actually signed a share transfer form to this effect and given it to her agent who took no further action. Here, however, John has not even signed the transfer form and it is submitted that this distinguishes the present case from **Pennington v Waine**[11] and so the trust was never constituted and thus the shares form part of John's estate and pass to the charity.

[11] Note how we have stressed the essential point of difference between this case and *Pennington* v *Waine*. Clear analysis like this will always gain marks.

(c) Finally, John telephoned his Uncle Jack, telling him to hold his interest under a trust fund of £500,000 for his sister Amy instead. In **Grey v IRC** [1960] AC 1 HL it was held that this is a disposition of a beneficial interest under a trust and as such it must comply with section 53(1)(c) of the LPA 1925, which provides that a disposition of an equitable interest or trust must be in writing signed either by the settlor or by his authorised agent. Failure to comply with section 53(1)(c) makes the disposition void. As the disposition was oral, it does not comply with section 53(1)(c) and so as it is void John's interest in the trust fund will still form part of his estate and will pass to the charity.

✓ **Make your answer stand out**

- Look in more detail at the reasoning in *Pennington* v *Waine* and especially at the judgments of Arden LJ and Clarke LJ and contrast their reasoning.
- Read the judgments in this case and see if you can identify any policy reasons for the decision which you can integrate into your answer.
- Read and refer to the note on *Re Gonin* at (1977) 93 LQR 448.

! **Don't be tempted to . . .**

- Plunge into the answer too quickly! This really is one area where careful planning will help your answer as you need to disentangle the different areas of law which appear in the question.
- Spend too much time on any one area. In particular, avoid the temptation to spend too long on the certainties point at the start.
- Make sure that in each case you go back to the fundamental question at the end: will the property go to the charity or to the intended beneficiaries?

 # Question 2

Anita has recently taken over as Chair of the Trust which provides pensions for employees and former employees of the Malvern Hills Mining Corporation. She asks you for advice on the following points:

(a) The trust has a standard clause stating that 'trustees are under no liability for loss or damage to the trust fund or its income unless such loss or damage shall be caused by the actual fraud of the trustees'. She has heard that some of the beneficiaries under the trust are considering claiming against the trust for negligence in its investment strategy and asks your advice on the extent to which this clause would protect the trustees in the event of negligence being proved.

(b) The accountant to the trust, Horace, has absconded taking with him £10,000 in bribes paid to him by investment companies in return for Horace agreeing to recommend to the trust that it invests with them. Anita asks you if the sum of £10,000 representing these bribes can be recovered from Horace who is now insolvent.

Diagram plan

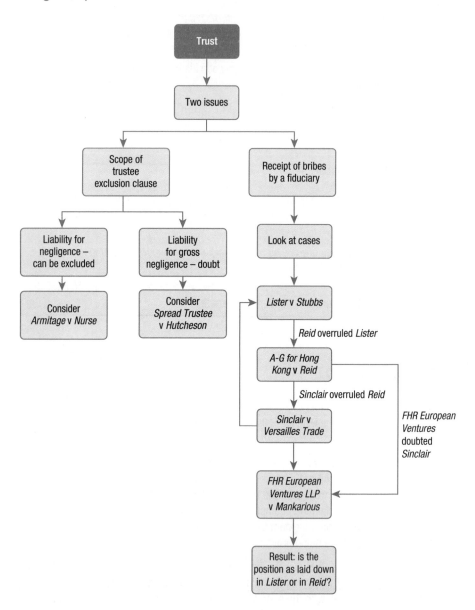

A printable version of this diagram plan is available from **www.pearsoned.co.uk/lawexpressqa**

Answer plan

→ Identify that this is a trustee exclusion clause and explain the decision in *Armitage* v *Nurse*.

→ Go on to distinguish between ordinary negligence and gross negligence; consider the decision in *Spread Trustee Co Ltd* v *Hutcheson*.

→ Refer to the dissent of Lady Hale in the above case.

→ Identify the remedies of the employer in cases where the employee has received a bribe.

→ Note that Horace is insolvent and so we need to consider trust remedies.

→ Trace the evolution of the case law in this area.

→ Conclude that Horace is not liable to hold the amount of the bribe on trust.

Answer

[1] There is a trap in this question for the unwary: you could easily discuss the issue of actual liability for negligence but of course you are not being asked this. Instead you must concentrate on the validity of the exclusion clause.

(a) This is a trustee exclusion clause[1] and the leading case is **Armitage v Nurse** [1998] Ch 221 HC where the wording of the clause was very similar to the one in this case. **Armitage v Nurse** concerned property including agricultural land and the beneficiaries' alleged negligence in its management. Millett LJ held that 'there is an irreducible core of obligations owed by the trustees to the beneficiaries and enforceable by them which is fundamental to the concept of a trust' and liability for this could not be excluded. As he pointed out: 'If the beneficiaries have no rights enforceable against the trustees there are no trusts.' Thus liability for actual frauds could not be excluded, but a clause could 'exclude liability for breach of trust in the absence of a dishonest intention on the part of the trustee whose conduct is impugned'.

[2] At this point you need to broaden your answer out. An average answer would just refer to *Armitage* v *Nurse* and say that the clause is valid. However, if you are aiming for a really good pass then you need to be aware of the ongoing debate on whether there is a separate category of gross negligence and, if so, whether it is possible for liability for this to be excluded by trustees.

It seems from the facts that no actual dishonesty by the trustees is alleged and so the clause could be valid but we need to go further. The actual degree of negligence alleged in this case is not clear: is it ordinary negligence or gross negligence?[2] This is important as there is a continuing debate on whether a trustee exclusion clause can exclude liability for gross negligence or only ordinary negligence. In **Armitage v Nurse** Millett LJ held that trustee exclusion clauses could cover gross negligence and held that a sharp distinction has always been drawn between negligence, however gross, on the one hand, and fraud, bad faith and wilful misconduct on the other. Clearly a clause could not exempt from liability for the latter.

[3] This case must always be discussed in an answer on trustee exclusion clauses.

In **Spread Trustee Co Ltd v Hutcheson** [2011] UKPC 13[3] the beneficiaries claimed that the trustee had been grossly negligent in failing to identify and investigate breaches of trust on the part of previous trustees. A clause in the trust instrument exempted the trustee from liability for breaches of trust arising from his own gross negligence. It was held that the parties could lawfully agree to exclude a trustee's liability for breaches arising from negligence or gross negligence. Lord Clarke in effect agreed with Millett LJ in **Armitage v Nurse** and said that 'To describe negligence as gross does not change its nature so as to make it fraudulent or wilful misconduct.'

[4] This where your hard work in researching cases can really pay off with those extra marks. A mediocre answer would mention *Armitage* v *Nurse* and leave it at that. A better answer would show awareness of recent cases such as *Spread Trustee* v *Hutcheson* but only mention the reasoning of the majority. A really outstanding answer would go on to look at the dissenting judgments.

However, Lady Hale dissented and felt that trustee exclusion clauses should not be able to cover liability for gross negligence.[4] She pointed to the Law Commission's Consultation Paper No 124, *Fiduciary Duties and Regulatory Rules* (1992) which said that 'it seems that a trustee may not exclude liability for "wilful default". There is however uncertainty as to whether liability for gross negligence can be excluded' (paragraph 3.3.6). She also gave the example of a case where the guardian of the estate of a minor might seek to rely on a clause exempting him from liability for gross negligence, which she felt any English lawyer would regard as unacceptable.

[5] Do not forget to end your answer by coming back to the original question – the advice to Anita.

The advice to Anita[5] must be that if only negligence and not fraud is alleged, as seems to be the case, then the trustees are protected by the clause, but the law is still developing and it may be that in future we will reach the stage where clauses exempt from liability for ordinary negligence but not gross negligence.

[6] This is very important. There is no point in rushing in and considering the possible imposition of a constructive trust if the money can be recovered as, in effect, a simple debt. You need to show that you are aware of this.

(b) The accountant to the trust, Horace, has absconded taking with him £10,000 in bribes paid to him by investment companies in return for Horace agreeing to recommend to the trust that it invests with them, and Anita asks if the sum of £10,000 representing these bribes can be recovered from Horace. There is no doubt that it could be recovered under ordinary civil law.[6] The receipt by Horace of a bribe is a breach of an implied contractual term that he will act in good faith to his employer, and the employer can claim an account of any secret profits which the employee made through the breach. One example is **Boston Deep Sea Fishing and Ice Co v Ansell** (1888) 39 Ch D 339 HC, where a managing director of a company, who had made secret profits out of his position, was liable to account for them to the company.

However, we are told that Horace is insolvent[7] and so we need to consider if we can claim a proprietary remedy so that Horace will have received the bribe as a fiduciary and so be liable as a constructive trustee to return it to the trust. If we can, then the claim of the Malvern Hills Mining Corporation will have priority over Horace's ordinary creditors.[8]

Horace was in a fiduciary position when he received the bribe as he was the accountant to the trust. However, in **Lister & Co v Stubbs** (1890) 45 Ch D 1 CA it was held that a bribe received by a fiduciary from a third party was not held on trust for the principal. The reasoning was that proprietary claims (i.e. those founded on trust) were only available where the principal seeks to recover property which belonged to him *before* the breach of fiduciary duty. A bribe, by contrast, is not the property of the principal but is property held by the fiduciary in breach of fiduciary obligation. Here the relationship between the fiduciary and principal is that of debtor and creditor, not trustee and beneficiary.

However, this principle was reversed in **Attorney General for Hong Kong v Reid** [1994] 1 AC 324 PC which held that benefits obtained from a third party in breach of fiduciary obligation, such as bribes, belong in equity to the principal from the moment of receipt. On this basis we could argue that Horace does hold the bribe on a constructive trust and so it can be claimed from him.

Sinclair Investments (UK) Ltd v Versailles Trade Finance (In Administration) [2011] EWCA Civ 347 changed the position back to what it was before **Reid** and so **Lister v Stubbs** is once again good law and there are only personal remedies available against defaulting fiduciaries, as in this case. However, although this represents the current law, in the latest case, **FHR European Ventures LLP v Mankarious** [2013] EWCA Civ 17[9] the court was not happy with the principle in **Sinclair**, which it managed to distinguish, and invited the Supreme Court to consider

[7] Although the previous paragraph was vital you now need to recognise the significance of this: in fact, in problems on trust exams, those against whom claims are made are often insolvent. This is to make you focus on trust remedies, as contractual ones, although needing a mention, will be useless as there will be no money to satisfy the claim.

[8] Do stress this point.

[9] Do note how keeping up to date with the latest cases has improved your answer.

[10] Make sure that you do not get so carried away by discussing the cases that you forget a conclusion!

'whether **Sinclair Investments** was right to decide that **Lister** is to be preferred to **Reid**'. Thus it may be that the law reverts to what it was before and under the authority of **Reid** the Malvern Hills Mining Corporation may be able claim a proprietary remedy against Horace.[10] All we can say is that here the law is in a state of flux.

✓ Make your answer stand out

- Trace the evolution of the case law in both situations and in both do not just list the cases but show how the law has changed and developed from case to case.
- Research why the Trustee Act 2000 did not regulate the use of trustee exclusion clauses.
- Read and refer to two articles on the decision in *Sinclair Investments (UK) Ltd* v *Versailles Trade Finance*: one by Hicks (2011) and the other by Hayton (2011).
- Note the suggestion by Hayton (2011) that as a result of the decision in *Sinclair* many trust deeds will now provide that any bribe or other secret profit received by the fiduciary will be held on trust for the relevant beneficiaries or the other contracting party.
- Watch for the decision by the Supreme Court when it considers *Sinclair.*

! Don't be tempted to . . .

- Only mention one case in each situation: in both (a) and (b).
- Forget that negligence can be ordinary negligence or gross negligence and that there is an ongoing debate on whether trustee exclusion clauses can apply to gross negligence.
- Overlook that in (b) Horace is insolvent – there is no point in considering trust remedies here unless contract remedies will not work.
- Just list the cases on receipt of bribes; instead show how the law has developed.

Question 3

'The appeal of maxims, so far as judges are concerned, is that they are capable of bearing what weight the judge chooses to ascribe to them.' (Watt, 2009, p. 93)

Do you agree with this limited view of maxims as a predictive factor in judicial making in equity?

Answer plan

→ Outline what the idea of equitable maxims is and explain that you will make a selection from them to illustrate your answer:

→ 'He who comes to equity must come with clean hands.'

→ 'Equity will not assist a volunteer.'

→ 'Equity will not allow a statute to be used as an engine of fraud.'

→ 'Equity looks to the intent and not the form.'

Diagram plan

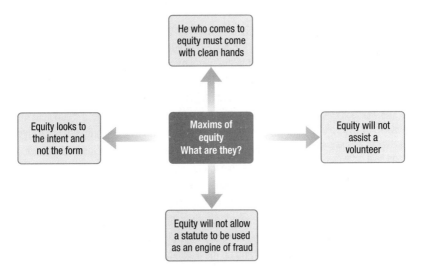

A printable version of this diagram plan is available from **www.pearsoned.co.uk/lawexpressqa**

Answer

[1] Reference to another slightly different view here will add to your marks.

This statement indicates that maxims are not to be taken as rules or even general principles which guide decision making in equity. Hanbury (2012) gives them slightly greater importance:[1] 'They are not rules which must be rigorously applied in every case but are more in the nature of general guidelines illustrating the way in which equitable jurisdiction is exercised' (p. 29). What is clear is that the maxims of equity describe, rather than define, some of the main principles that guide equitable intervention but their importance should not be over-stressed.

[2] This question is about equity today, so you should not give a long historical account. This sentence, however, is essential to put the maxims in their historical context.

[3] This sentence is the pivot on which this answer hangs: what would be really dreadful would be an answer which went through every maxim and said what it was, gave an example, and then went on to the next one. There would be no discussion or engagement with the issues raised by the question and the answer would almost certainly fail. You need to make a selection from the maxims.

[4] This is also vital: you can pick up marks by using one illustration for more than one maxim and gain extra marks.

[5] This is a particularly good maxim to choose to illustrate an answer as there is plenty of scope for discussion and opportunities to display your knowledge of case law and so earn extra marks.

[6] This sentence scores in two ways: it shows how the maxims relate to each other (and gets you away from that dreaded list of maxims!) and also gains you credit by your reference to an important recent case and judgment.

They consist of brief, pithy phrases which remain easily in the mind but in fact judges today do not use them so often. Their historical importance is greater because they began to be formulated in the time of Lord Nottingham C (1673–82)[2] and were one of the reasons why equity changed from being based on the general notion of conscience to a more formal and predictable system.

There are many maxims and I will illustrate this answer by referring to four in detail[3] although as the maxims are not rigid rules the application of one maxim can also involve either another maxim[4] or an equitable presumption. One of the best modern examples of this is ***Tinsley v Milligan*** [1994] 1 AC 340, where the maxim 'he who comes into equity must come with clean hands' was applied by a minority of the House of Lords whilst the majority applied the presumption that contributions to the purchase of property which is then placed in the name of another will lead to the presumption of a resulting trust. The issue was a claim to a beneficial share in a house because of contributions made to its purchase. The house was in the claimant's name only in order to facilitate a fraudulent claim to housing benefit by the defendant. The majority held that the issue of illegality was irrelevant: the defendant's claim was made out by proving the existence of a common understanding concerning ownership and she had no need to refer to the reason why the house was conveyed into the claimant's name alone. The minority, however, held that once the court was aware that the claimant did not have clean hands it should refuse any relief even though the claim could succeed without relying on the illegality, as it could here. This shows the truth of Watt's statement in the question: maxims are really capable of bearing whatever weight the judge chooses to give them.

Is this always so? One significant maxim is that equity will not assist a volunteer.[5] Thus where a trust is not constituted, equity will not, with certain exceptions, assist a beneficiary who has not provided consideration to enforce it (known as a volunteer) and this underlies the law on constitution of trusts. This is actually an example of another maxim, equity follows the law, as was pointed out by Arden LJ in ***Pennington v Waine*** [2002] EWCA Civ 227.[6] Thus the common law insists on the presence of consideration for the making of a contract but equity goes further than the common law, as it regards marriage consideration as consideration, and the husband, wife and issue of the marriage together with more remote issue, e.g. grandchildren

7 What we need to do is bring
in a case where equity has
applied the maxim that it
does not assist a volunteer.
In order to make our point we
need a case where there is
a specifically *equitable* form
of consideration and this is
why we have used marriage
consideration.

(***Macdonald v Scott*** [1893] AC 642 HC), are within marriage consideration.[7] Thus they can enforce a promise to transfer property to be held on trust.

However, if the parties are not within marriage consideration then they will be volunteers. In ***Re Plumptre's Marriage Settlement*** [1910] 1 Ch 609 HC the beneficiaries seeking to enforce the covenant were not the issue of the marriage, the wife having died without issue, but the wife's next of kin. The court in effect applied the maxim and held that, as they were not within the marriage consideration, they were volunteers and thus could not enforce the covenant. One could say that this maxim rests on more solid foundations as although there are exceptions in its application, it does provide a foundation for equity's rules on constitution of trusts.

Another equitable maxim which illustrates this question is 'equity will not allow a statute to be used as an engine of fraud'. In ***Rochefoucauld v Boustead*** [1897] 1 Ch 196 CA the claimant had mortgaged land but was having difficulty in repaying the mortgage. The defendant bought it and orally agreed to hold it as trustee for the claimant but treated the land as his own. The claimant was held entitled to an account of profits made on the land because, although the trust in the claimant's favour, not being in writing, did not satisfy the requirements of what is now section 53(1)(b) of the LPA 1925, it would be a fraud on the defendant's part to take the profits for himself.

8 It is vital at this stage of your
answer to refer back to the
question, not only to remind
you of what it is about but
also to tie your answer into it.

The courts have applied this maxim not as a rule which must be rigorously applied but more as a general guideline.[8] This is shown by ***Midland Bank Trust Co Ltd v Green (No 1)*** [1981] AC 513 HL, where an option granted by a father to his son to purchase a farm had not been registered as required by the Land Charges Act 1972 and the father, having changed his mind about the sale, then carried out a 'sham' sale to his wife, defeating the son's option. The son's claim failed, Lord Wilberforce observing that 'it is not fraud to rely on legal rights conferred by an Act of Parliament'. Thus the policy consideration of preserving the integrity of the system of registering rights against land[9] overrode the application of the maxim.

9 Note that we did not say:
'the land registration system'
as such, as title was not
registered – a small point but
you can lose marks for even
relatively minor inaccuracies.

A final maxim to consider is that 'equity looks to the intent and not the form'. Thus, equity will hold that a trust has been created even though the word 'trust' was not used as in ***Paul v Constance*** [1977] 1 All ER 195 CA. A bank account was opened in Mr Constance's name only because they would have been embarrassed by having a joint account in different names. Various sums were paid into it and Constance said to the claimant: 'the money is as much yours as mine'. These words, and evidence of the transactions in the account, established that Constance intended to declare himself a trustee of the money in it for himself and the claimant. However, where it is clear that there is no intention to create a trust then of course equity will not intervene as in **Jones v Lock** [1865] 1 Ch App 25 HC,[10] where a father produced a cheque made out in his name for £900 and said, 'Look you here, I give this to baby', and placed the cheque in the baby's hand. The court held that there was no evidence of a declaration by Jones that he now held the cheque on trust for the baby.

[10] The inclusion of this case gives balance to your answer by contrast with the previous case.

Thus an examination of the cases shows that the maxims still apply in the application of equitable principles and that although Watt is correct in implying that they do not have a clear predictive value in judicial decision making he is slightly overstating the case by saying that they are capable of bearing what weight the judge chooses.[11]

[11] We have engaged with the question in our conclusion and slightly disagreed with Watt's view. An excellent end.

✓ Make your answer stand out

- Look at the judgment of Arden LJ in *Pennington* v *Waine,* which shows how the maxim 'equity will not assist a volunteer' really just follows the common law.
- Read and refer to Watt (2009) especially pp. 92–104. You will find that his discussion of the place of equitable maxims can really 'lift' your answer.
- Read Gardner (1995), who argues that reasoning based on a maxim can lead to unarticulated value judgements. Read further and then consider whether you agree.

! Don't be tempted to . . .

- Fail to show how cases you mention illustrate how the maxims work.
- Look at the maxims in isolation. Instead, show how they relate to each other.
- Give too many cases. Instead, give fewer cases but in more depth.
- Fail to show how the cases demonstrate differences in approach by the courts.

📓 Question 4

'Does equity have a future?'

Critically evaluate the arguments for and against this statement.

Answer plan

→ Set the scene: does equity have a future; does it have any distinctive ideas?

→ Explain briefly that of course equity and common law are separate systems.

→ Are there distinctive features which are not present in the common law but are in equity, and vice versa? Evaluate the arguments.

→ Examine whether equitable doctrines could sit alongside common law doctrines.

→ Conclude by evaluating the likelihood of increased convergence between the two systems.

Diagram plan

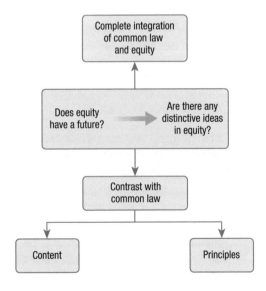

A printable version of this diagram plan is available from **www.pearsoned.co.uk/lawexpressqa**

Answer

[1] This introduction is saying two things, one obvious and the other less so. The obvious one is that this question is asking if equity has a future and of course the examiner will expect you to deal with this. However, it then asks another less obvious question: are there any distinctive ideas in equity which have a future? It is in your answer to this second point that you should aim to score those high marks!

[2] Note that there are two points here.

[3] You do need to mention something briefly about the relative position of equity and the common law today in order to give your answer a starting point but you should not go into too much detail on this.

[4] We have set the scene in the first paragraph and now we come to the main issue.

[5] This is an essential point which you must make in this essay and you need to support it with examples.

[6] This is an important point to make: there is no doubt that in many areas equity has undergone a resurgence.

This question is asking whether equity has any future as a separate legal system and also whether there are any distinctive ideas in equity which can be carried forward to the future.[1]

The first question really links to the fusion debate as the issue is whether equity and the common law can and ought[2] to survive as separate systems of law. There is no doubt that on the level of actual content, equity and the common law are different[3] in that they look at legal issues in different ways and their outcomes in the shape of their remedies are different. For example, the rules on the running of the burden in freehold covenants differ in common law (see ***Austerberry v Oldham Corporation*** (1885) 29 Ch D 750 CA) from those in equity (see ***Tulk v Moxhay*** (1848) 1 H & Tw 105 HC), as at common law the burden does not run at all, but in equity it does run where the covenant is negative. Moreover, equity has different remedies from the common law, for example specific performance and injunctions, and these, unlike common law remedies, are granted at the discretion of the court (see ***Patel v Ali*** [1984] Ch 283 HC).

However, the argument that equity and the common law have distinctive features at present does not answer the question of whether this will be the case in future.[4]

It can be argued that there are distinctive features which are present in equity but which are not present in the common law.[5] This is the view of Millett J (as he then was), who wrote (1998) that: 'The common law insists on honesty, diligence and the due performance of contractual obligations. But equity insists on nobler and subtler qualities: loyalty, fidelity, integrity, respect for confidentiality, and the disinterested discharge of obligations of trust and confidence.' One could go further and mention the equitable concept of the fiduciary. In ***Bristol and West Building Society v Mothew*** [1998] Ch 1 at 18, Millett LJ said that a 'fiduciary is someone who has undertaken to act for or on behalf of another in circumstances which give rise to a relationship of trust and confidence' and this concept has no counterpart in the common law.

Moreover, it is clear that in recent years the courts, particularly in Australia, have been reasserting the jurisdiction of equity as based on conscience.[6] For example, in cases involving claims to a beneficial interest in the family home they have asserted that the jurisdiction is founded on unconscionability (see **Baumgartner v Baumgartner** (1987) 62 ALJR 29) when English courts are still wrestling with the question of the extent to which they should give effect to the intentions of the parties (see **Lloyds Bank plc v Rosset** [1991] 1 AC 107 HL and **Stack v Dowden** [2007] UKHL 17).

[7] You will obviously gain a lot of credit for mentioning journal articles but the examiner will be especially impressed by evidence that you have actually understood the arguments in an article and have not just taken an isolated quote from it.

Duggan (1996) looks at equity from the perspective of what he calls the 'new equity rhetoric', which 'asserts that the function of modern equity is to raise community standards by requiring people to act selflessly in their dealings with others'. [7] A short term for this is, he suggests, 'moral altruism' and the quotation from Millett J (above) could be taken as an example of this. However, he suggests that in fact equity is no more or less concerned with promoting 'moral altruism' than the common law and instead equity, like the common law, is interested in efficient outcomes. He gives as an example the Australian case of **Hospital Products Ltd v United States Surgical Corporation** (1984) 156 CLR 41, where X persuaded Y to appoint him as exclusive Australian distributor of their products but his purpose was to capture Y's share of the market in the sale of their products. This was clearly a breach of X's contract with Y and so X would be liable for common law damages, but Y claimed that X was a fiduciary as he wanted to hold him liable as a constructive trustee. The Australian court refused as it felt that the terms of the contract excluded the existence of a fiduciary relationship. Duggan's point is that if equity is about promoting higher standards of altruism then this was exactly the case for it to intervene.

[8] In an essay such as this which is obviously dealing with general ideas you should try and use ideas such as these and get away from just a recital of cases. The ability to engage with more generalised concepts is the hallmark of a really good student.

Gray and Gray (2003, pp. 204–80, especially pp. 238–43) argue that there are 'meta-principles' in property law which are of general or idealised content which operate as overriding concerns. [8] They suggest that sexual equality is an example and that environmental protection will increasingly be one of these and, in the context of landlord and tenant law, the 'enhanced residential protection for the indigent tenant'. The point for us is that alongside these they suggest the equitable doctrine of the trust and the 'conscience laden premise of equitable intervention'. One example of the latter is estoppel and, for example, the judgment of Oliver J in **Taylor Fashions v Liverpool Victoria Trustees Co Ltd** [1982] QB 133 HC, who spoke of 'whether it would be unconscionable for one party to be permitted to deny that which, knowingly or unknowingly, he has encouraged another party to assume . . . '. Thus there will be themes which will pervade the whole of property law and some of these will come from equity. One could then take the argument a stage further and suggest that if this is so then although equity may still be seen in a separate light it will in time simply be seen as just one amongst several themes and will lose its distinctive place.

⁹ This is using the arguments made by the authors whom you have quoted to support your conclusion. You could of course come to the conclusion that greater convergence is neither possible nor desirable and this would be equally valid so long as you give reasons.

The conclusion could be that there will be continued integration of the fundamental doctrines of equity with those of the common law so that, although equity does have a future it will be increasingly as part of a unified system of law.⁹ This is the argument of Worthington (2006), especially in Chapter 10), who suggests that it is time for cohesive substantive integration of equity and the common law. If that is so there is much work to be done. For instance, it is still the case that the principles governing common law and equitable damages are different (see **Target Holdings Ltd v Redferns** [1996] 1 AC 421). What is essential is that the idea of a conscience-based jurisdiction, whatever name it takes, should not disappear from our legal system.¹⁰

¹⁰ This picks up the point made at the start of this answer: the question is whether we ought to have separate systems of law.

 Make your answer stand out

■ Look at the arguments made by Worthington (2006) and in particular look at how she argues that the common law is also changing with increasing reliance on such concepts as reasonableness.

■ Look at other areas where common law and equitable doctrines do not run together, for example there cannot be a tort (common law) of procuring a breach of trust (equity). (See *Metall und Rohstoff AG v Donaldson Lufkin & Jenrette Inc.* [1989] 3 WLR 563 at 615–623.) Would there be any advantages in common law rights and remedies being available in such a situation?

■ Look at the converse argument: that there is no need to consider the possible coming together of equity and common law. Instead, could equity grow and start to influence public law as well and introduce notions of controlling unconscionable behaviour by public bodies – or is there a need for this?

Question 5

'Equity is a roguish thing. For law we have a measure . . . equity is according to the conscience of him that is the Chancellor, and as that is longer or narrower, so is equity. 'Tis all one as if they should make the standard for the measure of the Chancellor's foot.' (*Table-Talk of John Selden*, 1856)

Is this still true of equity today? Discuss critically.

Diagram plan

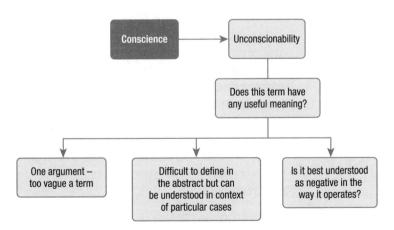

A printable version of this diagram plan is available from **www.pearsoned.co.uk/lawexpressqa**

Answer plan

→ What is meant by conscience?

→ Contrast this with unconscionability.

→ Critically consider whether it is possible to arrive at a workable definition of conscience, and contrast different ideas.

→ Consider cases where the notion of unconscionability has been applied and evaluate whether this term has helped in developing the law or not.

→ Conclusion – is the term unconscionability of any value to lawyers?

Answer

[1] This start pulls us away at once from what would be a tiresome essay on the over-familiar theme of whether equity is less certain in its application than the common law. This sort of answer would be heading for an average mark at the most. Instead, we have grasped the point at once: the real issue behind the question is whether the term 'conscience' can have any certain meaning and we then develop the essay to look at *unconscionability* and ask whether this really does depend on the whim of the individual judge.

[2] This is a good example of how knowledge of the history of equity can improve your answer. Although you may not get questions on the history of equity you will be able to use your knowledge of history to add detail to this type of question – and of course gain those extra marks.

The assumption which underlies this question is that any attempt to use 'conscience' as a means of deciding liability is doomed to failure.[1] This essay will seek to show that, although the notion of 'conscience' as a vehicle for determining liability is unsatisfactory, in reality the courts have not used this for many years and indeed it is arguable that it was never used. Instead, it is the concept of 'unconscionability' which sprang from conscience which is used and this essay will see if it is possible to give any clear meaning to that.

The term 'conscience' can be seen as the inner private voice of a person. If conscience was ever used in that sense to decide cases then the jibe in the quotation would be correct. However, it was not. In early equity, cases were heard by the Chancellor, who was an ecclesiastic and applied 'conscience' based on natural or universal justice.[2] Later, around the time when the Chancellors were lawyers, conscience meant the King's (or Queen's) conscience as the Chancellor was known as the Keeper of the King's (or Queen's) conscience. Lord Nottingham said in **Cook v Fountain** (1676) 3 Swans 585 at 600 that the courts were not conscience '*naturalis or interna*' but the conscience by which he would proceed was '*civilis et politica*'. Thus, conscience was not seen in the sense of an internal, private voice but in the context of society.

The courts today use the term 'unconscionability' and not 'conscience' and it is suggested that this is really the same idea of conscience as mentioned by Lord Nottingham (above). The question is then whether it is capable of having any certain meaning or whether it depends on, in that over-used phrase, the length of the Chancellor's foot.

The late Professor Birks felt that it did not and likened lawyers who dealt in unconscionability to the ornithologist who was content with 'small brown bird' as a descriptor of 'avian form' (Birks, 1996, pp. 16–17). Lord Nicholls in *Royal Brunei Airlines Sdn Bhd* v *Tan Kok Ming* [1995] 2 AC 378 at 392 HL observed that 'if unconscionability is to be the touchstone for liability . . . it is essential to be clear on what . . . unconscionable *means*' (his emphasis). This is precisely the point. In fact 'unconscionability' as a tool of equity passed into disuse for many years and has only fairly recently gained renewed prominence.[3]

[3] This is an essential point to make and then leads you on later to look at how, in the context of actual cases, unconscionability has been grafted onto established equitable rules.

Watt (2009) makes the important point that unconscionability cannot be defined in the abstract but can only be understood in the context of particular cases. He adopts the words of Deane J in the Australian High Court in *Commonwealth of Australia* v *Verwayen* (1990) 170 CLR 394 at 441, who referred to unconscionability as 'involving the use of or insistence upon legal entitlement to take advantage of another's special vulnerability or misadventure . . . in a way that is unreasonable or oppressive to an extent that affronts ordinary minimum standards of fair dealing'. Watt himself also suggests the touchstone of conduct which is 'not routine' in the sense that it is 'non-routine reliance on a routine reading of law' (at p. 108).

[4] You really do need to include a concrete example at this point to explain how the theoretical ideas might work in practice.

He gives as an example the situation where a landowner evicts a non-owner from his land.[4] In routine cases this would be perfectly fair as where the non-owner is simply a trespasser. Suppose, though, that the non-owner has built a house on this land in reliance on the land-owner's promise to allow the non-owner to occupy the house for life? (See, for example, *Inwards* v *Baker* [1965] 1 All ER 446 CA.) One could argue that the owner's conduct was 'non-routine' and in the formulation of Deane J (above) it would be 'unreasonable or oppressive to an extent that affronts ordinary minimum standards of fair dealing'. Thus, it brings the familiar equitable concept of estoppel into play.

[5] This approach will earn you a really good mark, as you are showing that you are thinking about the underlying idea of unconscionability by comparing the thought of one author with that of another.

This attempt by Watt to give clarity to the term 'unconscionability' can be set alongside the idea of Delany and Ryan (2008),[5] who feel that 'even the questionable approach of the Court of Appeal in *Pennington* v *Waine* [2002] EWCA Civ 227 appears premised on an understanding of the principle as essentially negative in character, a fallback weapon in the judicial arsenal to be used when harshness must be "tempered" rather than an instrument for inculcating any particular values of fairness'. This understanding of unconscionability as essentially negative is not inconsistent with Watt's analysis or that of Deane J. For example, where a non-owner in the example quoted by Watt (above) relies on the landowner's promise to allow him to occupy the house for life, the non-owner is using the unconscionable conduct of the owner in the negative sense of defending himself from a claim to evict him.

[6] You need to do this as well as outlining the theoretical discussion, as this essay requires a balance between both theory and actual cases.

With these theories in mind let us look at how unconscionability has actually been applied in equity.[6] In **Pennington v Waine** it was applied by Arden LJ in the context of a purported transfer of shares in a company which did not comply with the rule in **Re Rose** [1952] Ch 499 CA, as the transferor had not done all in her power to effect a transfer. She had told a partner in a firm who acted for the company that she wished to transfer some of her shares and later signed a share transfer form. Arden LJ held[7] that it would be unconscionable to allow the transferor in view of all that she had done to transfer the shares, to then change her mind and say that they were not the transferees' shares. The notion of unconscionability has been grafted onto an established rule but it is not clear if, in Watt's term, this was to deal with non-routine conduct or if it was unreasonable or oppressive conduct as outlined above by Deane J in **Commonwealth of Australia v Verwayen**. It could be argued that the conduct of the transferor was neither. In **Yeoman's Row Management Ltd v Cobbe** [2008] UKHL 55 the Court of Appeal applied unconscionability in an estoppel claim but in the House of Lords Lord Scott held that the Court of Appeal had been influenced too much by the fact that it regarded the behaviour of the company as unconscionable without requiring the essential elements of proprietary estoppel to be present.

[7] The point is that other members of the Court of Appeal did not use this term. If you hope for high marks it is vital to be precise!

[8] This essay obviously needs a conclusion but on the facts given and the arguments presented it can only be a tentative one. This will not lose you marks. Sometimes it is the very black and white conclusions which lose marks as they betray a superficial understanding of the law.

Thus, it is not clear whether unconscionability has played any real part in developing equity today or whether it simply confuses the law as it just adds to existing doctrines which are already capable of doing equity.[8]

Make your answer stand out

- Look at the article by Delany and Ryan (2008) mentioned in the answer and note how the authors look at use of the term 'unconscionability' by the courts in a number of different contexts – research these.
- Consider the rejection of 'unconscionability' as the foundation of liability in cases of dishonest assistance in a breach of trust.
- Could 'unconscionability' be more appropriate where it is sought to develop the law rather than add a gloss to old doctrines as in the examples in this answer? Consider whether it could be the basis for unifying proprietary estoppel and constructive trusts.

! Don't be tempted to . . .

- Fail to distinguish between 'conscience' and 'unconscionability'.
- Spend too long on history. A paragraph will be enough.
- Spend all of your time looking at cases – you must engage with the theoretical issues.
- Forget that when you do mention a case you make sure that you look at it from the point of view of how it illustrates the use of the term 'unconscionability'. This means that you will not necessarily be concerned with the actual decision.

www.pearsoned.co.uk/lawexpressqa

 Go online to access more revision support including additional essay and problem questions with diagram plans, You be the marker questions, and download all diagrams from the book.

Bibliography

Andrews, G. (2002) Undue influence – where's the disadvantage? *Conveyancer and Property Lawyer,* 66: 456.

Baker, J.H. (2002) *Introduction to English Legal History* (4th edn). Oxford: Oxford University Press.

Baker, P. (1993) Land as a *donatio mortis causa. Law Quarterly Review,* 109: 19.

Baughen, S. (2010) Performing animals and the dissolution of unincorporated associations: the 'contract-holding' theory vindicated. *Conveyancer and Property Lawyer,* 74: 216.

Birks, P. (1996) Equity in the modern law: an exercise in taxonomy. *University of Western Australia Law Review,* 26: 18.

Borkowski, A. (1999) *Deathbed Gifts: The Law of Donatio Mortis Causa.* Oxford: Oxford University Press.

Brown, J. (2007) What are we to do with testamentary trusts of imperfect obligation? *Conveyancer and Property Lawyer,* 71: 148.

Brown, J. and Pawlowski M. (2012) Testamentary trusts and the rule against capricious purposes: an underlying rationale? *Tru. L.I.,* 109.

Browne, D. (ed.) (1933) *Ashburner's Principles of Equity* (2nd edn). London: Butterworths.

Burn, E. and Virgo, G.J. (eds) (2008) *Maudsley & Burn's Trusts & Trustees: cases and materials* (7th edn). Oxford: Oxford University Press.

Chambers, R. (1997) *Resulting Trusts.* Oxford: Oxford University Press.

Chambers, R. (2013) Constructive trusts and breach of fiduciary duty. *Conveyancer and Property Lawyer,* 3: 241

Chan, B. (2013) The enigma of the Quistclose trust. *UCL Journal of Law and Jurisprudence,* 2(1), 1–39.

Charity Commission (2008) *Speaking Out: Guidance on Campaigning and Political Activity by Charities.* London: Charity Commission.

Clements, L.M. (2004) Bringing trusts back into the twenty-first century. *Web Journal of Current Legal Issues,* 2.

Conaglen, M. (2005) The nature and function of fiduciary loyalty. *Law Quarterly Review,* 121: 452.

Conaglen, M. (2007) *Fiduciary Loyalty.* Oxford: Hart Publishing.

Critchley, P. (1999) Instruments of fraud, testamentary dispositions and secret trusts. *Law Quarterly Review,* 115: 631.

Davies, D. (2004) The integrity of trusteeship. *Law Quarterly Review,* 120: 1.

Delany, H. and Ryan, D. (2008) Unconscionability: a unifying theme in equity. *Conveyancer and Property Lawyer,* 72: 401.

Dixon, G.L.H. (2009) Proprietary estoppel: a return to principle. *Conveyancer and Property Lawyer,* 73: 260.

Doggett, A. (2003) Explaining *Re Rose*: the search goes on. *Cambridge Law Journal,* 62: 263.

Dowling A. (2011) Vendors' application for specific performance. *Conveyancer,* 3: 208.

Duggan, A.J. (1996) Is equity efficient? *Law Quarterly Review,* 113: 601.

Dunn, A. (2008) Demanding service or servicing demand? Charities' regulation and the policy process. *Modern Law Review,* 71(2): 247.

Emery, C.T. (1982) The most hallowed principle. *Law Quarterly Review,* 98: 551.

Etherton, T. (2008) Constructive trusts: a new model for equity and unjust enrichment. *Cambridge Law Journal,* 67: 265.

Finn, P. (1992) Fiduciary law and the modern world, in E. McKendrick (ed.), *Commercial Aspects of Trusts and Fiduciary Obligations.* Oxford: Oxford University Press.

Fletcher, R. (1996) Charities for the advancement of education. *Law Quarterly Review,* 112: 557.

Gardner, S. (1995) Two maxims of equity. *Cambridge Law Journal,* 54(1): 60.

Gardner, S. (2010) Reliance-based constructive trusts, in C. Mitchell (ed.), *Constructive and Resulting Trusts.* Oxford: Hart Publishing.

Garton, J. (2003) The role of the trust mechanism in the rule in *Re Rose. Conveyancer and Property Lawyer,* 5: 364.

Garton, J. (2007) Justifying the *cy-près* doctrine. *Trust Law International,* 21(3):134.

Gray, K. and Gray, S. (2003) The rhetoric of reality, in J. Getzler (ed.), *Rationalizing Property, Equity and Trusts: Essays in Honour of Edward Burn.* London: LexisNexis.

Green, B. (1984) Grey, Oughtred and Vandervell: a contextual reappraisal. *Modern Law Review,* 47; 385.

Griffiths, G. (2008) An inevitable tension? The disclosure of letters of wishes. *Conveyancer and Property Lawyer,* 4: 332.

Hackney, J. (2008) Charities and public benefit. *Law Quarterly Review,* 124: 347.

Halliwell, M. (2003) Perfecting imperfect gifts and trust: have we reached the end of the Chancellor's foot? *Conveyancer and Property Lawyer,* 67: 192.

Hanbury, H.G. (2012) *Modern Equity* (19th edn). London: Sweet & Maxwell.

Harding, M. (2008) Trusts for religious purposes and the question of public benefit. *Modern Law Review,* 71: 159.

Harris, J. (1971) Trust, power and duty. *Law Quarterly Review,* 87: 31.

Hayton, D. (1994) Uncertainty of subject-matter of trusts. *Law Quarterly Review,* 110: 335.

Hayton, D. (2001) Developing the obligation characteristic of the trust. *Law Quarterly Review,* 96: 117.

Hayton, D. (2011) Proprietary liability for secret profits. *Law Quarterly Review,* 127: 487.

Hicks, A. (2011) Constructive trusts of fiduciary gain: Lister revived? *Conveyancer and Property Lawyer.* 1: 62.

Hodkinson, K. (1982) *Conveyancer and Property Lawyer,* 228.

Honoré, A. (2003) Trusts: the inessentials, in J. Getzler (ed.), *Rationalizing Property, Equity and Trusts: Essays in Honour of Edward Burn.* London: LexisNexis.

Iwobi, A. (2009) Out with the old, in with the new: religion, charitable status and the Charities Act 2006. *Legal Studies,* 29: 619.

Ker, B.S. (1953) Intermediate income. *Conveyancer and Property Lawyer,* 275.

Kodilinye, G. (1982) A fresh look at the rule in *Strong* v *Bird. Conveyancer and Property Lawyer* 46: 14.

Law Commission (1992) Consultation Paper, *Fiduciary Duties and Regulatory Rules* (No 124).

Law Commission (1999) Report, *Trustees' Powers and Duties* (No 260).

Law Reform Committee (1982) Report, *The Powers and Duties of Trustees* (Cmd 8733).

Luxton, P. (1997) Variations of trusts: settlors' intentions and the consent principle in *Saunders* v *Vautier. Modern Law Review,* 60: 719.

Luxton, P. (1998) Are you being served? Enforcing keep open covenants in leases. *Conveyancer and Property Lawyer,* 76: 396.

Luxton, P. (2007) Gifts to clubs: contract holding is trumps. *Conveyancer and Property Lawyer,* 274.

Martin, J. (1996) Certainty of subject-matter: a defence of *Hunter* v *Moss. Conveyancer and Property Lawyer,* 60: 223.

Mason, A. (1985) Themes and prospects, in P. D. Finn (ed.), *Essays in Equity.* Sydney: The Law Book Company.

Matthews, P. (1984) A heresy and a half in certainty of objects. *Conveyancer and Property Lawyer,* 48: 22.

Matthews, P. (1995) A problem in the construction of gifts to unincorporated associations. *Conveyancer and Property Lawyer,* 49: 302.

Matthews, P. (1996) The new trust: obligations without rights?, in A. J. Oakley (ed.), *Trends in Contemporary Trust Law.* Oxford: Oxford University Press.

McInnes, M. (2008) Charity and sport: a Canadian perspective. *Law Quarterly Review,* 124: 202.

McKay, L. (1974) *Re Baden* and the third class of certainty. *Conveyancer and Property Lawyer,* 38: 269.

Meager, R. (2003) Secret trusts: do they have a future? *Conveyancer and Property Lawyer,* 67: 203.

Millett, P.J. (1998) Equity's place in the law of commerce. *Law Quarterly Review*, 114: 214.

Mitchell, C. and Watterson, S. (2010) Remedies for knowing receipt, in D. Mitchell (ed.), *Constructive and Resulting Trusts*. Oxford: Hart Publishing.

Moffat, G. (2009) *Trusts Law* (5th edn). Cambridge: Cambridge University Press.

Nolan, R. (1996) The triumph of technicality. *Cambridge Law Journal*, 55(3): 436.

Panesar, S. (2013) Title deeds to land and *donatio mortis causa*. *Conveyancer and Property Lawyer*, 70.

Parry, N. (1989) Trusts for masses. *Conveyancer and Property Lawyer*, 53: 453.

Pawlowski, M. and Brown, J. (2004) Constituting a secret trust by estoppel. *Conveyancer and Property Lawyer*, 388.

Perrins, B. (1972) Can you keep half a secret? *Law Quarterly Review*, 88: 225.

Perrins, B. (1985) Secret trusts: are they dehors? *Conveyancer and Property Lawyer*, 49: 248.

Picton, J. (2011) *Kings* v *Bultitude* – A gift lost to charity? *Conveyancer and Property Lawyer*, 1: 69.

Ridge, P. (2008) Justifying the remedies for dishonest assistance. *Law Quarterly Review*, 124: 445.

Smith, L. (2003) The motive, not the deed, in J. Getzler (ed.), *Rationalizing Property, Equity and Trusts: Essays in Honour of Edward Burn*. London: LexisNexis.

Swadling, W. (2008) Explaining resulting trusts. *Law Quarterly Review*, 124: 72.

Swadling, W. (ed.) (2004) *The Quistclose Trust: Critical Essays*. Oxford: Hart Publishing.

Thompson, M. P. (2003) Mortgages and undue influence, in E. Cooke (ed.), *Modern Studies in Property Law*, Vol. 2. Oxford: Hart Publishing.

Turner, P. (2006) The High Court of Australia on contracts to assign equitable rights. *Conveyancer and Property Lawyer*, 390.

Virgo, G. (2003) Restitution through the looking glass: restitution within equity and equity within restitution, in J. Getzler (ed.), *Rationalizing Property, Equity and Trusts: Essays in Honour of Edward Burn*. London: LexisNexis.

Virgo, G. (2012) *The Principles of Equity and Trusts*. Oxford: Oxford University Press.

Watt, G. (2004) Publication review: W. Swadling (ed.), *The Quistclose Trust: Critical Essays*. *Conveyancer and Property Lawyer* 418.

Watt, G. (2009) *Equity Stirring: The Story of Justice Beyond Law*. Oxford: Hart Publishing.

Worthington, S. (2006) *Equity* (2nd edn). Oxford: Oxford University Press.

Index

INDEX

Tried and tested

What law students across the UK are saying about the **Law Express** and **Law Express Question&Answer** series:

'I personally found the series very helpful in my preparation for exams.'

Abba Elgujja, University of Salford

'Law Express are my go-to guides. They are an excellent supplement to my course material.'

Claire Turner, Open University

'This is the best law Q&A series in my opinion. I think it's helpful and I will continue to use it.'

Nneka H, University of London

'These revision guides strike the right balance between enough detail to help shape a really good answer, but sufficiently brief to be used for last-minute revision. The layout is user friendly and the use of tables and flowcharts is helpful.'

Shannon Reynolds, University of Manchester

'I find them easy to read, yet very helpful.'

Rebecca Kincaid, University of Kent

'The information is straight to the point. This is important particularly for exams.'

Dewan Sadia Kuraishy, University of Manchester

'In the modules in which I used these books to revise with, generally the modules I found the most difficult, I got the highest marks in. The books are really easy to use and are extremely helpful.'

Charlotte Evans, Queen Mary University of London